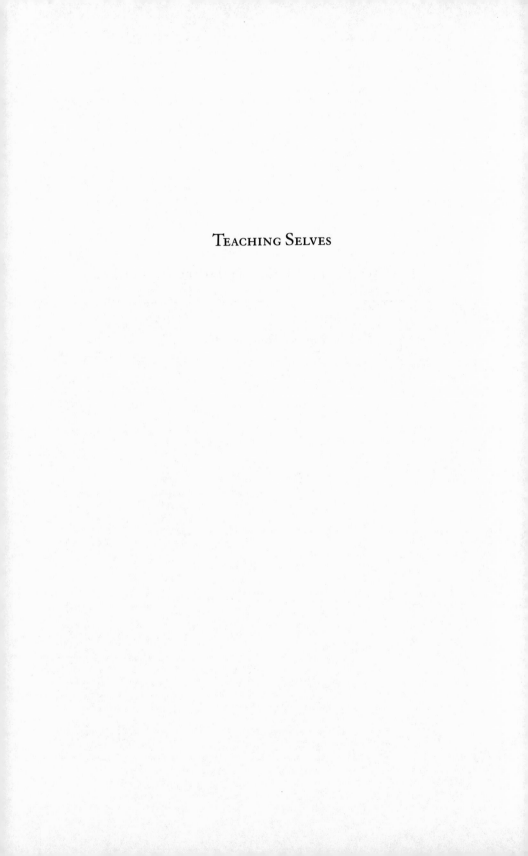

TEACHING SELVES

SUNY series,

TEACHER PREPARATION AND DEVELOPMENT

Alan R. Tom, editor

TEACHING
SELVES

Identity, Pedagogy, and Teacher Education

JANE DANIELEWICZ

STATE UNIVERSITY OF NEW YORK PRESS

Cover art: Sherri Wood, art quilts, *Cog*, 1995

Published by
State University of New York Press
Albany

© 2001 State University of New York

All rights reserved

Printed in the United States of America

For information, address
State University of New York Press,
90 State Street, Suite 700, Albany, NY 12207

Production, Laurie Searl
Marketing, Michael Campochiaro

Library of Congress Cataloging-in-Publication Data

Danielewicz, Jane, 1952–
   Teachingselves : identity, pedagogy, and teacher education / Jane Danielewicz.
      p. cm.—(SUNY series, teacher preparation and evelopment)
   Includes bibliographical references and index.
   ISBN 0-7914-5003-1 (alk. paper)—ISBN 0-7914-5004-X (pbk : alk. paper)
      1. Teachers—Training of—United States.   2. College Students—United States—
   Longitudinal Studies.   I. Title.   II. SUNY series in teacher preparation and development

LB1715 .D32 2001
370'.71'073—dc21   00-054793

10   9   8   7   6   5   4   3   2   1

For John

who had enough patience

I was aware of the fact that identity is an invention from the very beginning, long before I understood any of this theoretically.
—Stuart Hall, "Minimal Selves"

That all crossings over are a way of knowing, and of knowing we don't know, where we have been. . . .
—Robert Haas, *Sun Under Wood*

Talking about pedagogy, thinking about it critically, is not the intellectual work that most folks think is hip and cool.
—bell hooks, *Teaching to Transgress*

I don't feel it is necessary to know exactly what I am. The main interest in life and work is to become someone else you were not in the beginning. If you knew when you began a book what you would say at the end, do you think you would have the courage to write it?
—Michel Foucault

CONTENTS

_____

ACKNOWLEDGMENTS

This book about how identities arise explains the continuous process of how others, through words and actions, make us who we are. I would like to acknowledge some of the many people who have created me, the writer, by contributing to the enterprise of self that this book represents.

As my husband John McGowan described it one day, I wrote this book on the strength of my own convictions. He is the one responsible for letting me know that such a thing was possible. For years, John has gone around telling people about my inventiveness as a teacher. Though it took a long time before his comments hit home, I am grateful for his repeated suggestion to write about the occupation that fuels my everyday life—the practice of teaching.

Without my students and colleagues in the School of Education at the University of North Carolina, there would not have been anything to write about. They are the reason this book exists. Since I joined the faculty in 1992, my work with prospective teachers has been electrifying. I recall clearly the first day of the first course I taught in the basement of Peabody Hall. Though I was a seasoned veteran, I had never encountered students like the twenty-six undergraduates who sat before me—intense, driven, committed, and eager (even desperate) to know how to be teachers. For me, it was a teacher's heaven. The first group was not an anomaly; each subsequent year I encountered more wonderful students. I have tried hard to live up to their high expectations of good teaching, which is how the pedagogy I describe in this book got started.

My passions are not limited to teaching; I also love to talk (and to talk about teaching). I thank my colleagues in the School of Education for being such engaged conversational partners. Working with Dwight Rogers on an interview and observation project sparked the idea of doing something similar with my own students. But not only the idea transferred. Dwight's interviews are splendid. His informal instruction in the art of interviewing helped me develop skills crucial to the essence of this book. George Noblit, through good example, a bit of proselytizing, and sheer force of personality, has kept ethnography (and those of us who want to write it) alive and well in the School of Education.

But it was Alan Tom who made the book real, gave it physical form, made me stop talking and start writing. Though we had many conversations, I remember one day in May, years ago, sitting in the front window of a café on Franklin Street. While I was gazing out at the spring-green trees and the light-dappled lawn of the quad across the street, he was talking about my book. Hands chopping through air, cutting planes in imaginary space, he would say, "Here's a chapter." Then talking and gesturing a bit more, he would add, "That's a chapter." By the time we had finished our coffee, I had a book in my head. Eventually, everything came to pass, just as he said it would. But to write the book, I needed his vision first.

Of course the manuscript would never have become a book at all without the generous guidance of Priscilla Ross, editor in chief at SUNY press. I hope the book lives up to her expectations. Many thanks goes to Laurie Searl who managed the production of my book with care and patience.

There is no adequate way to thank the six students whose stories make this book alive, genuine, important, relevant, vital, compelling, and worth reading. As testimony to their pursuit of teaching lives, this book is my gift in exchange for their hours of talk, prodigious energy, simple hard work, serious introspection, and abiding affection. Though I cannot reveal their identities, I hope the book reads true to them. Our work together has forged life-long bonds, and I look forward eagerly to hearing the stories of their futures.

Writing this book has not been a solitary affair, not in the least. My writing group has been nothing short of fabulous. Its current members—Judith Farquhar, Megan Matchinske, Marisol de la Cadena, and Joy Kasson—have read every page of every draft. As I wrote, they were always in my heart and mind. Their familiar faces, a gentle, waiting audience, would often float into my mind's eye. Sometimes, imagining the table where we sat and shared our work was provocation enough to write on a slow day. My book bears the distinctive imprint of each of these women, who, through their motivating comments, judicious critiques, and simple love, made it the best one I *could* have written. Its limitations are purely my own.

I am grateful to William Andrews and to Laurence Avery (chair and former chair) for their steady support and to the English Department for granting me a research and study leave. Thanks goes to Ruel Tyson and Peter Filene at the Institute for the Arts in Humanities (and to the other fellows) for a faculty fellowship and a productive semester. I am indebted to Mr. and Mrs. William J. Armfield IV, for offering their mountain home (complete with back porch rockers) in Roaring Gap, North Carolina, as a writer's retreat open to Fellows of the Institute. Janie Armfield's generosity prompted me to take several trips; I always returned to Chapel Hill with a great deal more of the book written, plus renewed energy to carry on.

My friends are the backbone. Without Lynn York, neighbor and fellow writer on the block, my life during the past few years would not have been half as much fun. We have spent hours talking, shared children and chores, laughed loudly over nothing much, and even written together. I am especially grateful to Lynn's parents, Mr. and Mrs. Van York, who lent us their house at Hilton Head for resting and writing. In addition, the Yorks' generosity enabled me to complete final segments of my fieldwork.

Laurie Langbauer, teaching companion and literary theorist extraordinaire, gave me the courage to move in the direction of writing personally. The autobiographical sections after each chapter allowed me to connect in an immediate and visceral way to the work of writing my students' lives. In addition, Laurie's ideas about theory and her suggestions about conceptual organization were invaluable in the development of the chapter on pedagogical principles. My affectionate friend, Carol Mavor, inspired me every day by demonstrating how pleasure is the result of responding creatively to the habitual, often overwhelming, demands of ordinary life. Finally, to friends I can no longer distinguish from family, who encouraged and loved me, I extend my sincerest thanks: Nancy Jesser, Kevin Parker, Della Pollock, Jacqueline Hall, Carol and Bill Malloy, Jim Hevia, Pamela Downing, John Warasila, Irene Papoulis, and David Brehmer.

To my family, I owe everything. My husband John (an academic and writer himself) understands the discipline a book needs; he did everything in his power to help me through: managed the kids, cooked the dinners, tolerated my moods, answered all my theory questions, and urged me, continually, forward. My son, Kiernan, cheerfully relinquished the family's computer whenever I was working at home. Invariably, upon leaving the room, he took the opportunity to fling a sarcastic comment over his shoulder, a practice I found endearing. He seemed to be saying, in case I hadn't noticed, he had become a teenager while I was busy writing. I treasured these moments of contact between us. Apart from the mutual recognition they afforded, his words infused the situation with much-needed humor. My daughter, Siobhan, with a simple act of joyful enthusiasm, made sure I finished the book. Sometime last year when she realized what I was up to, she ran out to the cul-de-sac and announced proudly to all the neighbors, "My mom is writing a book!" In those moments of deepest discouragement, her words kept me going. I could never have allowed her to lose face with the neighbors! My parents cultivated in me a strong will and fierce determination, two traits necessary for a writing life. And my mother held the faith, always.

INTRODUCTION

This book is about becoming—the process of how a person becomes someone, particularly of how students become teachers. In it, I propose a pedagogy for identity development. I describe the qualities that must characterize our teaching in order for the students we encounter to become something other than students. Education is about growth and transformation, not only of culture, but of persons too.

Teachers

Whenever I announce I am a teacher in a crowded party of strangers, talk stops. In seconds I discover myself at the center of a small circle of radiating quiet. Encountering someone who identifies herself first as a teacher arrests the conversation. Perhaps this happens because each of us has powerful, yet complicated and uneven histories with those individuals who have been our teachers. Some may have changed us, altered in large and small ways our future paths. All have passed judgments about our behavior and abilities and maybe even acted in ways to fix our place in everyday life more firmly than we thought anyone would ever have the right to do. Yet since in America we must all go to school, no one can avoid relationships with teachers. Few of these relations are chosen; they are mandated, the result of national laws that regulate compulsory education in the United States.

Some teachers impress us deeply. We remember those teachers who noticed and praised us, whose behavior and eagerness edged open the seamless quality of life's surface to reveal other worlds, textures, and ideas, the power of which transfixed us and set us on paths we never dreamed were there. Nor are the teachers who hurt or discouraged us ever forgotten, who through ignorance, intolerance, or simple boredom taught us the wrong things the wrong way. Like stories about our families, teacher stories are common stock, indulged in and re-told, or revisited when an explanation of a quirk in our personalities is required.

Even now in middle age, a time when I once imagined my life would be settled, I have outgrown neither the memories themselves nor my need to re-member the formative episodes involving the teachers who inhabit my past. The narratives continue to change me as I repeat and, in so doing, relive them. There's Miss Margaret, who terrified me in second grade with her strict rules, her adept-ness at public humiliation and ruler-slapping corporal punishment. The real hor-ror happened in fourth grade, though, when she reappeared as my teacher the year our class was housed in the dark depths of the convent basement. Periodi-cally she got out the broom to chase the mice from the classroom corners and into the cloakroom, an impassioned performance that reinforced my long-held conviction that she was a witch. The Wicked Witch of the West did not die when the house fell on her; she was resuscitated, come back to life, and had reap-peared in our midst as a teacher. At the age of nine, as a well-trained Catholic I fully understood and believed in the miracle and possibility of resurrection.

But I also recall Sister Margaret Miriam, a Sister of Mercy, her face framed in starched white cotton overlaid with several pinned but shifting layers of black veiling, the habit she wore a visible emblem of a chosen life that was holy, mys-terious, and other worldly. I remember the tremor in her voice and her visceral transport out of our dull classroom and into life somewhere "out there" the first time she read aloud Dylan Thomas's "Fern Hill" in my sophomore English class. To me, a student in a small-town high school in Pennsylvania where ambition for girls was linked mostly to marriage, the way she lived represented something else, something other. She embodied imagination; and in so doing suggested that dreams, visions, words, and the ecstasy that accompanied them, could be perfectly reasonable, worthy, even necessary qualities of one's everyday life.

These, and all my teachers, through their daily acts and their demonstra-tions of self, helped define who I am, made me aware of preferences and talents of which I was previously unconscious, reminded me of life's limits, and directed me by way of example to either accept selflessly or to wholeheartedly work against the daily impediments I was certain to encounter. Both models were im-portant. Against the conservative ones, I rebelled and discovered who I did not want to be. On the other hand, the imaginative teachers made agency viable: they showed me that it was possible to think and to speak and to act, to be someone.

Teaching Selves

And now I replicate this work in a redoubled sense: I am a teacher of teachers writing a book not about the acts of teaching but about the process of how stu-dents become teachers. I undertake this work gladly, passionately, because teachers occupy positions in the public domain in America where it's still possible to effect change, to improve the lives of others. Education is transmittable capital; its value and power can pass from teachers to students.

If we need teachers who effectively educate (a fundamental requirement for any optimism about the future), then we need to know how the best teachers have become themselves. What makes someone a good teacher is not methodology, or even ideology. It requires engagement with identity, the way individuals conceive of themselves so that teaching is a state of being, not merely ways of acting or behaving.

I regard "becoming a teacher" as an identity forming process whereby individuals define themselves and are viewed by others as teachers. Two questions are central: How does "becoming" happen and how can it be encouraged? A good teacher (I have no specific practices or qualities of teachers in mind here) is an invested teacher, someone who identifies him- or herself as a teacher. To be effective, to be really good, to retain a vision of success and intellectual development for one's students in social climates not conducive to such endeavors, to persist despite the low regard our culture has for such work—then one must *be* a teacher, not just act like one. This happens when one sees oneself and is seen by others as a teacher. Instead of playing a role, teaching entails a greater investment—one's identity must be on the line. For me, then, the classroom is a compelling and serious place where the stakes are high. Not only do I wish to be remembered as one of the good ones who transformed and inspired, but also as one who helped her students to become teachers in their own right.

This conception of a teaching self entails much more than simply playing a role, taking up a profession, or accepting a job in a school system. In using the term "identity," I am referring to how individuals know and name themselves (e.g. "In regard to race, I am a white person.") and how they are recognized and regarded by others (e.g. "She is a white person."). All identity categories, even those that seem biologically designated like gender or race, are processes under construction. They are not unified or fixed entities that exist permanently inside individuals. This process of becoming is what I call identity development. As persons in the world, we are continually engaged in becoming something or someone, such as parent, woman, white person, old person, teacher. Because identities are conditional, restless, unstable, ever-changing states of being, they can never be ultimately completed. Though identities are fluid, individuals do have recognizable selves. We might think of a person's identities as points of fixation, temporarily arrested states, that are achieved moment by moment in the course of relations between individuals.

Though I focus in this book on a single identity—becoming a teacher—I wish to emphasize the fact that individuals are composed of multiple, often conflicting, identities. For instance, not only do I view myself as a teacher; also

I am a woman, a mother, a friend, a writer. These identities are constantly under construction as they are reformed, added to, eroded, reconstructed, integrated, dissolved, or expanded. Each of these conceptions of "self" exists simultaneously and fluidly, with varying degrees of importance or relevance given any one time or place. Likewise, my students possess a variety of other defining identities that figure into the way they develop as teachers. As an educator, I find hope in this view of identity as malleable, subject to invention, created by individuals and others, flexible and sensitive to social contexts. It means that I can affect how students become teachers by paying attention to pedagogy, to ways of structuring activities and environments that facilitate social interaction, the medium and milieu of identity construction.

Teaching Stories

This enterprise of teaching teachers, of constructing identities, is central to my work as a faculty member in a secondary teacher education program at the University of North Carolina. The teacher education program is the context in which my study is situated, not the object of my analysis. My goal is to focus on pedagogy—how best can we teach our students in the individual courses that comprise the program—rather than on curriculum or structure—what is the best kind of teacher education program? Instead of offering a critique or suggestions for reorganization, this book describes an approach to teaching in the form of general principles that promote identities within the confines of a fairly typical teacher education program.

Because of factors such as institutional history or the relationship between the university and the public schools, teacher education programs often present less than perfect conditions for learning. The curriculum can be fragmented into discrete areas such as "adolescent psychology" or "methods," and the required set of courses may be disconnected, with little overlap among them. Instruction may occur mostly on campus, with students spending little time in the public schools. Teacher mentors in the field may have very little connection with program faculty, which inhibits the development of personal relationships. Without a cohort structure, there may not be a strong group identity among the students, making the program feel impersonal. While acknowledging all conceivable limitations, I am insisting that it is still possible to teach effectively and to foster teaching identities, despite the constraints of any particular program.

Although I have much to say about how best to make teachers, I will eschew my recommendations for now. Advice gravitates toward conclusions— where the book will end and where the real work begins—and not the point where I wish to start. Instead I will tell stories—often as they were told to me—of how people become teachers by learning to see themselves that way. Inevitably, some stories are about when that identity doesn't work too, when people, no matter how much they hoped to, find they cannot regard themselves as teachers.

When all is finished, my position, if it convinces, will do so because it derives from the words and worlds of others. For more than two years, I have worked with six undergraduate students enrolled in a two-year teacher education program with the intention of being high school English teachers. The evidence for how teaching identities develop will be based on the life stories of these six individuals as represented through interviews, observations, and collections of their written work. These texts reveal the expressed desires, thoughts, reactions, experiences, and processes that occurred during their two final years as undergraduate university students, while taking courses and completing a semester-long teaching practicum, and includes events from the year following their graduation. The long-term relationships I've established with these students through this work are not the norm in teacher education programs. But our relations have been so fruitful and expansive in so many ways that we ought to try making the model of sustained contact standard rather than anomalous. For teachers and students alike, the consequences have been astounding. Furthermore, as a teacher myself, my role in this work is not (and could not have been) neutral or abstract. This personal commitment ensures that my stories, especially accounts of my teaching self, will occupy their own place in the book.

Reasons for Teaching

In these difficult economic and vicious political times in the United States, when difference and culture are places of conflict and dissent, it is hard to imagine wanting to be a teacher, let alone enrolling in a teacher education program, completing a practicum, and accepting a job in a public school. Because of these adverse conditions, we are reduced to imagining only moral arguments—social responsibility, youthful idealism, missionary zeal—as reasons why someone should become a teacher. And, in the end, the full responsibility for defending such a choice, of holding out against the money and prestige one might theoretically accrue by working in business, is left up to the individual who receives little if any support from friends, family, or institutions. (In fall of 1998, beginning teachers in the Chapel Hill school district, one of the state's most prestigious districts, were offered a salary of $23,258, well below the national average.[1] Around the state salaries are lower and working conditions more difficult.) No wonder there are teacher shortages state and nationwide. No wonder that recent legislation (passed in 1998 in North Carolina and in other states) relaxes certification standards so that holding a B.A. without any teacher preparation qualifies that person to teach in a public school. With regard to teachers, we are in desperate straits.

To those students under my care who have chosen to pursue teaching over other careers, I feel exceedingly grateful and highly responsible. Viewing identity development as central, making selves the point in teacher education programs, is a way of supporting and validating these aspiring teachers. This book partly represents my efforts to create a world where it is not only acceptable but is laudatory to be a deeply invested teacher, to be a knowledgeable and articulate person, to feel like a fully useful and necessary citizen, and to have the respect of the nation for being committed to a life in the classroom.

CHAPTER ONE

IDENTITY AND PEDAGOGY

Getting Ready

It is a Tuesday morning at the end of August (hot, already the temperature in 80s at 9 A.M.), and soon to be the first meeting of my course Education 153: Literacy in the Content Areas. Sitting in my office (chilly, the air supercooled), rattling my papers, shifting their paper-clipped stacks into order, gathering enough 5 × 7 index cards for free-standing name plates, I imagine the room where I will teach, Peabody 311, large and bright, with movable tables that we'll arrange in a square around which we can all sit comfortably. Eyes closed, I visualize the near future.

Apart from the furniture, the other contents of this third-floor room will be a useful distraction for the students during the few extra minutes I stall, waiting for stragglers, before beginning. The room's wall shelves spill untidily with leftover out-of-date textbooks, partial sets of basal readers, and antiquated, cast off, audio-visual equipment, including filmstrip projectors that no one uses anymore. They're a novelty. Amid the litter of a different sort of educational past as a backdrop, we will enact performances of our potential teaching futures. And so standing there during those few wasted moments, I will be anxious. Inside, in the silence that precedes the words, I'll hear my pulse pounding. The easy beats I'll count slowly, not wanting to start too soon, too loudly, too urgently. In that moment of almost beginning, knowing what will surely come of working with these twenty-six college juniors, I am extremely happy.

That is what I dream as I sit expectantly in the office. My hands are calm now. There are ten minutes left before I climb two flights of stairs. The photocopied papers, in crosshatched piles, are ready to go. If I could see outside (the office is windowless), I'd spy the new students crossing the quad, heading north toward the building, or getting off the bus at the corner by the Carolina Inn, students who have high hopes that my class will act as a powerful agent to transform them into teachers.

After four years of this ritual anticipation, I now understand that students enter the room with expectations and desires that differ significantly from my own sense of what we will do and learn in the course. Because my students and I share the same goal—for them to be teachers—it was not obvious when I began teaching this course (required for all students in the secondary teacher education program), that our views of how their teaching identities were to come about differed so radically. In fact, the very notion that identities construction is the goal is something they'll discover rather than anything I can count on them knowing in any direct way at the semester's start.

They are waiting when I enter the room promptly at 9:30. In the midst of rearranging the tables and chairs, I recognize a handful of students from my other classes, Richard Lambert and Elizabeth Tavey from "English Grammar," Lauren Elkins and Donna Rogers from "Rhetoric and the Teaching of Writing." And sitting with them are Howard Dempsey and Michaela Morris, two new faces, students I will meet in a few minutes, though they're obviously English majors since they sit with the others.[1] Students unconsciously cluster together by academic discipline on that first day.[2] Without preamble, but after I introduce myself, pronounce my unpronounceable name, we begin: "Take out a piece of paper and something to write with. Now we'll write for about five minutes or so about why you're in this class— what you expect, want, or need. And after we write, then we'll talk." Every semester it's always the same. The business of staking out the territory— sharing their goals and desires, generating a steady stream of questions that I keep on turning back to the class to answer (to gauge what they know or don't know as fast as possible)—takes up most of the hour and fifteen minutes of class time. In the last five minutes, I rush to pass out the syllabus, much of which they've unknowingly intuited during the productive and engaged conversation we've just had. A few students trail me back to the office with more questions. Good, I think, persistent. With a lot to say. They'll make it as teachers.

Insisting on Identity

When they arrive in my classes, however, these students are not yet teachers. They have expressed the desire to become teachers by enrolling in a teacher education program, and I have undertaken the job of helping them get there.

But what does this goal entail? What are the implications for students? Furthermore, what educational experiences will foster the transition from student to teacher? As I stated at the beginning of this book, becoming a teacher involves the construction of a person's identity. In regard to the individuals portrayed here, this involves the transformation of their identities over time. They began the program thinking of themselves as "students" (an identity category made salient by their status as undergraduates), but by the end of the program they ought to identify themselves primarily as "teachers." My aim as their teacher is to create a curriculum that promotes this identity development. But before moving onto pedagogical issues, I'd like to define what I mean by identity and describe in theoretical terms what the process of identity development looks like. In subsequent chapters, these assertions and theories about identity will be explained, critiqued, and modified as my students tell their stories.

Here is my claim: becoming a teacher means that an individual must adopt an identity as such. I take this strong position—insisting on identity—because the process of teaching, at once so complicated and deep, involves the self. One way of approaching this task—that of imagining themselves differently—is to ask students to develop personal theories of action—how they might act if they were teachers. Experienced teachers develop theories of action (which Gail McCutcheon describes as "sets of beliefs, images, and constructs" about people, learning, and knowledge) through practice (1992, 191). Encouraging students to create these action theories before they've had the opportunity to practice in the field has several benefits. First, they realize that teaching is complicated and that it is a generative process. Second, they are able to feel how theory and practice are yoked together. Without much effort, they can see why they must link the methods they adapt to their beliefs. Finally, proposing theories of action forces students to integrate the whole range of variables involved in any teaching situation rather than operating from one perspective alone.

Teaching is a complex and delicate act. It demands that teachers analyze the situation, consider the variables of students, texts, knowledge, abilities, and goals to formulate an approach to teaching, and then to carry it out—every day, minute to minute, within the ever-shifting context of the classroom. It requires having empathy for students, a knowledge of one's field, a sense of how learning occurs, the ability to generate a practice out of an idea, and the power to evaluate instantaneously whether it's going well or needs adjusting. Moreover, teaching depends on the teacher's capacity to constantly think ahead, to follow hunches, and usually, on top of all this, to perform convincingly for an audience, sometimes lecturing but always being the leader, directing activities and managing time efficiently. To do all this well, one must inhabit the classroom as if it is the most natural place in the world. One must be tolerant of the bureaucratic and otherwise ethically compromised situation of the teacher within a school. These abilities suggest that teaching demands nothing less than identity to accomplish these tasks; this is more than just playing a role.

In her work with prospective teachers, Deborah Britzman (1991) describes the qualitative difference between achieving an identity in contrast to playing a role: "The newly arrived teacher learns early on that whereas role can be assigned, the taking up of an identity is a constant and tricky social negotiation" (54). Roles are flimsy and superficial, transitory and easily adopted or discarded. They seem to be whole and complete, like a ready-made set of clothes that one can put on before class and take off after. I wouldn't be a very good teacher if I felt I was playing a role (and neither, I believe, would my students). Identities require the commitment of self to the enterprise in a way that acting out a role does not. A teacher must rise to the occasion time after time; the self goes on the line every day.

Defining Identity

Identity is our understanding of who we are and of who we think other people are. Reciprocally, it also encompasses other people's understanding of themselves and others (which includes us). Theoretically, the concept of identity involves two notions: similarity and difference. So identities are the ways we relate to and distinguish individuals (and groups) in their social relations with other individuals or groups.

Of course identities can never be unified or fixed; they are always in flux, always multiple and continually under construction. Yet this doesn't mean that selves don't exist or are unrecognizable; there are moments and conditions of coalescence. First, we have real physical bodies and we often experience our consciousness as unitary and existing inside the body. Second, others react to and recognize us as individuals, not only by how we look but also by who we are depending on the context. So while identities are constructed through social interaction, identities (realized as the "I" of the self) are attached to individuals and their physical bodies. Furthermore, no one has only a single identity. Every person is composed of multiple, often conflicting, identities, which exist in volatile states of construction or reconstruction, reformation or erosion, addition or expansion. The bottom line is that no matter what the context, we are continually engaged in becoming something or someone.[3] So how do identities develop?

The Role of Discourse

Individuals are constituted subjects; their identities are produced through participation in discourse. As active participants in a variety of discourses, individuals have agency to shape selves. On the other hand, discourses (and all other participating individuals) affect the development of those identities. Identities then are the result of dynamic interplay between discursive processes that are internal (to the individual) and external (involving everyone else). The sociologist Richard Jenkins describes identity as "a practical accomplishment, a process" the direct result of the "dialectical interplay of processes of internal and external definition" (1996, 25). In concrete terms, this means that students are making themselves into teachers, for example, by taking education courses, and that students are being made into teachers by virtue of the effect these courses have on them. It is the interplay of internal and external forces in the midst of social interaction that allows for the construction of identities.

By discourse I am referring to the "ways in which language functions in specific social or institutional contexts and on the social and ideological relations which are constructed in and through language" (Williams 1983, 39). Discourse, which is manifested through language, consists of a system of beliefs, attitudes, and values that exist within particular social and cultural practices. Engaging in these language practices (such as conversing, analyzing, writing reports) shapes an individual's identity. Discourses are powerfully constructive of identities because they are inherently ideological. Many discourses are multiple and simultaneous; at any one time an individual can be involved in many different discourses. Discourses are not only various; they are also hierarchical. Sometimes participation in one discourse conflicts with or counteracts membership in another. In some instances, individuals have the opportunity to choose between competing discourses. These choices have significant ramifications in terms of identity. In addition, some discourses carry greater social value and prestige compared with others. Thus, identity development depends on social interaction through engagement in multiple discourses.

The concept of identity then has several dimensions, one aspect having to do with a single person—individual identity—and the other with groups—collective identity (Jenkins 1996). For instance, being a teacher is certainly an identity I would claim for myself. Inside, I believe I am a teacher. Fortunately, in my daily life at the university, others—students, staff, and colleagues—also see and react to me as a teacher. Both these pressures—from the inside out and from the outside in—act in concert to build and sustain my identity as a teacher. Others make me even as I'm in the act of making myself. Thus, Jenkins suggests that the entity we refer to as our "self" is an "ongoing, and, in practice, simultaneous synthesis of (internal) self-definition and the (external) definitions of oneself offered by others" or, in other words, "the internal-external dialectic of identification [is] the process whereby all identities—individual and collective—are constituted" (25). Both dimensions of identity evolve as prospective teachers go through the teacher education program. In describing the identity development of the students who are the center of this book, I will show how certain contexts and practices (for instance, composing a philosophy of teaching) promote the individual dimension while other situations and persons (for instance, the teaching practicum) contributes to the collective aspect of a teaching identity.

If my job is to help others *become* teachers, and if I regard being a teacher as an identity, then I have to understand how identities are formed so that I can create through my teaching in a conducive atmosphere. I am acutely self-conscious that discourse is simultaneously a set of practices to be taught, a medium of instruction, and the very material substance out of which identities arise. Given that the internal and external dialectical processes of identification construct identities, then what would an effective teacher education program look like? What kind of pedagogy could we employ at the university that would in fact promote these identification processes?

The Secondary Teacher Education Program

At UNC Chapel Hill, the program to certify high school teachers consists of a series of six courses taken during a student's junior and senior years of undergraduate study in the School of Education.[4] In addition, at the same time, students are completing an academic major in an appropriate field such as mathematics or English. Besides a semester-long teaching practicum (in everyday speech referred to as "student teaching"), in their senior year students take courses in learning theory and adolescent development, in social foundations of education, and in methods, which includes a course called Literacy in the Content Areas. It was the initial and continuing challenge of teaching this course that was my original impetus for writing this book.

The purpose of the literacy course is to introduce future high school teachers to concepts about learning and literacy along with techniques and methods for enhancing literacy in their students no matter what the subject area, whether it be mathematics, English, or biology. (The rationale for the course—designed long before I started teaching it—grew out of theoretical

and practical concerns similar to those underlying the writing-across-the curriculum movement.) Literacy was very broadly defined to include traditional
conceptions—reading and writing—and extends to encompass broader notions such as computer literacy, cultural literacy, content literacy (strategies to
acquire knowledge in a discipline), and literate thinking (the ability to think
analytically about information). With this knowledge, for example, students
were supposed to integrate literacy-enhancing activities and practices into a
month-long unit of study in their discipline that included daily lesson plans
(a course project).

When I first taught the course some six years ago, I assumed students
would be receptive to knowledge and methods they could *use* as teachers. (All
the students enrolled in this class are undergraduate Education majors, mostly
juniors, who will be certified high school teachers by the time of college graduation.) But I discovered that students had difficulty connecting to information
or focusing on methods because they were grappling with the whole notion of
becoming teachers in the first place. In response to their reactions, I began slowly
to recast this course, focusing more on the process of teaching, subsuming the
content and methods as means not ends, with the result that students learned
more. On course evaluations, they rated these process-oriented activities as
more "relevant," "satisfying," and "interesting" compared with the ratings of activities by their peers in prior semesters.

When I began to reflect about how and why I was changing my approach
in the course, the answer pointed in the direction of identity (something I
called "self" at first). It seemed that knowing information, techniques, or strategies that enabled students to "pass" as teachers was not enough to calm their
fears or to lessen their anxieties about who they were at the moment and how
long it would be before they felt they were (as they often put it) "truly teachers."
Besides this course in the School of Education, I was also regularly teaching
two others required for the English education majors: English 31: Rhetoric and
the Teaching of Writing, and English 36: English Grammar. This meant that
I became well acquainted with the English education majors in particular,
many of whom took all three courses with me (although other faculty also offered them). I noticed how dramatically students changed their attitudes and
ideas about teaching from one course to another. This longitudinal contact enabled me to see more clearly the dilemmas and issues that preoccupied them as
their education progressed.

With an eye toward improving my teaching, I decided to take a closer
look. This resulted in the design of a formal study based on observations and
interviews that would entail studying a small group of students while they
were enrolled in the teacher education program and following them for at least

one year after graduation. In the spring of 1996, I solicited students who were English-education majors to participate in the study.[5] Six agreed. Of this group, by the time of graduation, Rick and Lauren had taken three of my courses, Donna and Elizabeth two, while Howard and Michaela had taken only one—the literacy course—which they all took together that spring.[6] (The participants will be reintroduced in detailed profiles in Chapter Two.)

The Idea of Pedagogy

At the time I began the study, it was clear that no amount of methods, tactics, or everyday support and encouragement ("You'll do just fine!") would be forceful enough to resolve my students' questions about who they were and who they were going to become—questions of identity. Furthermore, certain aspects of their "selves" (as they described them, such as being a Christian or being gay), affected, influenced, interacted with, and conflicted with their attempts to become a teacher, to develop a professional identity.

During the three years of working with prospective teachers, I had become increasingly intrigued with the process of identities construction and wondered whether one pedagogy or another might create classroom climates where identities could flourish. Preparing teachers was a significantly different long-term goal for me as an instructor compared to previous courses I had taught at other institutions, for instance, where I attempted to make students better writers. Though I didn't know exactly what I was searching for, it was during my first semester of teaching courses for education majors that I started closely attending to how I taught my classes.

While I reflected on both the good and bad days, it was invariably the classes that did not go as well as I had hoped that absorbed my attention. No matter the thousands of hours spent satisfactorily teaching, one poor class made me question my abilities to pull off whatever activities I had planned and compelled me rethink the convictions that lay at the heart of my practice. Some days were mentally easier to fix than others. Sometimes with small, practical adjustments in mind for next time (like tweaking the groups to capitalize on heterogeneity or writing in class every fifteen minutes or so to trace how opinions coalesce) I would finally believe that things might go better tomorrow. However, on particularly knotty days, my critiques lasted longer and went farther. The bad day I would evaluate in light of the week or month—how's it going generally? I might consider broader goals—what was the point of group work? It was a neat idea, but did it affect the class the way I had imagined it would? I tried more experiments and simultaneously invited extra feedback "in the moment" from students through short reaction pieces written in class.

Mainly, though, I kept asking students what they wanted more of and why, all the while keeping track of my reactions to their requests. Which ones did I resist? On what topics did I agree? What happened when I talked about my responses to their requests in class? After a lot of analysis I discovered something.

At the crux of large and small defeats lies the impulse to theorize, to reflect on what happened and to make provisions for changing or adjusting things in the future. I had been involved in the secondary teacher education program for about a year before the real and impossible reason students were taking my classes surfaced. They were soon to be in classrooms teaching and they had to learn to become teachers. I inquired about other courses. "Oh, you're not supposed to worry about that," one of my colleagues told me outright, "Just make sure they know about jigsaw grouping before they get to my class."

Nevertheless, I continued to be much engaged with my students' concerns even though paying serious attention to pedagogy seemed neither easy nor attractive as a line of research to many faculty (and was perhaps even dangerous pursuit for an untenured professor). As bell hooks remarks in *Teaching to Transgress*, "Most of us are not inclined to see discussion of pedagogy as central to our academic work and intellectual growth" (1994, 204). For me, it was a powerful draw, that process of thinking theoretically, inventing activities, and trying them out the next time in class. In short order, things changed. In my classes students were talking and writing more, which I regarded as a positive turn. More often than not the designated seventy-five minutes sped by. There were even occasions when no one noticed that time was up for the day; we just kept on rolling. Once two other faculty members curious about my teaching (I talked about nothing else in the hallways) casually dropped in to check out one of my classes but no one (including me) noticed because we were so involved with each other (that day—working in small groups, sharing and critiquing writing-to-learn activities designed the night before). Afterward, I was teased, but not unkindly, about my intense involvement.

Over time, after I reflected on what worked and what didn't in my classes, and in response to the reactions I received from students, I came to believe that pedagogy, when it's good, means everything. In the broadest terms, good pedagogy means putting into practice one's theories about learning and teaching. It requires teachers to conceive of and to structure their classrooms as social settings that promote interaction and to invent activities that invite students' deepest engagement. Pedagogy is absolutely not synonymous with methods, a collection of decontextualized practices described as a series of steps that can be handed from one teacher to another like so many tools in a kit. Mariolina Salvatori, in a book that traces its history, defines pedagogy as "an always already interconnected theory and practice of knowing, that in order to be effective must 'make manifest' its own theory and practice by continuously reflecting on and deconstructing it" (1996, 7). The best pedagogy gets its shape and force from its theoretical roots: a teacher puts what she knows into practice while considering the material conditions and needs of her students. Then begins the cycle of reflection and reconception. Teaching is an act that once started is never over.

Proposing a Pedagogy

As a matter of course, I keep an informal record of what works and what doesn't in my classes so I can revise assignments and activities in subsequent semesters based on students' reactions. These notes were especially important during the first several years of teaching new courses in teacher education. One project that appeared frequently in my notes (and went through many iterations as a result) involved students writing their philosophies of teaching. It was a project that started on the very first day (though students did not at first perceive that activities such as focused-freewriting would turn into something as formal as a philosophy) and was finished on the day of the final exam. One innovation that made a huge improvement was my stipulation that anything they proposed in their philosophy had to be explicitly connected and apparent in their integrated units designed to teach specific content, e.g. American literature. Or, to imagine the task another way, I insisted that their instructional designs couldn't just be a collection of neat activities no matter how clever or appealing. Instead, everything they planned had to be motivated by a rationale, and there had to be a logic to the progression of the unit from one activity, one day, one week to the next. Doing a good job meant that a person reading someone's instructional plans should be able to intuit the philosophical beliefs of the teacher who designed it.

As I mentioned, this interweaving of activities throughout the semester improved the basic quality of both unit designs and teaching philosophies in general, but it had even more significant outcomes. Many of these prospective teachers developed a sense that there are such things as overarching principles of learning, development, and pedagogy. Furthermore they realized that once understood, these principles could be reliably called upon to figure out what to teach and how to teach it—no matter what the conditions, the characteristics of the students, or the nature of the academic content. Those students who caught on to this idea and the process became more confident and better at sizing up the formidable task of teaching during the practicum the following semester. And later, after enough time had passed for some students to have begun teaching, when they returned for a visit, I was able to see that the idea of the overarching principle—ones they had devised personally and individually—was something they held on to because it had actually helped them to teach.

But my understanding of what was going on with my teaching is the result of hindsight, the product of a great deal of note-taking and written reflection; I wanted to know what worked and why. These were the questions that mattered. The folders of teaching notes grew. Then one day, because of a teaching award, I was asked to write a description of the literacy course and what amounted to a teaching philosophy. This context forced self-conscious analysis (something else I learned). It was in the act of doing almost the same task I had devised for my students that I became aware of underlying theoretical principles and their power, about those I was relying on and why. When I read back though my notes, the connections between activities and their origin in a guiding principle became apparent. What I had previously done unconsciously could now be more widely applied, and the process itself could be made explicit and offered to students. A whole world opened: I could create many different open-ended structures based on a single theoretical idea (i.e., that certain contexts engender articulation). Each contained the latent possibility of encouraging students to learn whatever they needed in order to become teachers.

The six students who participated in this study (in addition to those students who enrolled in my classes and who by virtue of their presence affected my thinking) provide both evidence and testimony for what I have learned.[7] Thus, I end this book with a proposal that describes a set of principles (ten in all) that, taken together, constitute a pedagogy for identities construction. They include discourse richness and openness, dialogue and a dialogic curriculum, collaboration, deliberation, reflexivity, theorizing in practice, agency, recursive representation, authority, and enactment.

The principles of pedagogy comprise two categories: structural principles (the first five) and performative principles (the last five). Principles such as "dialogue" or "collaboration" refer to the way the social environment of the classroom is structured, designed or arranged, as well as to the nature of interactions that occur there. Principles such as "agency" and "authority" refer to individuals and their actions or performances as well as to the implications of action in particular social settings. For instance, we can promote our students' sense of themselves as teachers in classrooms where the mode of interaction is dialogic (as opposed to monologic) and where agency is valued, i.e., students' participation is meaningful and their behavior has consequences.

All principles depend on the theoretical notion that discourses themselves and everyday discursive practices are what construct selves and fashion identities. Obviously, the concepts are not my inventions. In proposing this pedagogy, I have assembled a collection of well-known ideas or theories and suggested their usefulness for teachers whose goal is to develop their students' identities. Although the pedagogy has its roots in my work with prospective teachers, it has broad applications. These principles can be used by any teacher in postsecondary education to derive practices for teaching in the service of whatever identities are at issue, whether that be historian, writer, competent citizen, or teacher. Moreover, since developing identities or becoming persons who are active and effective agents is the real point of a college education, this pedagogy may appeal directly to college and university faculty in all disciplines.

The flexibility of this pedagogy lends it great power. The principles are entirely open-ended. They concern the process of teaching and are meant to generate the overall structure and the interactional dynamics of classroom life, not to describe curriculum per se or define academic course content. Teachers may build an individualized pedagogy around one or more principles, any of which are transformative. Combining several principles (all ten are not necessary) intensifies and magnifies their effects.

For now, however, my explanation and development of this pedagogy must remain necessarily abstract with the promise of satisfying all curiosities about theory by the end of the book. Instead, I would like to refocus attention on the heart of the matter. What happens to students who enter a teacher education program with the goal of becoming a teacher?

REFLECTIONS

Rapture

Hurrying in front of Greenlaw, the English department building, to cross the quad, get to my car after a quick trip in to check mail, fax a draft to a colleague, and pick up some library books left inadvertently on my desk, I see Jason, a student from last spring a year ago, who has just finished student teaching (high school English), now finally a graduating senior. "Hey, Dr. Danielewicz," he calls out. I stop, check my long steps, shake my shoulders to relieve the weight of my bag of books. He opens his arms, saying "Can I give you a hug." "Sure," and I hug him back. "How's it going this semester? Everyone has really missed you, since you're not teaching, especially grammar." "Yeah, I know. Sorry. And I'm afraid I won't be teaching next year since I'll be director of the writing program." "You're not teaching at all?" he asks. "Well, no, I'll be teaching some class, but I don't yet know what. We're changing the secondary program entirely so there's no more Ed 153." "Oh," he says, "That's too bad. It was such a great class."

I flashback to Jason in class on a day when students designed "writing centers" for their peers. He's sitting in the back of the room, in a small circle of desks, three others with him, and he's got them holding tight to a small branch he's brought to class, their eyes closed, while he reads aloud—nature poems by Frost, essays by Thoreau. Afterward, the students write about how their sensory experience interacted with their interpretations of the literature Jason has read to them. The little group in their concentrated activity did appear to transcend at least place (a dirty, dingy, cluttered room, full of leftover books, odd chairs and tables) if not time, physical bodies, philosophical biases, and whatever else.

Suddenly I realize Jason is standing there expectantly, waiting for me to say something. "What's that you're wearing?" I ask, pointing to a scrap of dark purple ribbon, folded into a loop with tails, pinned to his shirt. "Oh, that's to show solidarity. It's Women's Week and there will be a march and rally tonight." Jason's shirt is tie-dyed, his long hair is caught up in a big, round crocheted cap that sags in the back like a tired, rainbow-colored chef's poof. The hat rims his face, top to bottom; the prominence of his forehead, so unobstructed, reminds me of a baby's face, how, looking at an infant, we are struck by the fact that a person's eyes do occupy the midposition, not upper third, of their face, halfway between chin and hairline. He looks vulnerable.

I wonder how he made it through student teaching. I wonder if I was a good teacher. I wonder if the class helped him to be a teacher, or whether it was just fun relative to the other required courses, or whether he learned anything of significance. I think about hugging him, how easily he asked and how comfortably I complied, about how many students I've hugged (mostly at graduation), about the crowd of his friends who stand a few feet away on the upper terrace watching us. In their jeans, braids, hats, and beads, they're unlike the majority of other UNC students, those who look "straight" or "preppy," though most students do not come from prep schools or from privileged families. To signify their aspirations perhaps, they wear clothes that come from catalogs, J. Crew or Tweeds, and name brand polo shirts, Tommy Hilfiger and Ralph Lauren. In this respect, Jason was a minority student in my class. But he liked the class, and so did the others. I want to know why.

What kind of a teacher am I? Why am I different? What do they see in me? Student evaluations done for institutional purposes are not very revealing on this subject. My own appraisal of what comes through in my teaching goes something like this: I am a romantic, prone to fusions of thought and feeling, to rapture even, certain there is more to life than has been presented, even though such details and situations as I can apprehend appear perfectly solid and without anything missing. The poet Adrienne Rich says that "sensual vitality is essential to the struggle for life"; this truth I live. My classroom is not immune from my personality, nor from the characters of my students who diversely and deliberately inhabit its space.

When I walk into class, what's real—the chairs and tables, the students themselves—is not what occupies my attention. Rather I'm drawn by what has yet to happen, about what might happen once things are stirred into motion. On good days, I lose myself in the action, listening to what students are saying, joining a small group designing a lesson, revising the second activity of the day since students are engrossed still in the first. I imagine that what we are doing now might someday be happening then, in another classroom, theirs, each of them teachers. I foresee what is conceivable. Not in reality, for I am no psychic, but in theory. Because, more than anything else, the whole time I'm there, I act as if I am seeing possibilities. This imaginary envisioning energizes me and my students, bringing to life the time and place of the classroom.

CHAPTER TWO

Aspiring Teachers

A Teacher's Past

It was almost accidental circumstances (familial entanglements and professional temptation) that led me to become so deeply invested in teacher education. In graduate school, I had been trained as a linguist to conduct educational research in the field of rhetoric and composition, with an emphasis on the teaching of writing. My first real academic job was at a small college in upstate New York, in the English department, where I invented curriculum and taught in the undergraduate writing program. To be a writing teacher is to exist as a member of the lowest academic caste. Often, people think of language, especially written language, as a mere tool, a skill to acquire, an instrument to be used to accomplish other tasks. Thus, teaching writing can be a challenging and often thankless job. But its difficulty and complexities can also be engrossing, and I found myself fascinated by the troubles that writing posed to proficient speakers. Furthermore, I discovered that I was good at helping students become writers; accomplishment added satisfaction and pleasure to the process of teaching.

One particular insight made me successful: Students found it easier to write, and so wrote more and eventually improved, in classroom environments where writing was real. When writing mattered, it was difficult to imagine the result as mere rehearsal. When students had something to say, the writing process made sense: If at first one wrote to discover a position or list evidence, then a second go-round was obviously necessary to shape the piece into a form that convinced the reader. Creating a communication-based classroom, where writing is everything, turned out to be feasible. For me, this was powerful and widely applicable knowledge. Not only is classroom context malleable, but it is also incredibly consequential in terms of what and how students learn—regardless of the discipline being taught.

This idea migrated with me when several years later I found myself moving from a small private college in the Northeast to a large state university in the South to take up a position split between English and education. The differences between these two institutions and what I was asked to accomplish were as vast as the geographical distinctions between Rochester, New York, and Chapel Hill, North Carolina. Whereas everyone in my first twelve-member English department had routinely taught writing in one form or another, I was now a member of two departments, each composed of over fifty faculty, where it was primarily the role of graduate students to teach the undergraduates to write.

As faculty, I was expected to instruct the graduate students to become effective writing teachers, and I was also assigned undergraduate courses related to the certification of high school English teachers. I remember just after the move in early August of that year, unpacking my books into a new office, scanning the titles to arrange them conveniently, piling as usual the writing books low on the shelves. A thought suspended the motion of my uplifted arm. In my hand was Donald Murray's *A Writer Teaches Writing*, a blue-covered and dog-eared book, one of my favorites. I saw through this arranging what had happened. These, I realized, are no longer the books I will be reaching for because I had become someone else: a teacher of teachers.

As it happens (or perhaps it is my urgency to forge such a connection that makes it so), writing and teaching are both processes that involve selves-under-construction. What I had learned about fostering writers could be applied, I imagined, to developing teachers. Writing and teaching both entail an investment of self, and neither transition occurs spontaneously or without extensive feedback and social interaction. And though I wasn't certain at the time, I hoped that my prospective teachers would be as responsive to classroom context (if I could devise an appropriate one) as my novice writers had proven to be.

Moreover, I was not without other resources. A second conviction about learning and teaching remained strong and clear: Language in its many forms is determining. As individuals, we use language to represent thought and to make meaning, but language is not an individual's universe since it exists exclusively in a social context. Its form is derived through interaction between individuals. A discourse community is constituted and its members identified by those who "speak the same language." Our common linguistic practice generates both tools (syntax or rhetorics) and users (writers and speakers), both communities and persons. This reciprocal action— that we make language and language engages us—determines what gets learned, how much, and by whom. Participating in multiple discourses, as we all do simultaneously, (on the streets, in classrooms, at home, in churches) alters not only the individual but also the social communities within which we are always situated.

Newcomer

The classroom is a familiar and comfortable place; I am at home there. I entered my first class at the University of North Carolina with the usual curiosity about whom I would find seated before me, anticipating what my students might make of me, their professor, a newcomer about whom no underground gossip had yet accumulated. The differences (compared to the homogeneity of the small, private institution I had just left) were obvious, some immediately so, like the sound and patterns of students' speech which represented a wide range of regional, national, and international varieties of English.

Other distinctions were not immediately observable but instead palpable. I could sense these underlying qualities but I could not see them. How would I get a better view of my students, how would these differences be manifested, what bearing would they have on my teaching? It seemed to me that these were questions about identity and its formation, issues that became apparent because of the diversity between the New York and North Carolina students. In the ever-constant process of identity construction, it is the ways that we are like and unlike others that make and mark our identities as individuals.

On the first day of any class I teach, I survey the group before me, making superficial judgments about who they are, discriminations that will be refined and changed as I get to know them better. I greet them initially as students and by default as members of the university community. Other identity dimensions are less readable but nonetheless active and present; of these I try to be constantly appraising. Each student occupies regional and national positions; every one of them exhibits gendered behavior which may or may not be conventionally consistent with visible physical characteristics; their sexual preferences (while often private) exist nonetheless and affect their personas; all have grown up as members of racial and/or ethnic groups their relation to which is not reliably observable; many profess religious affiliations; each person exists in a matrix of familial connections, immediate or widely branching: child, grandchild, sibling, niece or nephew, wife or husband—sometimes parent or even grandparent; they have all been shaped by the social class background and economic conditions of their families. These existing identities affect, influence, interact with, and often conflict with an individual's attempt to become a teacher, to develop a professional identity.

Six Students

It is undoubtedly a cliché to say that individuals are distinctive. But in the world of education we need to be reminded of this basic truism—that every person is unique and responds differently and unpredictably to events (even the same events) in the world. There's plenty of evidence to suggest that in educating groups of students we lose sight of just how important individual differences are. For instance, in designing courses and curriculum (and teacher education programs are no exception), we typically create one structure of tasks and expect similar responses from our students, no matter how wide-ranging their abilities or interests are. But after working several years in the field of teacher education I became more and more interested in how individuals reacted to my courses and less concerned with how the class in general rated my teaching (which is how I had always previously judged my effectiveness as a teacher). This shift in my attention occurred because I realized what really mattered was not the short run—whether students had learned anything by the end of the semester—but rather the long view: did they actually seek jobs as teachers after graduation? Were they sure enough of themselves as teachers to survive the initial challenges of real jobs?

To find out, I conceived this project; it focuses closely on six students to trace their development through the teacher education program and to understand the choices each ultimately made after graduation. All six were generous participants who, once they had consented to join the study, agreed to many hours of taped interviews, shared their journals, teaching philosophies, unit plans, and other written materials. They also permitted me visit them during school placements and stayed in touch with me through letters, phone calls, and visits for more than a year after graduation. Allow me to introduce them.

Howard Dempsey

Howard fidgets in the chair across from me, hooks one ankle to the opposite knee. The chair's arms confine him as he talks rapidly during the interview, shifting his weight from side to side with each burst of speech. His words come easily, giving me a chance to listen instead of needing to plan the next question. "I'm from Person County," he explains, "the northeast corner of North Carolina near the Virginia state line." He regards the place where he grew up as "a strange mix, a real rural town, but it does have a college." Apart from two or three gas stations, the Hardee's, and a block-long remnant of Main Street with one remaining restaurant—Joe's Grill, open for lunch only—the town exhibits few signs of prosperity. A paper mill between

Murfreesboro and the next town over, plus peanut, tobacco, and now soybean farming, support most of the families who live there. But not Howard's. What I learn about his family makes his arrival at the university not in the least surprising: "Both my parents teach college English. My sister is a math teacher now at my old high school. Both my parents swear they did not want us to ever do this . . . that we should have noticed that they had no hours for anything and no money to go anywhere . . . but that's what I was going to do . . . get a Ph.D. in English."

However, Howard entered the university with a teaching fellowship, one that stipulated working in the public schools. After briefly considering an environmental science major, he "somehow got sidetracked into English" where he found himself "happy to go to classes here and just read for the sake of reading, of learning and talking about the literature." At twenty-one, a senior, Howard is preparing to become a high school English teacher. He wears a beard, favors tee-shirts printed with images of literary figures (like the one of Shakespeare he is in today), professes fascination for American literature and history (especially the period of Westward migration), and is writing an honors thesis on the film *My Private Idaho*.

When he talks about books, it is clear that Howard's intellectual commitments are serious and pleasurable, yet he believes his temperament—easygoing, patient, relaxed, a self-proclaimed comic and game-playing enthusiast—orients him in other directions: "I'd actually want to work with toddlers. I've decided that is a gift I have or something. I am going to try high school for a while . . . for some reason the idea of teaching has always appealed to me." Judging from appearances or even knowing the serious Howard in an academic setting, it might be difficult to visualize him connecting with small children. But he is right. One night at my house, the semester's end potluck dinner, Howard spent his time entertaining my children, inventing a personality and voice for my five-year-old daughter's stuffed dog and inviting everyone to construct and perform an oral dialogue. After this performance (not to mention the Americana trivia game he made up along with my nine-year-old history-besotted son), the kids begged thereafter to have that "big guy Howard" invited back.

Although he expresses a desire (to work with toddlers) that conflicts directly with his intended future (as a high school teacher), there is nothing insubstantial, contradictory, or confused about Howard. He lives comfortably with contradiction at one level because he is certain on another. Regardless of who or what he teaches, Howard knows he's capable of being a teacher. When I ask what makes him well suited to teaching, he replies: "Fairness. I can be really fair, really patient with people. And then just generous. Or hopefully a generous attitude giving time, giving energy." "Why

English?" I inquire. Howard says simply, "I have a love for literature that I want to share. An infectious love. I want to show people why English is important. Literature is just such an all-encompassing realm. You have all of humanity put into it."

Elizabeth Tavey

At the end of her senior year, the semester following student teaching, Elizabeth wrote an autobiographical and ethnographic account of her attempt to be a whole language teacher. She concluded with the following idea: "To be successful, teachers must decide what they wish to accomplish as teachers, what their goals are, and finally, they must determine how they are to teach. The method must stem from the underlying tenets of a teacher's inner self and be congruent with what he or she believes about the world and life. Otherwise, it will be just that, a method to be followed, not creed to be lived."

By the time Elizabeth formulated this conclusion, I knew that these forceful words stemmed in part from the experience of her teaching practicum in a small town high school, apprenticed to (in her view) a conservative and egocentric older male teacher who was openly hostile to her philosophical stance, to what he called her "progressive and liberal ideology." However, Elizabeth's call for integrity as the root of tolerance eloquently represents her person. Even sitting in the back of a classroom crowded with academically gifted undergraduates (as she was at our initial encounter), Elizabeth attracted my attention. She spoke with authority, a quality that struck me immediately when she answered a question in my English grammar course. Though its source was unknown to me, I was impressed by her possession of voice, an astuteness that I wished all students could develop.

Later, when I had the chance to ask Elizabeth how she became an English education major, she replied: "I'm definitely not someone who has known from the time they were able to dress up and play teacher that they wanted to. There are so many people like that and when I'm around them I question how you can be really that certain about something that's so difficult and so complex. And so I'm not that."

More than a year prior to the interviews, Elizabeth had sought me out to discuss how she felt differently from other students: "Writing is what matters to me. Can you be interested in language without being a teacher? Writing," she said, "is about the only way to discover what you're thinking. It helps to express things on paper." She returned to this theme later. In contrast to writing in high school, where "there was an absence of thinking and an absence of authority and ownership," some writing projects in college made her feel that her thinking was "legitimate." She realized "that no matter what you are writing, whether it's a poem or an essay, if it doesn't come from inside, it's not going to be good. If it's something that's imposed on you, it's not worthless, but it's not good writing."

Though it's typical for students to seek faculty mentoring, Elizabeth was direct about her search for a female role model. She had grown up in Winston-Salem, N.C., had one sister and a great father—but her mother had died of cancer when Elizabeth was fourteen. Though I could not read all the ways Elizabeth had been affected by her mother's death, clearly she had not given in to devastation. The person I saw across the office was a determined and deeply resolved young woman, nearly six feet tall, with blond hair to her waist, and the posture to intimidate (should it be necessary) even the strong among us.

Donna Rogers

Donna has a question that she asks everyone. Her manner gentle, her voice subdued to a whisper, her eyes wide and dark: these traits add urgency to the words and alert her listeners to take care in replying. The question, somewhat elaborated, comes to me on a tiny greeting card written in minute script (orange ink) with a bag of cookies, which she leaves at my office door in thanks for a letter of recommendation. "Dr. Danielewicz, how does your philosophy of life complement your philosophy of teaching? Have you identified your purpose in life? Is it well defined? You know my love for you compels me to wonder about your relationship with God. Do you believe He exists? If so, do you commune with Him? How?" Though she is not there to hear my answer, I say out loud, "I'm an atheist, Donna!" (But I do have a mission, a secular desire to teach without holding back, as if my work counts, as if words pronounced in a classroom have the potential to change everything or even anything).

Our first discussion on the topic of God had occurred some months prior and was at my invitation: "Please come to my office, Donna. There's something we need to talk about." As a public institution, the University of North Carolina and its faculty are bound by the U.S. Constitution's insistence on the separation of church and state. Whatever my religious beliefs, I am forbidden to proselytize about religion in class when performing my role as instructor, a paid employee of the state. Donna, in preparing to become a public high school teacher, needed to understand and abide by this edict.

While certain Donna is aware of this issue, I was unclear, after receiving her first writing assignment concerned with influential teachers, about how and where she positioned herself. Her paper began, "When considering how God could possibly use my life to expand His kingdom, I am reminded of two high school English teachers." Did Donna know what constituted an open profession of faith? Did she draw the line in the same place others would? My concern arose less from ideological vehemence than from personal uneasiness and a desire to protect her: I did not want her to be reprimanded or possibly dismissed for what she might say or do while teaching.

Despite a demure appearance and quiet mannerisms that invoke her teachers' protective instincts, Donna doesn't need any more or less guardianship than any other twenty-year-olds instructing teenagers. Her student teaching supervisor (an older male professor) came to me worried about her choice of placement. Donna had requested a Durham high school, one serving an inner-city population where drug busts, drive-by shootings, and juvenile arrests are daily events, almost to the point of their being unremarkable. Sensing he'd been taken in by a first, false impression of her vulnerability, I shook my head in disagreement, "Don't worry about Donna," I told him, "She's got a core of steel and a disposition that in the end will prevail."

The first week of student teaching Donna reports feeling "tremendously blessed," describes her cooperating teacher as "phenomenal" and "on fire." She says about her seniors: "They are called 'average' but they are not . . . they are really tough. We've only been in school for three days, and I've already had to break up fights. I have to be prepared to be tough because that is what is required. It will just take some artfulness in knowing how to reach them." Artfulness! She both amazes and convinces me with this assessment, and I think her success will stem partly from this same source. Her students will be so surprised by her actions and novel responses that they'll be interested in spite of themselves, wondering what she'll say or do next.

Richard Lambert

Even to native North Carolinians used to locally distinct linguistic styles, Rick's dialect—the rhythm and intonation of his speech—surprises and charms. The first question I asked him myself "Where are you from?" I've since heard others repeat. In response, Rick always laughs, tilts his head back and to the left as if to accommodate his widening grin, and replies, "Oh, a place you've never heard of—Woodland. In Northampton County. Northeastern North Carolina. It's toward the coast, near the Great Dismal Swamp. Know where that is?"

I do now—and know as well much about Rick's family, not only his parents, sister, but aunts and uncles too, cousins at all removes, and the girlfriend from back home (sweethearts since sixteen and going on their sixth anniversary). Long fascinated by stories ("in first and second grade") and amazed at the number that can accumulate in a single day, he tells them whenever he can. On a spring afternoon as the light coaxes early green from the trees, he comes to office hours to say thanks for a great class: "I went right home and called my mother to tell her about today." The stories keep Rick together; they bridge the miles and the cultures between the university and his home county. Also the stories cross the deepest boundaries between Rick, a white, middle-class, sweet natured boy (his own description) whose guileless naïveté so amuses people that doors open automatically ("He'll be the success story," I heard a fellow faculty member announce) and others who without these "God-given" traits, unearned tickets to success, might reasonably resent him.

Rick is thrilled by the idea of teaching, though openly nervous: "To be honest, I'm scared as hell." He starts off telling me he's "been preparing kind of mentally for the interview, trying to figure out why, I'm about a month away from student teaching, how did I get here?" A few provisional explanations proceed this response: "I believe the study of literature, of English, is one of the few liberal arts subjects that teaches you compassion. It's one of the few outlets compatible with your daily life." At first his reasons sound stiff and even contrived, but later I understand that to him they are profound.

Rick attended a private high school with a graduating class of twelve. Puzzled, because he lived in a barely populated rural county with parents of moderate income, I ask why. He is very intense in the telling: "I'll be honest with you. It doesn't reflect my parents' views or my views. In the late sixties when integration happened, all the white families would form a school and that's exactly how the school formed. If you look at the date, 1967, right at that time. And because the county is, I think, 86 percent black and the public high school is like 93 percent black. And that is why the school is there. The reason I went was every one of my friends in the community were going there. That was the big reason. All my parents' friends sent their children there."

Minutes after the O. J. Simpson verdict was announced, heading to class, I walked across the quad, circling the trees as usual, and threading my way among small groups of African-American students, gathering in places and in groups unlike any I had seen previously in the years I had taught at UNC. At Carolina, these students are a minority, and shamefully so; we enroll far fewer than we could considering the state population. In class on this day, Rick writes: "I see so much segregation on this campus. This 'imaginary racial wall' does not begin at Carolina, but is a microcosm of what the students have been brought up to believe and have experienced in the past. Sometimes racial boundaries are formed not by deep-rooted prejudice, but by the sheer ignorance of not knowing or understanding where the actual human being is coming from."

Michaela Morris

"Writer, actor, director . . . yes. And teacher—that too. I *am* in the teaching fellows program," Michaela explains. She sits forward in her seat and then back again, the movements changing in a syncopated rhythm with each major topic shift in conversation. She speaks eagerly and doesn't relax for a moment; pure energy, not anxiety, feeds her body's tension. As she talks, I am drawn in by her springy excitement but equally fascinated by what she says. It is habitual for Michaela to analyze everything automatically. After a single day of observing the teacher who will mentor her, Michaela describes how each of them approaches living: "I have a lot of things I want to do with my life besides being a teacher. Whereas I think Miriam Long *is* a teacher and that is what her life *is*. I think in that way we really differ because her life is teaching, whereas I will be a teacher and there will be other stuff too.

Even though her ambitions diverge—"I've been doing creative writing for the last two years . . . and I feel that that is more my calling than teaching is. But then I feel called to be a teacher as well"—Michaela gives off the impression that she will pull it off. She will shape events and interact with individuals to get everything she wants. I intend no criticism here but instead admire her insistence. It is not at others' expense but rather in conjunction with them that Michaela proceeds. Besides, the things she wants are so invariably good: "My strong point is sharing what I think and feel about reading and writing and getting students fifteen, sixteen, seventeen, eighteen years old excited about reading a book, writing a story, or writing a letter."

She confesses many difficulties, yet with such a cheery ruefulness I can't help thinking she isn't really disturbed by anything she's been asked to do or by the stressful and demanding situation of her current life: I think Miriam Long keeps trying to scare me. On Thursday we were eating lunch with this guy who's a second year teacher, and she turns and looks at me and says, 'Do you have any idea how much *work* this is?' And I said, 'Well, I have a pretty good idea it's *work* all the time.' And she said, 'You just don't look panicked enough.' So I said, 'I'm sure that will come. Trust me. I'll panic, I promise!' " Such assurance, and an ability to be an equal conversational partner, distinguishes Michaela from many of her peers in the teacher education program who approach student teaching with skepticism and even fear.

Michaela is not unaware of her distinctiveness. "I feel like a maverick, the Tom Cruise teaching fellow," she tells me when I ask about her experiences as a member of this group. (In North Carolina, high school seniors who wish to become teachers compete for generous and much sought after four-year scholarships to the university. In return, fellows are obligated to teach the same number of years in a public school or repay their scholarship, a hefty debt, after graduation.) But it is on the grounds of disliking elitism that she prides herself on being a radical. "I never felt like it was my thing. It never mattered to me especially that I was a teaching fellow and somebody wasn't. I never felt like 'Oh, I'm a teaching fellow and I should get more benefits.' But you do get a lot of perks. God, I am treated differently by administrative staff in high schools and at job fairs if they know I'm a teaching fellow." This is true, I tell her, assuring her that she will have her pick of the jobs in the spring. She laughs. Whether to agree with or to challenge my assumption about her future I'm not sure.

Lauren Elkins

Although she has been completely invested as a student at Carolina (with a high grade point average as evidence), Lauren is eager and ready to graduate. She tells me it has been easy to plan her future since teaching seemed like a natural choice for her: "I made the decision because I really enjoyed high school a lot, and I felt really comfortable there. I couldn't imagine working in an office or anything like that. I just didn't feel like that was my element. So I had some teachers who helped influence me and that I really looked up to." Other aspects of her life fell into place without complication, which is what Lauren prefers, "Simple, no fuss." She and her fiancé Mathew (also planning to teach, specializing in instructional technology) will marry the summer following graduation. They intend to move back to Lauren's hometown a little west of Charlotte and apply for jobs in the area. Already they have been buying furniture and stockpiling it at her parents' house in anticipation of having their own apartment.

"But for now," she says a month before student teaching, "I'm looking forward to getting my own classroom." Then she adds, "I've been very nervous about going into a high school because I look young. I know I look young. People tell me that all the time. And so I cut my hair and I bought these different clothes so I wouldn't look like a student, I bought a different bag to carry, not my backpack. All summer I have been preparing to go into the classroom and I went for the first time last week and they didn't see me as a student at all." She is visibly relieved. Without reservation about her career choice, Lauren is plagued by worries about how she will teach and her ability to relate to students. When she rereads her journal from my class, she finds that her writing contains "many expressions of doubt or apprehension."

Two beliefs keep her firmly anchored even through the times when she feels overwhelmed by her inner fears. First and foremost, Lauren's approach to teaching is centered on an ethic of care: "I do want to show them that I care about their lives and what's going on. I don't just want to teach my students English . . . I would like to be able to relate to them on a personal level and to help them out." One of her former teachers, her band instructor, remains in Lauren's memory the epitome of the ideal teacher. "I just loved him. He was one of those sarcastic kinds of people who can cut up with you all the time. He was down at the students' level. We didn't have to reach to find him." In contrast, she remembers being afraid of her junior English teacher while liking the class itself because it was a challenge: "I worked very hard for my A. But there was just something about her that was intimidating. She had a reputation. She went to Duke apparently and was like really brilliant. But in school, she was feared almost and had a great hold on her students." Lauren has no impulse to intimidate but rather wants to be there to help.

The other touchstone for Lauren lies in what constitutes teaching English as a discipline. By teaching skills, especially reading, writing, and even grammar, Lauren aspires to making a pragmatic contribution to her students' lives. In attempting to articulate a philosophy of teaching, Lauren arrives at the following insight: "I will not only be a teacher of writing; I will also be a teacher of living. Few, if any, of my students will become world-famous novelists. All of my students will have lives beyond the classroom. Whether they wish to be auto mechanics or analytical chemists, writing will have a place in their lives. My job is to send them off with life skills that will be relevant in any occupation."

Positions

These profiles are patchwork portraits of difference and diversity. They reflect the everyday contingencies and circumstances, the constraints and opportunities that collaborate to make a person. During the interviews, my students (as we all do) adopted a commonsense way of talking about themselves as if they were always the same person at all times, in all contexts, and in every social encounter. But we know this foundational self does not (and cannot) really exist. It is, however, a convenient and enabling fiction in our narratives, both mine and those of my students. As the cultural theorist Stuart Hall (1997) has pointed out, it is how we are represented by the positions we adopt (or are forced to adopt) at different times and places, and the social roles we play in each varying circumstance, that make us (momentarily) who we are. The next chapter shows how this theory is borne out, revealing how the different positions each student occupies at any one time and place forms the path and journey each takes toward becoming a teacher.

REFLECTIONS

Never

Elizabeth says that another teacher inspired her to consider becoming a teacher: "My senior English teacher was the first time I ever even gave teaching a thought, after I had been in her class a while and knew her outside of class." This reason—that someone in your life impressed you so much you want to be like him or her, even choose the same profession—is one my students often tell me when I ask "Why teach?" It demonstrates how teachers and teaching are dominant and powerful realities in our culture, ones that shape individuals' destinies. After all, how many of us grow up wanting to be parents because our parents were so great? It's more than luck, a gift, to have a teacher who's wonderful or impressive. And it seems specially significant that such exemplars can have so much influence. If students' stories are credible, then choosing a life as a teacher depends in large part on having had a conversion experience with a teacher.

"This, I think, is exactly what happened to me" I begin writing, confident that I'm in the thick of my story here. But the forward momentum of my words falters; my fingers stop typing. No it's not. This is not how it happened. It is yearning that motivates this story. I wanted so much to have had a teacher who recognized me and acknowledged my name as I have Elizabeth's. For the most part my teachers were uninspiring, persons memorable more for their peculiarities than for anything intellectual. My desire to teach began with envisioning teaching as something that would sustain me economically; a salary that could lift me out of the lower middle class; it was the time-honored profession that women could legitimately and easily enter. In actuality, my boyfriend (whose family was rising up through the middle class) suggested it one night as we sat in a dark movie theater waiting for the film to materialize up front. It was no big rational decision on my part; I was his girlfriend. It was not something I was really attracted to. The desire I could not voice was to be a writer, an English major at least. Certainly books were then as they are now one of my passions, but it is only now that I'm in my forties that I can say I wish to write, I am a writer, I do write. But who knew what desires lay hidden in any putative heart of hearts when only eighteen? There must have been something else besides a boy's suggestion that made me do what I did.

The Fifties

I never wanted to be a teacher. I grew up in a fifties brick split-level house, a new suburb on the edge of a pre-Revolutionary town near Philadelphia. The crescent of houses built only on the one side of the street replaced a wooded hillside and part of an apple orchard, the remains of which our house overlooked for a year or so until they built more houses. My father, a tool-and-die maker, paid hoarded-up cash for the house. He was the sort of man who did not trust his future or his money to anyone. We were subjected, my brothers and I, at the dinner table (the meal served nervously by my mother at 5:00 P.M.

on the dot every workday) to my father's stories about food shortages during the Depression and how real estate was cheap then, easily had by ready cash. Working-class immigrants, his family had lost their candy store when my father was a teenager. He managed to finish high school. Good with his hands and fond of order and precision, he found a decent factory job, skilled labor, a bench in the tool crib.

My father's skill as a machinist kept him out of World War II, making him one of the few young men left at home. Working in a munitions factory, he met my mother who was running a drill press on an assembly line producing bazooka rockets. Though she told me she refused him at first, they eventually had a wartime wedding, borrowing sugar coupons from neighbors, enough to make a wedding cake. Like everybody else after the war, they fled the city and started a family. In her smart and modern house, my mother wore aprons, hung out laundry in neat rows in our yard, cleaned, straightened, and sanitized for hours on end, encouraged us children to eat vegetables, and regulated our small lives with daily doses of vitamins and books she read aloud with great expression.

I never wanted to be a teacher. My mother, a half year ago, told me that I swore as a teenager that teaching was the last thing I wanted to do. She says this to *me*, her daughter, a middle-aged woman, a professor, a teacher. And *now*, why now? I was shocked when she recalled this adolescent disclaimer, no memory of which I can recover. My first impulse was to deny her recollection, then to question her for more details: when had I sworn myself against teaching, at what age, what was I wearing, and how often had I mentioned it?

I did none of these things. I tried to forget it. My father was two weeks away from death the day we had this conversation in my parents' bedroom, standing in front of the mahogany highboy, a place that inspired serious or intimate exchanges. I don't know why this was true, except that our efforts at this kind of talk, my mother and I, were always rushed, even furtive, short bursts of something important, an item kept alive on one or the other of our minds until the moment arrived when we found ourselves squeezed together in the two feet between the bed and the chest, both heavily carved, ornate, dark wood, much too big for the small room, and fashioned for a house of an earlier era, not their split level, modernist, brick and wrought-iron-railed suburban house. It was in getting by each other, my mother to check herself in the mirror, or me trying to make it to the doorway past her, that we'd stop to negotiate our bodies through the channel and find the words and breath to say what we'd been saving up.

CHAPTER THREE

SEEING THEMSELVES AS TEACHERS

Explaining Selves

We've been talking about an hour, sitting face-to-face in my narrow office, when I ask Michaela to describe her state of mind about teaching before taking the required courses in education. "Coming here," she begins, "I didn't know what kind of teacher I wanted to be. I knew that I loved my subject, and that I could teach it just because I care about it." Michaela's comment reveals that we don't just become someone overnight and forever. Making and living our identities involves action and process, occurs in real time and depends on our connections with others, on what we do and say, and how we feel about it. Michaela's words are passionate—love and care; in everyday encounters she is deeply and personally invested in becoming.

An identity is never fully or finally achieved; we are always actively being and becoming. As Richard Jenkins puts it, "Identity is not 'just there'; it must always be established" (1996, 4). Furthermore, creating identities is not an individual undertaking, but involves others, especially groups or collectives connected to social institutions as well as the discourses associated with them. We make our "selves" through activities and practices like classification (she is a teacher), association (I am like her), and identification (I want to be like her). Conversely, our selves are made for us through similar processes enacted by other persons, discourses, and institutions. Though individuals are not entirely autonomous and cannot simply "choose" specific identities, we do seem possessed of some agency in the matter of which identities we gravitate toward and cling to as opposed to those we ignore. And, although our different positions in the world result in our having conflicting identities, we tolerate, integrate, and balance these different selves because we could not live otherwise: "Identity gives us a location in the

world and presents the link between us and the society in which we live"
(Woodward et al, 1997, 1).

Although in theory there is no limit to the identities we might imagine,
in practice, we appear interested in a limited, though not fixed, array of possibilities. Even though individuals are distinct and different from one another,
housed as we are in separate skins, we share many of the same social positions—friend, professional, parent; we may be Jewish, a Southerner, African-
American. The identities that individuals develop within and around these
positions are culture specific and easily recognizable through the presence of
social institutions that support and perpetuate them. For example, many individuals identify themselves as teachers. Not surprisingly, there exists a rich collection of social institutions such as schools of education, teacher unions, and
the public schools that employ teachers that, along with their discursive practices, continuously construct individuals as teachers.

This is what happens in theory. But in actual lives, how do these processes
work? At the time they entered the School of Education as college juniors, what
did my students feel and believe about themselves as prospective teachers? Without a doubt, whatever my students thought about their teaching "selves" at this
stage resulted from the interaction among many factors and conditions, including
family patterns, educational histories, personal character traits, national and regional affiliations, social class background, and a lifetime of social encounters. Perhaps the one major commonality is their desire to be teachers; although, among
them, even this goal is neither uniformly defined nor similarly motivated. Each
has crafted a unique vision based on the many diverse experiences typical of everyday life, few of which at this point in their life have been especially geared toward
influencing them as teachers. Now that has changed. Their declaration to be education majors has initiated contact with an institution whose mission includes
teacher education. These students are encountering what social theorist Pierre
Bourdieu (1984) would call a new "field," a collective group or an institution that
has a material context, both a place and a space, and includes a set of symbolic resources and routine practices through which individuals make their identities.

But while becoming a teacher is the goal, the outcome is unpredictable.
Any one student occupies multiple positions simultaneously and makes different social meanings relative to the others in the same group or program. In
terms of the features that will bear significantly on their teaching lives, differences (e.g. family histories) far outweigh similarities (e.g. age, or years of education). There are few constants among the small group of six students who
were part of this study. Even the degree of contact each has had with formal
institutional structures related to teaching varies. Three (Michaela, Howard,
and Lauren) received undergraduate teaching fellowships and as a result have
been visiting or working informally in the public schools since they arrived on

campus as first-year students. The others (Rick, Elizabeth, and Donna) have had no regular or formalized opportunity to connect with schools since they arrived at the university. In regard to their formal education, all will be taking a series of six required courses. While coursework will certainly influence their evolving visions of themselves, in most ways, the program will end up being more variable than consistent. Thus when I encountered these students as they entered the secondary program, I could only speculate about whom among them would become teachers.

This chapter focuses on the period of my students' initial immersion into the institutional structures of teacher education. Later in the program, when they become interns in the public schools, the students will be subject to many intense shaping forces, ones they have hitherto not experienced while taking courses in the teacher education program. For one thing, they will enter into relationships with their mentor teachers who have considerable power when it comes to determining the fate of novice teachers. Power differentials create special problems for the interns: on the one hand, they must accept the authority of their mentor teachers, and on the other, they must develop authority in order to be teachers in their new placements. The student teaching situation is undoubtedly formative (and formidable). In this respect, school contexts are equally significant as university contexts in forming identities. However, the scope of this study does not allow for an in-depth analysis of the public school setting. My overall goal in this book is to improve the quality and type of experience students encounter while they are in the teacher education program at the university to ensure they will be more successful when they do move into school contexts.

Toward that end, this chapter explores some the personal and idiosyncratic factors that my students believe affected their fledgling identities as teachers, and it traces the interactive processes by which, according to their reports, their identities further coalesced. The first half of the chapter illuminates my students' sense of themselves as aspiring teachers, and draws on their impressions and memories of how they became attracted to the idea of teaching. The latter half considers how the School of Education both as an institution and as an affiliated group of people influenced the construction of students' identities as teachers.

Why Teach?

Deciding

My students had no hesitation in responding to questions about becoming teachers. Some claimed it was one they had been thinking about constantly. After all, they were in college, and having declared themselves education majors, and they intended to enter the world as somebody, as teachers. When I asked during initial interviews, "How did you decide to be a teacher?" one said, "It was very gradual" (accretion); another replied, "I got sidetracked into English" (accidental); "Nothing else appealed to me and nothing turned me away from it" (accommodation). Others had quite dramatic reasons: "My life plan changed" (a conversion); "I have an inner teacher just dying to get out" (personal destiny). General conditions affected some students: "I really enjoyed high school and felt comfortable there" (a good fit); "There was the Teaching Fellows scholarship" (economics). Relationships played a role: "I really looked up to some teachers" (admiration); "It was growing up around academics" (all in the family).

The responses students provided are all different; none are definitive or simple. Furthermore, these are (and can be) only partial reasons. They're certainly not the whole story. At times, I suspect these first-uttered answers; they seem so often to be automatic, unreflective responses, ones students have rehearsed by virtue of having been asked repeatedly about their postcollege futures. But the conditions of the interview—having plenty of time, being singled out, opportunity to focus, direct attention, one on one from a professor, feeling comfortable, their familiarity with me, a willingness to participate—counteracted this automaticity, allowing students to say more than the first thing that came to mind.

The longer students talked about themselves as teachers, the more intricate, interconnected, even tangled their responses became. In analyzing the transcripts I discovered that there was no easy way to categorize or reduce them into definitive answers. Such a process obscured the underlying architecture that resulted in each student's decision to teach. The interviews once transcribed resemble blueprints, sketches, musical scores in which appear rhythms, repetitions, emphatic moments, lost and rediscovered threads, patterns of argument. I was certain there was structural meaning in the coded transcripts, the sections marked with colored highlights, the scribbled margin notes, the bracketed segments connected by lines drawn from one page to another.

But what meaning emerged from the abstract marks I laid over and on top of the words? The coded transcripts did seem to be physical representations of a metaphysical process, visual portraits of each student's experiences and inclinations, the converging environments that resulted in a decision to teach. It occurred to me that identity must be something like this, a structure that results from an assembly of factors, overlaid, and overlapped. No two persons ever display the same factors (though many are shared), plus how they are assembled varies, some more tightly integrated than others, some more precious, some porous, some indestructible.

Indisputably, our identities have social origins. We come to know who we are through social relationships with others. However, since we are discrete individuals, our identities are manifested in what we regard as the self, that internal state of consciousness we refer to in everyday speech whenever we say "I." The word is simple and primary, but the way we experience the individual self is not. On the one hand, we perceive the self in daily life to be consistent over time and place (e.g. Whether I am describing myself as a child or as an adult, I refer to the same person—Jane). But, on the other hand, we know that selves change (e.g. Jane the adult is not identical to Jane the child). Thus we daily experience an evolving "I," a condition that enables us to recognize and acknowledge the self as a malleable, ongoing, and collaborative work in progress.

The self then depends on a dialectic of identification: self-definition and definition by others, both of which are necessary (Jenkins, 1996, 49–50). In becoming teachers, my students define themselves in any way that signals this emerging identity. Conversely their sense of themselves as teachers is further developed as others (teachers, parents, faculty, institutions) see them as such. The way that others respond to an individual's presentation of self is also crucial. In treating someone who wishes to be a teacher *as* a teacher (even though he or she is not yet), we acknowledge and reinforce the claim, making it more and more real for the individual who internalizes the judgments and reactions of others. Note that here I am describing a general process. There is nothing to guarantee or predict the reactions of the individual relative to feedback received from others. Negative judgments can result in positive identification with an emerging identity on the part of the individual just as well. The process—presentation of self, reaction from others, internal response—is cyclical, and affects how the individual represents him- or herself in the next encounter, thus starting a new, progressive cycle.

To further complicate matters, not only do the judgments of others affect an individual's developing identities; it also matters just who those others are. Some people, depending on their social positions, have relatively more power and authority, especially in regard to specific identities. However, power is never a given but depends very much on the nature of the individuals involved in the encounter. For instance, as a faculty member and a teacher, my opinion may hold a lot of weight with some students in education, but, because I am a woman faculty member and teacher, this authority may be compromised for certain other students. Fortunately, our identities don't ever depend solely on the influence of single individuals. For most of us, on any given day, the opportunities to encounter many different others in a variety of situations is boundless. Thus, we collectively share the responsibilities and pleasures of fashioning one another.

Like the process of identity itself, the decision to become a teacher resulted from a resolution of contingencies. It depended on each person's

assembled different factors, the force or weight of each factor, how factors interacted—one leaned up against another, one variable bled into another, one
condition in their lives made another position untenable. In representing my
students' decisions, I have chosen individual words or specific terms that students used to describe their motivations. Rather than single attributions, they
always ascribed to multiple reasons; however, no student mentioned all described here. Furthermore, the analysis, though valid, is necessarily partial because it depends on what students offered in the interviews. Despite these
limits, my students' comments reveal the dialectical process by which identity
positions are achieved.

1. *Always known.* Simply put, being a teacher is something some of my students feel they've always known about themselves. Howard describes this
position of intrinsic knowledge: "For some reason the idea of teaching has always appealed to me." Although he mentions family background as one potential factor, he is adamant that it is not *the* determining one: "Both my parents
teach college English. My sister is a math teacher now at my old high school."
But his inclination toward teaching doesn't result from family pressure: "Both
my parents swear they did not want us to ever do this. . . ."

For Howard, teaching is not a matter of becoming someone in the future,
but a trait he already associates with himself. "Even as a student, I never felt it
as a hierarchy. Certainly I defer to any instructor but in class when talking with
my classmates I always felt that we could *always* teach each other. I guess I have
always had that feeling. I am a teacher." Furthermore, he insists that teaching is
a kind of generic orientation toward everyday life: "I don't know if there are
times when you're not!" It is my question that sets off the process of self-
reflection. When he thinks about his prevailing attitudes and typical behavior,
he concludes that he is now, and always has been, a teacher.

In a similar fashion, Michaela feels that being a teacher is somehow
inherent, a previously existing condition: "I have been thinking lately about
whether or not I consider myself to be a teacher. I think I have been my
whole life in some sort of capacity. Not so much like the bestower of knowledge. But if I know something that somebody else needs, I'll share my
knowledge with people. I think I've *always* been like that." Michaela adds: "I
would be a teacher whether or not I was in a classroom. No matter what career I was to go into, I still feel like I would be a teacher of sorts." Although
Michaela describes teaching as an intrinsic part of herself, she doesn't believe it has to be her destiny: "There have been times in my life—and a lot
of them are occurring more recently—when I am a teacher. But I don't know
if I want to be a teacher as a career, like a high-school-teacher teacher."
Michaela insists on the distinction between being and doing, between innate

feeling and public enactment. She conceives of "being a teacher" as an ordinary way of relating to others. Her view doesn't necessarily imply she will seek a job as a teacher. Michaela believes she can be a teacher without earning a living as one.

2. Difference between feeling and being. However, separating identity (being a teacher) from role (a teaching job) makes Michaela uncomfortable: "There's a difference between feeling innately teacherlike and in being a high school teacher. There's a discrepancy there." Her uneasiness stems from an analysis of the pragmatic conditions of teaching, not from any doubts about her abilities or inclinations: "If you're a good teacher, and you educate students the way the public wants you, then you don't ever quit working. You can't hang up with your last client at five o'clock and go home. You stay and you go to soccer practice, and then you go to the ball game, and then you go home, and you grade papers, and then you get up at six o'clock in the morning and go to school."

She continues, quite agitated: "It's very disturbing to me how you can run on that kind of energy year, after year, after year, when you are still just keeping your head above water? So I teach for thirty years and then I'm making twenty-eight thousand dollars a year! Those aren't the kind of incentives that are going to make me want to stay especially when I go to school, and there are people toting guns around, and I have to break up fights and that sort of thing." Michaela isn't sure about her future and during the time before graduation, Michaela wants to feel she has options about who she will become. Given the real drawbacks of being a high school teacher, she's not sure she can commit herself under such conditions. While she feels like a teacher on the inside, she is hesitant about representing herself that way in public.

3. Role models. "In high school I had some teachers I really looked up to. So that's when I decided to do this," Lauren eagerly reported to me one day. Elizabeth had been similarly influenced. Both students described their relationships to other teachers as the most compelling reason for becoming teachers. For Elizabeth, it was knowing her teacher outside of class, some personal contact. Likewise, Lauren admired her teacher's ability to be "down at the students' level. We didn't have to reach to find him." She was impressed by knowing "there was somebody underneath this persona in the classroom."

The process of strongly identifying with someone to the point of wanting to adopt their profession happens not only in actual encounters between students and teachers. Representations of teachers appear to be as powerful as actual ones in instilling a conviction to teach. Rick sheepishly reports, "the changing point in my life, this may sound cheesy or melodramatic, was the movie *Dead Poets Society*." After seeing the film as a high school student, Rick "immediately decided to become an English professor at college." Though he has modified the original vision, his primary goal of becoming a teacher, born in vivid moment of identification, still persists.

What made these teachers impressive? Lauren and Rick agree that it's a matter of efficacy; these were teachers who transformed students' lives. Lauren still visits her former teacher and considers him a friend. When she envisions herself teaching, she says, "I want to have that kind of influence on other people." Rick describes his intentions similarly: "It was teaching, from the turning point of the movie, watching the Robin Williams character change these boys' lives." For Rick and Lauren, what attracted them to teaching was the possibility of being a teacher capable of changing the lives of others.

4. Teaching as service. In having a defining moment plus school experiences that reproduced his ideal fantasy of teaching, Rick knew as a first-year student that he would definitely apply to the teacher education program. Before coming to college, Donna had also undergone a revolution in self-understanding, though unlike Rick's, it was not directly about teaching. "Senior year [in high school]," Donna reports, "my life plan changed. I realized that I had an interest in the mission field. Whereas before, whenever I thought about people who went abroad to share the gospel, I thought 'Oh, how dreadful,' I would hate that as my lifestyle. It was just not appealing at all."

With newly found faith, Donna evaluated her choices of major during her first college year, "wanting something that would be conducive [to mission work] in case I ever did that in the future." Teaching was to serve: "They need teachers all over the world, and in a lot of countries they don't allow missionaries, but they do allow people to come in if they can help the society as a whole." It was equally important to Donna that her chosen major would enable her "to have lasting results," like sharing the gospel, which endured "not just during this lifetime, but for eternity." She decided on teaching as the perfect "option." As an afterthought, she added the proviso, "And I love English so much." Thus, Donna's decision to teach was an offshoot of another, more primary identification of herself as a Christian destined to be a missionary. To teach, for Donna, meant to serve.

5. Loving English. Sometimes the first loves of our lives turn out to be glorious but short-lived. Then in moments sudden clarity, we realize the true object of our affections has existed, unnoticed, the whole time. Howard describes that his original intention as an incoming college student was to go into science: "I applied to Carolina because it was the best college in the country for public health. I was going to be an environmental scientist." The need to major in chemistry and the attitude of the science majors he encountered as a first-year student discouraged Howard: "That wasn't me. English is where I should have been all along."

What motivates some students is not at attraction to teaching per se, but a intense love for English as a discipline—reading books, studying literature, critical and creative writing. At the risk of sounding trite, Howard admits to an earlier predisposition: "I remember in fourth grade or fifth grade, deciding that I wanted to be a writer."

Like Howard, Donna discovered her love of English after she entered college. She reports telling everyone who inquired in high school about her intention to be a pediatrician. "I was convinced I was going to be a doctor. I was registered as pre-med . . . which I see now does not suit me at all." But Donna rejected her first major on the grounds of being ill-equipped to handle the discipline: "I was so disenchanted at the prospect of taking chemistry, biology." She finds a truer match in English, remembering "being fascinated by the literature because of the way my teachers presented it." Once she began thinking about English, other teachers from her past appeared very influential to Donna: "Senior year my writing improved dramatically because [the teacher] wanted us to make our papers a piece of art."

Donna's attitudes about her spiritual life and professional future were changing independently during the transition year between high school and college. "My freshman year I was undecided [about a major] the whole year. I didn't know for sure what I wanted to do." She had rejected the pre-med track, knowing she "wanted to be involved in English somehow." Although she was undergoing a spiritual conversion during this same time, it had no immediate bearing on her thinking: "I didn't know how that [English] would apply to what I'd do after graduation." Donna's decision finally to be an English teacher was the outcome of a union between what had previously been two separate aspects of her self: religious beliefs and notions about career.

6. *Altruism.* Prevailing cultural images of a high school teacher's life are mostly negative. In popular books and films (*Dead Poets Society* is a good example), teachers control high-energy teenagers all day, deal with violence and drugs that pervade school environments, and cope with bureaucratic paperwork and endless paper grading while trying to connect with kids to impart information, teach critical thinking, and instill disciplinary practices. Despite the prevalence of such unappealing images, my students are attracted to teaching because of their very commendable (if idealistic) humanitarian motives. Teaching remains a profession where it's possible to work toward goals like social justice, equality of education, and literacy for democratic citizenship. In spite of the numerous negative conditions associated with schools, the vision of themselves as grassroots agents of social

change remains for my students a compelling reason for pursuing a teaching career.

Drawn by the "idea of teaching" and personally connected to English, Howard takes a pragmatic view about what he has to offer: "I know there is better way to do it." Howard sees himself as a willing volunteer; teaching is a worthwhile job, one that needs doing, one he can do well.

Lauren envisions teaching primarily as a moral act, a profession in which she can make a difference to her students: "I do want to be a friend to my students, show them I care about their lives and what's going on. And if they are having a problem, that I understand that people have problems. Because a lot of teachers don't do that." Two high school teachers influenced Lauren in profoundly different ways, one her band director, the other her junior English teacher.

Because she had a teacher who was intellectually dedicated to literature, Lauren discovered her interest in English as a discipline. Geared toward advanced placement classes, this teacher predominantly lectured, assigned frequent papers, and set very high academic standards for her students. Although Lauren "loved the class," she found this teacher "brilliant but intimidating." In imagining reasons for teaching, Lauren finds herself critiquing a teacher she once respected: "Why is this person teaching? She didn't appear to love it. She had a great *hold* on students . . . like she was feared almost. We never knew what she thought because she didn't share anything. It was just teach the work."

Lauren was most annoyed by the fact that her English teacher "didn't know her students very well" in contrast to her band director who, she felt, revealed his "vulnerabilities," which allowed students to know him. In an interview, I ask Lauren, "So do you think you are going to be demonstrative in that way?" She replies, "I won't be as demonstrative as he was. No. I won't be like that." But she goes on to insist that her strength as a teacher will be her ability to connect personally with students.

Michaela's reasons for teaching are ideological; she thinks human society is worth saving. It is her attitude toward such an enterprise that will make her a success: "I have a lot of empathy with the human condition. I really do. It sounds really goofy. But that is going to help me as a teacher because I don't have a rookie cop attitude about it." Michaela eschews the idea of control, preferring the image of her teacher self as "entertainer" instead of "parent or policeman." As a realist, she believes that "the acquisition of knowledge is very burdensome" and "there is a lot to be said for showmanship" as a means to an end. "The more you know the more you can understand the breadth of human experience, how much pain and suffering, how much joy there is."

Like the others, Michaela perceives of herself as a forceful individual whose actions will affect others and the social conditions of school: "I'm going in there with a good heart. I know that every student can learn. I don't believe in stupid people. I care about my subject and I care about what I am doing. I hope that will communicate itself to my students so they'll care about what they are producing and creating in my class."

For all six, teaching appeals for reasons of social justice. They speak about their commitments to students and to educational change with effervescent determination. From this position, being a teacher is akin to being a social worker, identities in which the self is characterized by altruism and commitments to abstract ideals such as equality and democracy.

7. *Saving grace.* "If you pick up the right book and it speaks right to you, then that is your saving grace for those four days or however long it takes for you to read it," explains Michaela, in telling why she feels "called to be a teacher." In school, it was not so much the teachers themselves who mattered, but rather the great books that Michaela's teachers managed to get into her hands: "Without books and without being able to write in high school I don't know what I would have done." Michaela and I connect through this shared feeling: "Yeah," I tell her. "When I was a teenager, I felt like I couldn't exist a single day if I couldn't read something." Michaela smiles and looks away, explaining her desire to teach stems from having "grown up loving reading and writing." Her "strong point" as a teacher is "sharing what I think and feel about reading and writing and getting students—fifteen, sixteen, seventeen, eighteen years old— excited about reading a book, writing a story or a letter."

Elizabeth also feels that language provided deliverance from the tedium of teenage life and even more strongly was a method of salvation, especially through the difficult years of adolescence. Trauma prompted Elizabeth to begin writing. When Elizabeth's mother died, shortly before her eighth grade graduation, she began to keep a journal, where "writing was an act of self-preservation, a tool for claiming and disarming the resentment . . . at the insecurity of motherlessness." Writing was how she became herself: "By translating the feelings into words and putting them in the journal . . . they became real and so did I." In the essay "Literacy in Three Metaphors," Sylvia Scribner (1988) describes one condition of literacy as a "state of grace." She means nothing religious in her metaphor but is referring to the circumstance when a "literate individual's life derives its meaning and significance from intellectual, aesthetic, and spiritual participation in the accumulated creations and knowledge of humankind, made available through the written word" (77). From her journal, Elizabeth received these benefits.

But being saved by writing also led Elizabeth to think she could be good teacher, one who could enable students to discover the state of grace literacy offered: "As I began college, I realized the journal was directly related to my desire to become a teacher." Having a real reason to write, her journal being "the place I made sense and meaning out of life, how I learned to be critical and introspective" provided Elizabeth with a real reason to teach. If she taught students to write with the goal "of using language to discover meaning and experience and to communicate it, they would want to learn." Elizabeth's conviction rested in self-knowledge: "Simultaneously I thought of the journal and teaching. I realized teaching writing wouldn't just be a stab in the dark. It was something I felt and understood."

8. A calling or . . . a job. During the last interviews I had with students just prior to graduation, we revisited the question of how they decided to become teachers and their current attitudes on the topic. Several reported feeling persistent ambivalence. Elizabeth, despite deep convictions about writing and its power, ideas that were reinforced by her work with teenagers, found she could not picture herself teaching English in a high school. The decision to enter the teacher education program "was so gradual it's hard to even describe a point where I was convinced. And still now [a month before graduation] there are times when I don't know if I want to be a teacher." Michaela is similarly torn: "I really feel that writing is more my calling than teaching is . . . I feel called to write because I don't ever remember a time in my life when I didn't want to write, and now I'm at the point in my life where I have to make a choice . . ."

Elizabeth describes her interest in teaching as "really a writing-based thing at first." Because she enjoyed the few classes focused on the history, theory, and practice of writing, Elizabeth recalls when she knew she wanted "to major in education." Since there is no such undergraduate major, Elizabeth chose English education, the closest option: "Nothing else appealed to me and nothing turned me away from it. Education more so than the English will let me pursue my real interest. Because in literature classes, you really are not writing. Well, you are writing, but it still wasn't the same."

Nevertheless, Elizabeth concludes she has made an honorable choice: "I tell people at home or old teachers, even if I don't teach for the rest of my life, I'm glad I majored in education because I'm glad I know what I know now." Michaela tells me she wants to spend time writing: "After I graduate I'd like to take off a couple of years and get together a collection of short stories to send out for publication." For at least two years Michaela has been taking creative writing courses. Her success in the excellent and demanding program at UNC makes her feel that "writing is more my calling than teaching is." She hastens to add, "But then I feel called to be a teacher and so . . ."

Of all the students, Rick has maintained the most consistent attitude about his resolution to teach. He repeatedly insists he's very "positive" and has "never questioned" his prior decision to enter education. However, he does have competing desires. After discovering the genre of fantasy novels "about sixth or seventh grade, I decided I wanted to become a writer." He laughs but admits to another deep commitment: "To this day, I still feel like I'm a writer trapped in a nonwriter's body." But this urge to write doesn't deter him from his intention "to get out and teach a couple of years." At the same time he insists he's "never had a doubt" about returning to the university in the near future for a "master's program in English education." The firmness of his decision to teach high school is reinforced by the fact that he's got other options about which he's just as secure.

Likewise, Howard imagines multiple alternatives. Although he plans "to try high school for a while," he remains dubious, not about teaching, but about high school. While he loves literature, and possesses an internal sense of being a teacher, Howard is skeptical about the paperwork and other hassles of high school life, claiming that "some of the bureaucratic things already turn me off." In making his decision, Howard is caught between thinking pragmatically about the downsides of teaching as an occupation, while at the same time feeling certain that teaching is something honorable and worth doing. What might help clarify and resolve this indecision?

Identifying

At this point in their lives, these students are attempting to make reasonable decisions about their still-distant futures. A wide variety of experiences, persons, and circumstances, in combination and with varying power, shaped each one's decision to major in education. Although they're not clear exactly about what being a teacher entails, they are aware that the decision to teach may have significant ramifications not only on what they do as adults but on the sort of person they become. For instance, Michaela refers to the "call" to teach, which suggests she understands that being a teacher will be a transforming pursuit. But in general my students' thoughts about these issues are very provisional and uncertain mainly because their material experiences of teaching, teachers, and schools is relatively limited. Furthermore, this past consists of memories for the most part unexamined, even, for some students, inaccessible.

One day I asked Michaela whether she was able to connect the theory presented in my class with the practices of any of her former teachers: "So when you're sitting there learning all this [theory], you don't immediately think, oh, such-and-such a teacher did that?" "No," Michaela flatly replied. "A lot of the past experience—I think back to my high school or middle school—those were unpleasant memories. I *don't* recall. So actually I'm sitting there, trying to make up a teacher that would do that sort of thing." Her response made me realize how difficult it was to learn abstract content in a context far removed from the situation in which the information might be used.

There are several ways that teacher education programs could facilitate students' decisions about becoming teachers. If identity happens through processes of identification, then students require avenues through which they can self-identify as teachers. This means discovering personal reasons for wanting to teach, reasons that no matter how far-flung or wide-ranging are recognized and affirmed by the program. Seeing themselves as teachers is one part. The other crucial aspect of the process is identifying with others who represent or embody the identity in question. Thus, opportunities to associate with other teachers (university professors, high school teachers) are necessary. Coursework can be useful in both aspects of the identification process. In addition to content and methods, academic courses can provide the elbow room students need to discover and develop their individual abilities and personal interests. In addition, if work in academic settings is linked to contact with real teachers in variety of school settings, then the notion that teaching is an identity as well as a profession will be made readily apparent to prospective teachers.

What Kind of Teacher?

Anticipating

Teacher education programs vary widely in terms of how many courses (professional education and academic content) are required of prospective teachers relative to the amount of field experience offered. Whatever the balance, however, the teaching practicum—at least a full semester, during which students take responsibility for teaching their mentor teacher's full load—carries great weight. Students regard it as the "trial by fire," the test of "real" experience through which they will finally know whether they can survive as teachers and an opportunity to reconsider their desire to even become teachers.

In our program, students are admitted to the School of Education as college juniors.[1] They take most of their professional courses during their junior year; the teaching practicum occurs in the senior year. All English education majors participate in student teaching in fall semester. The first month is taken up by an intensive methods course during which time students generally observe at their assigned high school and get to know their mentor teachers and future students.

This part of the chapter focuses on this pivotal period of my students' educational life as prospective teachers. They have spent a year learning about things as diverse as adolescent psychology, the role of literacy in content teaching, and the history of secondary education in the United States. Now, as they approach the beginning of their teaching practicum, they are preoccupied with the upcoming months, a state of mind that was evident from the interviews that occurred in the month prior to student teaching. All six talked eagerly about their school placements, raised concerns about their prior preparation, and expressed their anxieties, fears, and doubts (there were many) about themselves as teachers. This half of the chapter will explore their ideas as they anticipate being teacher interns, a hybrid position existing on the cusp between being known as students and/or as teachers.

1. Michaela: identifying with and beyond her mentor teacher. Michaela has been assigned to the recently opened, second high school in Chapel Hill. Its older counterpart enjoys a reputation for having excellent teachers (many with advanced degrees), maintaining strong academic standards, and graduating a large number of high-achieving students. The new school is expected to be equally superb by all standards. Her mentor teacher, Ms. Long, has twenty years of experience and is known for her talents in teaching the college-preparatory students. Except for a class of juniors, Michaela will be teaching all honors English sections, American literature, focusing on the classics including *The Great Gatsby, The Scarlet Letter, A Farewell to Arms,* and *Huckleberry Finn.*

Michaela maintains an eager, but levelheaded, attitude toward teaching, a position she attributes partly to being older than her peers, having taken an extra semester to finish college. She'll officially graduate in December as soon as the practicum is over: "I mentally graduated last May. I've overcome that little hump. I am ready to move on to the next phase of my life. A year ago, still twenty-one and still a little shaky, not completed with college, I would be scared as a jackrabbit about student teaching."

Rather than fearful, Michaela feels excited and confident: "I don't know when it happened but I got over the fear. I'm more excited now, though still nervous and get butterflies when I think about standing up in front of that classroom. The confidence comes from knowing I can do it and I'm ready to do it."

Most important, Michaela foresees an easy "transition from my life into the student teaching placement" because she identifies with Ms. Long's style and personality: "She's going in a thousand different directions! Which is fine with me because that is where I'm coming from. *So I just fit.*" By identifying with her mentor teacher, Michaela grows even more self-assured. When I asked her to elaborate, Michaela replied: "On Thursday, she breezed in, books everywhere, trying to figure out what to do that day. Her class walked in and she said, OK, I haven't figured out what I am going to do. Michaela, one thing you are going to learn about teaching is that you just have to get up there and wing it. And so she grabbed some notes about Nabokov . . ." Ms. Long's spontaneous approach based on an inner confidence appeals to Michaela who believes she's a similar kind of person. This match between mentor and intern validates Michaela's image of her teaching self as an "entertainer," and encourages her to believe that teaching can be a creative and improvisational performance. Further, her aspiration to be an actor can be satisfied to some degree by being a teacher like Ms. Long, making the identification process all the more powerful.

Despite the pleasure and intensity of connecting with Ms. Long in these ways, Michaela has serious reservations about her mentor's view of teaching as an absolute identity: "Whereas Miriam Long *is* a teacher and that is what her life is, I think *in that way we really differ.*" Michaela rejects the idea of teaching as a primary or overpowering identity, preferring to view teaching as one identity among others. She pictures herself having multiple professional identities. I gather from her words that she imagines that these identity positions *could* possibly coexist, richly and productively, without her ever having to choose among them.

The process of comparing ourselves to others allows us to discover similarities and differences. Both categories yield useful information to anyone who is engaged in developing an identity. In Michaela's case, the specific knowledge she gained by comparison with Ms. Long was identity provoking but not in any straightforward way. Michaela's strongest reactions were bifurcated: on the one hand, in regard to Ms. Long's style and personality, she was similar and "just fit." On the other hand, she couldn't picture herself totally invested in teaching, insisting "in that way we differ." It was impossible to predict at the start of the teaching practicum how these competing associations with her mentor teacher would affect Michaela's development as a teacher.

We engage automatically in these kind of associative processes—assessing how we are the same and how we are different from others—every day in many contexts. In a way that is powerfully constructive of self, Michaela is characteristically reflective in the interviews. She becomes the person who prefers one life "writing short stories" over another through the act of narration. She is very self-conscious and notices how she is alike or different from her mentor. My questions contribute to the reflective process and push her to see the ramifications of these distinctions, images of a future she hadn't yet articulated to herself or anyone else before the moment of our discussion. While the nature of her relation to Ms. Long shapes her identity, it is by no means determinate. Remember that Michaela is grappling with other positive and negative dimensions of teaching such as the ethical concerns she's raised about working conditions, salary and respectability.

2. Donna: Sharing with her mentor the goal to center instruction on students. The word *prophetic* aptly describes Donna's approach to life. She thinks about the world in fateful terms, trusting that God is looking out for her or that whatever happens was meant to be. When you talk to her, you get the impression that she's walking fearlessly forward into a life she knows is waiting for her. About her placement, she comments: "I thought the things I requested were contradictory. Somehow it has been arranged so that I've gotten exactly what I wanted." About the reputably rough, urban high school she's about to join, she says, "Harkins just seems top notch. I am really impressed with the faculty, with the way they interact, with the facilities, with everything." Overall, she begins the teaching practicum in a state awe and deep respect, especially for her mentor teacher: "The teacher I have is phenomenal. She's twenty-seven or twenty-eight, and has been teaching only for three years. What is most impressive is how she lets her students see her. I guess it's common for older teachers who've been doing it for a long time to be sort of burned out. She is not at all." About the practicum in general, the other five interns have mixed feelings; they are mostly wary and withholding judgment. None display Donna's fervor.

The sense of having a future makes Donna feel possessed of great agency; her main goal is to reach students and, in so doing, change them. After an initial visit to the school, she said this about her future students: "I still sense a boredom, blank faces, and I mean a lot of the seniors. In looking at each of them individually I saw that there was a lack of engagement." Her most immediate and pressing concern is a potential failure of "leadership": "My greatest fear is that we'd go through the motions, do the exercises that I had planned or whatever, and that they would leave maybe feeling a bit enlightened but not changed. I don't want that to be the case. I know there's only so much I can do to prevent that."

To meet this challenge, Donna enlisted the help of her mentor, Ms. Kearns. Whether it was because of age or temperament or a shared affection for students, from the beginning Donna and Ms. Kearns regarded each other as partners in the teaching enterprise. Although Donna respected Ms. Kearns, and acknowledged her authority as a mentor, Donna was not consumed by or worried about her relation to Ms. Kearns. Since their relationship was not at issue, both teachers were freed to focus their attention on the students, especially in terms of how to make instruction student-centered. Donna comments: "It's just going to require a lot of thought about how to provoke excitement because I see now that it's not really the way you are, necessarily, that makes students learn. Because Ms. Kearns is really energetic and is excited about what she's doing, but still you see people sitting there with blank stares. Some people you just can't stir them. So what do you do?"

When I asked Donna if she felt prepared to teach, she replied: "I knew the kind of influence I wanted to have on my students . . . to develop a passion for literature and for writing and for being intellectually stimulated. But the way of doing that was not concrete. I knew the basics but over the past year with a lot of exercises in your class that has become more concrete. And yet at the same time, there's only so far I can go into a child, there's only so much I can do. In developing units and designing lessons, I always keep the knowledge that I'm going to have to learn to allow God to be the one to deeply stimulate them and so I guess that's a comfort. It's not all my responsibility." In other words, Donna must be accountable for her choices and take responsibility, but not all responsibility. In many ways, Donna's faith is an extra resource that she draws on when needed. Because she feels secure, not alone, she is able to empathize with her mentor teacher and not panic about how difficult it is to reach these students.

Being possessed of an internal sense of security allows Donna to have an open stance toward her students: "I don't have everything preplanned because I don't want to go in with a preset structure and then enforce it on them." In describing how she would go about teaching, Donna assumes Ms. Kearns's involvement: "Definitely [through] observation, watching the way they interact, watching their expressions, watching how they respond to the different prompts, reading what they had written and how they'd written it. By doing all of that, I think we can assess what they need. Really just watching what is stimulating to them and what isn't."

When I ask her about how she'll approach teaching *The Scarlet Letter*, the next assigned text, she says, "I've been thinking much more about the process, teaching the students not just about the book itself, but how to study a book and how to be engaged in a book." Then she adds, "And that's really what she's interested in doing too. That hasn't been a struggle, knowing that's the way she is too." Donna's optimism as she begins her teaching practicum stems from believing she *can* teach students what's most important, "stimulating deeper thought about human nature and the way we interact with one another, about spiritual things," because she shares these values with her mentor.

3. Lauren: Being a teacher depends on other people's perceptions. A week into her teaching practicum, I ask Lauren how she's doing. "I feel pretty confident right now actually. I'm not freaking out." she says, then adds a qualification: "I have been nervous all summer at how the students would react to me . . . about how they would perceive me." She has definite ideas about the way she does not want to be viewed: "I didn't want them to see me as a buddy because I didn't want any discipline problems." However, meeting her students has been reassuring: "Now I've seen [their reactions] and I'm satisfied."

This was not the first time Lauren entered a situation where she was concerned ahead of time about other people's perceptions. The prior semester Lauren was assigned to tutor in a "predominantly minority, low-income" high school where "just about all the classes were totally African-American, maybe like one or two white people." Lauren feared that her effectiveness could be compromised because she would be seen as a "white," and therefore unlike the teachers and students: "I was worried about how they would see me, maybe, more than anything." In the end, student perceptions did matter, but not in the way Lauren imagined. Students saw Lauren as a caring teacher who treated them respectfully, which made it easier for her to be exactly that kind of teacher: "But they liked me at Hillside and I liked them. When I was teaching, if I said, 'Well, why do you think he did this?' And then [the student replied] 'I don't know,' then I said, 'Yes, you do, you know something.' That's how I treated students—"You do know something; don't try that with me"—and gave them a little credit. So caring is a big deal to me. That's a bigger deal to me than English." However, proclaiming herself a caring teacher is not sufficient to make it real. In order to feel that is who she is, Lauren needs the opinions and reactions of others to define, reinforce, and validate her way of being.

It was a relief for Lauren to discover that students would respect her even if she presented herself as a nurturing teacher: "I think my main purpose in teaching is to help students. It breaks my heart all the problems that students have today. The main thing is that I'm there. I want to be an adult in their lives who is dependable." Furthermore, Lauren believes this kind of relationship is mutually beneficial for everyone: students get attention and Lauren becomes the teacher they need. "I can't save everybody but maybe I can help some students. Sometimes students just need someone to say, 'Well, that's okay, I understand.'" Lauren's internal predilections are confirmed when students react positively to her approach.

It was not only toward her students that Lauren looked for external validation. At the start of her teaching practicum, she was focused naturally on her mentor-teacher and wished for her approval and support. Mrs. Jameson was an experienced teacher who, because of her talents as well as overcrowded conditions in the school, had a disproportionately heavy teaching load (142 students a day). So she needed an intern just like Lauren—someone who had prior experience with minority students and who was not afraid to act independently and take on teaching responsibilities as soon as possible. Lauren could not have been happier: "It was the third day of school and they are still trying to work out scheduling problems. And some other teachers, she introduced me to them, and they asked her, 'How are you going to deal with one hundred forty-two kids?' 'Well,' she said, 'we are going to work that out. We are going to find some ways to deal with it.' She said '*we* are,' like '*she* and *I* are,' like 'it's *our*' class. That really helped a lot, just saying things like that to me. And she said things like that to me throughout the day. That helped me to feel very comfortable and to feel like I was respected."

For Lauren, other people's opinions are powerful because they confirm and establish her identity. Her situation reveals how identity is not a fixed condition but rather an ongoing dialectical process occurring between the individual (internal states) and other people (external conditions). This dynamic of social identification is one routine that constitutes identity. Lauren's experience demonstrates Richard Jenkins's point about the role of others in making individual identity: "It is not enough to assert an identity. That identity must also be validated (or not) by those with whom we have dealings. *Social identity is never unilateral.*" (1996, 21, emphasis his).

4. Rick: Identity commitments are rooted in prior experience. There are any number of identity positions available in the culture that students like mine could potentially adopt. What attracts us to certain ones but not others? Why be a teacher? There is no general, overarching theory that can explain or predict what identities an individual will develop. Social factors determine some part. For instance, they define identity positions in general, but they cannot account for why an individual *invests* in one identity position rather than another. Students enter the program already deeply involved in multiple developing identities (son or daughter, man or woman). These values and inclinations, desires and preferences, when connected with these early developing identities, motivate their actions. We can better understand individual cases, accounting for why Lauren or Elizabeth or Rick were drawn to being teachers, in reference to their individual histories and personalities, including conscious and unconscious dimensions. External social pressures affect a person's interest in becoming, but these are not the sole determinants. Individual agency and personal commitments rooted in much earlier experience influence those identities a person ascribes to. What is the nature of the teaching identity my students wish to adopt and why? How can their attachment or passionate interest be explained? Rick's narratives reveal some of these connections.

In describing his first impressions and responses the first week of student teaching, Rick offers feelings, thoughts, and personal history as possible reasons for his reactions. One of his main teaching goals is "to help my high school students make contact with their childhood." He believes that the positive experiences of his childhood past may be reproduced: "I'm gonna try to let them go back into their childhood and catch a lot of the magic and emotion that they had." When I ask him about methods to accomplish this, he replies by saying: "To be emotional is what I'm going to strive for. Whether I get up there and start whimpering in class or start dancing in class, I want it to be emotional." But Rick knows it will be a challenge, given that he attended a small private school for twelve years, to teach at a large, public high school in ways that reflect these goals.

Rick recognizes that major differences between his school past and the current situation will mean changing the way he's always thought about teaching: "The two sad realizations I've come to is in a big public school like this, in the long run, I'm not teaching them to go to college. And that's a big change. I walked in there subconsciously thinking that I was going to be teaching every one of them to achieve college-level work. And the second one is the harsh reality of how separated the blacks and whites are in the classes. In eleventh grade American Lit, probably out of thirty students, there's ten or twelve African-Americans." Both these observations, especially since he has recognized them simultaneously, distress him. They appear to be related phenomena. He's shocked to discover and very afraid that there may be an immoral and illogical connection between race and educational opportunity. The "harsh reality" he's afraid of, something he definitely does not want to perpetrate by his own behavior as a teacher in the system, is that many African-American students attending public high schools are probably not college-bound.

Seeing how race is implicated in issues of educational opportunity in an actual situation ("I had read it in books and studied it in classes," Rick said) is enough to disturb anyone. But Rick's high school experience in an all-white private school haunts him. Though his parents "believed in public schools," and it had "hurt their conscience," Rick and his sister were sent to a private school because "the education system was bad." He continues: "We knew a lot of people in the public schools in my county and that's where they really believed I should be but, but . . ." I finish the sentence for him. "They couldn't do it—your parents." Rick is visibly upset as he speaks.

In the current decade, what he considers to be "years later," Rick is shocked to discover how little has changed. Although it is true that he is teaching in a large public high school, he has a special teaching assignment. His mentor-teacher is connected to the Seminar Program, a school within a school, "comprised of 100 to 200 students" whose parents work in the Triangle and wanted to send their children to an innovative hands-on program. They are college-bound students." Though he will teach some regular classes, his main experience will be in the seminar program. "And guess what?" Rick comments, "in the seminar program, there's one [African-American student] in each one of the two sections. Yeah." He looks unhappy and ends the conversation on saying, "It's scary because half the kids [in the school] are African-American and then you got kids with Confederate flags on their backpacks with "the South will rise again" stuff. You can just feel that something is going to blow up any day now." "What do you plan to do?" I ask. "For English," he replies, "I can teach them is basic writing skills and basic survival skills in the workplace." He pauses, "Hopefully there can be some type of open mindset taught too." We pause and look at each other. Neither one of us believes that will be nearly enough. But I know this issue will motivate Rick's choices, moving him in certain directions—whether that be teaching method or the sort of school he eventually teaches at—that will reflect his prior experience as white person who received a better education than his African-American peers.

5. Elizabeth: Developing identity depends on seeing a place for yourself. Elizabeth was unusual among my students because of a serious interest in theories of language and literacy. In advance of our conversations, I already knew something about Elizabeth's theoretical orientation from her prior work in my education classes. But it became clear during the interviews that she believed being an effective writing teacher was connected to understanding and appreciating how language worked. About teaching, Elizabeth postulated that students would learn more if they wrote to discover personal meaning.

Elizabeth's abiding interest in writing (as opposed to reading literature) stemmed from the positive effect of keeping a journal. This personal experience shaped her academic interests, influenced what she learned in education courses, and most important, affected her orientation toward teaching. Though she had taken the same courses as everyone else, which included writing a philosophy of teaching for English 31, Elizabeth described these experiences as "essential" and "formative." The books and articles she was asked to read reflected her inner thoughts and ratified her past experiences with writing as a process with the power to transform persons and things. These academic experiences changed the very way she thought about herself.

Thus Elizabeth approached the practicum with a very clear image herself as a teacher devoted to process. In her view, both reading and writing were meaningful activities that students should encounter as evolving and malleable processes. In part, she arrived at this position through course work and on account of the research she had already done to prepare for writing her thesis on whole language theory and process-writing. One influential source, she reported, was Donald Murray, a writer and pragmatist in the field of composition: "He defined writing as the process of using language to discover meaning and experience and to communicate it." She found that Murray's ideas explained the satisfactions and personal benefits she'd received from journal writing as well as had specific implications for teaching: "I could apply that to papers I had written and to writing in a journal or diary or whatever." Thus the reasons to write entailed discovering meaning, something Elizabeth believed in herself and something that she could teach to students.

Compared to her peers in the study, Elizabeth's situation was considerably more complicated. Our conversations had twin functions because she intended to write her thesis while she was teaching during the practicum semester. Both teaching and writing are demanding enterprises, but Elizabeth envisioned the two experiences as interconnected. She had requested to be placed with a mentor-teacher who was interested in process writing, and hoped that she could experiment while teaching. She was very directed in how she would approach each task—teaching and thesis writing—and about which she had many interrelated questions. During one interview, she flipped open a notebook and read out the following list: "How does that theory translate into practice? How do other teachers put it [process writing] into practice? When they make adjustments and shape it to fit public school curriculum, is it still true to this theory or this philosophy? What does it lose? Does it still work? What is it about public school that makes this way of teaching hard to implement? And how can those things be changed, or are they huge fundamental things that would completely alter American schools?" Though Elizabeth had several formidable tasks ahead of her, she appeared eager and well prepared.

At the outset Elizabeth's placement looked positive and workable. She was assigned to work with an experienced teacher who collaborated with two others in designing a curriculum informed by whole language theory. On the day she arrived in my office to outline her thesis, I also asked for a report of her first observation at the high school. She reported positively: "The three teachers 'have the same curriculum' with a 'shared planning period'"; "I saw this process-writing flow chart on the board"; "they had written a personal narrative the night before"; and "Mr. Collins is real open to this perspective." Nevertheless, she expressed concerns about having such definite views about teaching, and to want to teach writing more than literature in the public schools: "One question I keep coming up with is—there are other definitions of teaching writing. This isn't my sole definition. But does that definition work? When a student has to write a research paper in twelfth grade, if [process] is at the heart of what I really think writing should be, is that going to translate?"

Despite these worries, Elizabeth began the semester highly optimistic, without the misgivings of some of the others, basically because she envisioned a fit between her inner ideas and the outside world. At first she thought her experiences with journal writing were private and idiosyncratic, but then her views (and self) were validated through her academic work and by her teachers at the university. Furthermore, after meeting her mentor teacher and visiting her school, she has received other evidence that corroborated her hope that process teaching was a viable possibility. A significant factor in whether or not Elizabeth becomes a teacher has to do with the integrity of this internal perspective. What she believed implicitly has now been made explicit—without much modification. These correspondences between inner and outer experiences, occurring at different stages in her thinking, have encouraged and motivated Elizabeth. Not only have they influenced her decision to become an education major in the first place, but also what she sees so far in the educational world has reassured her at the start of the teaching practicum that she may very well have a place and a future as a teacher.

6. Howard: Being a good teacher depends on the freedom to do something different.
Howard has no interest in being a prototypical teacher, in being predictable or
like everyone else. In one interview, shortly after being assigned a mentor-
teacher, he comments: "I'm not sure if I'll fit the mold that they seem to want
to set us in." Furthermore, he defines himself as independent, creative, and opposed to traditional norms—"being a rule breaker and all." He has found his
university education to be "fulfilling" and "not disappointing." "I am happy," he
reports, "to go to English classes and just read for the sake of reading or learning on my own and talking about the literature." One reason he's attracted to
teaching is that it's an excuse "to talk about books."

However, Howard is realistic about students and realizes they may not
share similar pleasures. In an essay about teaching written for a class, he ac-
knowledges this potential difference: "I cannot afford to lose students by taking
their interest in my teaching subject for granted. I must engage my students
from day one." He is talking about academic (not personal) engagement, methods that focus students on ideas and concepts. For instance, in preparing a unit
on American literature for his practicum, Howard plans to include a wide range
of texts, activities, and genres, from poetry to music. On the first day of the
unit, he hopes that students will compare in writing "Cooper's 'noble savages' to
a description of 'white man's dog' in *Fools Crow*," followed by a discussion about
Native Americans and media stereotypes. Then they will read "Steven Vincent
Benet's 'American Names' and listen to 'American Remains' by the Highway-
men, focusing on the inclusion of Native Americans in these histories." Although ambitious, his ideas are novel enough to achieve precisely what he
wishes—attracting students and giving them a "purpose for reading" rather
than "because they say it is a great work."

This combination of strong individualism and passionate intellectual interests makes him believe he'll be a good teacher, one who won't lecture students. Instead, he imagines being that charismatic teacher who invites students
to join his open ventures into the world beyond the established curriculum. In
fact, Howard wants to be the kind of teacher he himself has loved best, and not
the teachers who "have sat behind their desks or hidden behind their podiums
while trying to force feed me lecture." "I learn best and most," he explains,
"when the teacher came out from behind the desk to be with the students and
to learn with the students." "Good teachers," he concludes, "are often taught
just as much as they teach."

His insurance against becoming "a dogmatic instructor controlling their
every minute" is to keep the pace fast and the material interesting: "I don't see
myself as a teacher who stands up at the front. I have to be moving. I like a lot
of action, and I can see a lot of group work." He calls his dream course "Literature of the American West." It involves twelve books, including *Bury My*

Heart at Wounded Knee (by Dee Brown) and *Gunfight at the OK Corral* (by Robert Utley), and numerous films, such as *Posse*, *The Man Who Shot Liberty Valance*, and *Little Big Man*. He imagines that designing curriculum will be a vital and sustaining part of his life as a teacher.

Howard feels confident that he can be a good teacher, "a coach," someone who "facilitates" as long as he can sustain the energy it takes to be that kind of teacher. To be the exceptional teacher, as Howard imagines it, depends on several conditions that he can only anticipate and hope for as he begins his teaching practicum. He will need some freedom to be creative with curriculum, some flexibility to use interactive rather than passive teaching methods, the opportunity to captivate students with ideas instead of controlling them by being "iron-willed" with "ruler-in-hand."

At the moment, a week after he has observed his mentor teaching and prospective students, he is upbeat and hopeful. Among the five classes he'll be teaching, "one freshman honors, two junior honors, two sophomore middle track," Howard will have to plan for "General, World, *and* American" literature. He's excited by the challenge of teaching so broadly. The interactions so far with his mentor-teacher have been especially encouraging: "She said it would be okay if I brought in some of the stuff on Native Americans I had done in your class." Basically, Howard is open to being a teacher because he anticipates doing the kinds of creative and imaginative work with literature and other cultural forms he feels are necessary to sustain him intellectually.

Piecing Together the Puzzle

Prior to the teaching practicum, before they have any sustained experience being seen by others as teachers or even as teachers-in-training, it is difficult for these students to make anything but provisional statements about being teachers. Much of this fuzziness and uncertainty will disappear over the months of the teaching practicum. But their present circumstances constrain what they can know.

What happened during the last minutes of an interview with Howard at the start of the teaching practicum illustrates this condition. Though he's easily answered all my prior questions, the one about personal theories of action stumps him despite my attempts to make the question concrete. "Teachers," I explain, "usually have theories about knowledge, students, or teaching in the back of their heads or somehow in their minds when they think about teaching." I illustrate with an example about why I ask them to design integrated units in the literacy class (of which Howard's was a perfect exemplar). Howard has already unconsciously answered this question in the past hour by explaining the benefits of theme-based teaching, the notion that engaging students actively improves learning, and that cooperative group activities are better than

informational lectures. But I want to know if he's aware of the ideas behind his
plans and actions: "Well, he replied, "I certainly never voiced any. I'm sure I do.
I just have my concepts and I've never really thought about vocalizing them.
Not sure really. Maybe I'll get back to you." However, I'm not content with his
response and pursue things a bit further: "Like I said, it's an odd question so
that's why I end the interview that way." Then Howard says, deliberately, "I
know that I have my thoughts about things. I have never really thought about
putting them together. I'm sure they do piece together into a puzzle. I have just
never really thought about fitting them that way I guess."

As twenty-year-olds, my students are forced to project how they will feel
as they imagine themselves in classrooms as teachers. In this future realm, for
some of my students, choosing to teach doesn't involve the high stakes connected to identity; they regard it (and understandably so) instead as a less complicated but still monumental life decision about a job or a profession. Yet their
attempts to articulate their positions and attitudes about being teachers is important because it reveals where they are, what they're concerned with, and
what it means to be a teacher from their perspective. We can improve our
teacher education programs by taking the variability of their positions into account. I am impressed by how different their views about teachers are, which
helps me to understand how complex identities can be to consider the variety
of forces that influence their development. Though we may be teachers ourselves, we cannot rely overly much on our own past histories to know what
being a teacher is or means for someone else. It always depends on so much
that is unknown and out of our control.

Furthermore, I now realize and more fully appreciate how resourceful
and opportunistic (in the best possible sense) individuals are in noticing and
using whatever resources are at hand—a role model, a book, an encounter in a
classroom, a conversation, a prior experience—in the processes of making and
remaking themselves. As we have seen, particular events, people, things (even
the same ones) can have very different ramifications for one individual compared with another. Plus there exists a vast array of dialectical processes involving social encounters that are ongoing and through which our selves come into
being. The ones that mattered to my students included internal conditions,
such as Elizabeth and her journal, or Donna's connection to the mission field,
as well as external forces, such as Lauren's connection to her former teachers or
Rick's private-school experience.

But are there any experiences or influences that do seem systematically
to make a difference in adopting identities? Certainly, other people, especially
if they are practicing teachers, appear significant some of the time. But there
is nothing definitive or generalizable given my students' stories. Are there,
perhaps, some situations or contexts that seem generally more powerful than

others in regard to identity development? The teaching practicum will certainly be important though it is impossible to say how or in what ways. We will have to wait and see. These are the questions that will be taken up in subsequent chapters.

Going Public

In theorizing about how selves are made, Goffman (1969) uses the term "presentation of self" to suggest that individuals have desires "to be" *and* "to be seen to be" someone or something. Furthermore, individuals have agency, or the ability to signal to others how they wish to be seen. However, these projections always occur in social contexts. No matter how free individuals are to project whatever images of self they desire, they cannot control how others will perceive or interpret them. In all social encounters, there are many kinds of unpredictable and uncontrollable forces at work. Even though individuals are energetically constructing "presentations of selves," they are not existing in a vacuum. Others are active too. Institutions, situations, actors—all features of the social world are involved and affect not only what selves get presented, but also how they are interpreted, taken up, or transformed by our social partners.

In referring to these conditions, the theorist Pierre Bourdieu (1990) describes the context of social life and the individual's participation in it as "improvisational." In other words, while individual action is possible and has the power to affect others, the trajectory of such actions is unpredictable and unreliable, open to modification and subject to appropriation. Furthermore, in every encounter, individuals not only act but are acted upon as well. Even in the simplest circumstances—one person conversing with another—the textures, connections, and patterns of the exchange are extraordinarily complicated so that deliberate control or even directionality seems impossible.

Yet identities do arise through participation in this haphazard, improvisational, and impromptu dance, in "the relationship which is struck between self-image and public image" (Jenkins 1996, 71). My goal in working with these students then is to think about ways of teaching that might maximize interactions and allow these relationships between self-image and public image to flourish. Even though my students are unable to make decisions about becoming teachers (in fact, identities are never the result primarily of a person's decisiveness), they can attempt to reveal their internal feelings or states of mind in public, to try out different presentations of self. Making things public is a way to participate in the identity-making process. Enrolling in a teacher education program, taking courses, going through the practicum are all ways of exposing the self to identity-forming processes. In contrast, those images of ourselves we don't ever expose can never be engaged or reinforced. So Michaela's innate feeling of being a teacher is not, and could never be in this nascent form, an identity. She has to go public. This is something she realizes quite explicitly when she talks about "feeling like a teacher" or "being a teacher." Thus, there is considerable value in persuading our students to actively pursue their identities as teachers but in a context we have specifically designed to offer many opportunities for public dialogue and involvement. This should be the pedagogical goal of all teacher education programs.

REFLECTIONS

Escape

I cannot remember my aversion or even any resistance to the idea of teaching once I went to college, where I enrolled in a teacher education program almost immediately. Oh, I *know* it was purely a matter of pragmatics and survival. I had to escape the dinner table, then and forever. Teaching, it appeared, was something concrete that I could do. With a teaching credential, I could get a job and support myself, and never have to go back to that house, that street, that town again. Not if I didn't want to. And I didn't, at eighteen, emphatically so.

Growing up I had been one of those kids who believed she didn't know anything, who was inward, a quiet, careful girl who led a secret life of desire, of flight into another world, the one that was in books. The act of reading was what all of life should be: sensual, risky, intriguing, sexual, upsetting, unpredictable, satisfying, endlessly variable, a place to play out my fantasies, to test my fledging desires to betray, evade, and disobey the rules of my Catholic background.

This difficult but interesting work occupied most of my childhood. From about the age of eight or nine until I went away to college, I sat for any available hours (and there were many, my mother deciding that I didn't really have to do housework as long as I demonstrated that I could do housework, her job of training achieved, and anyway, she affectionately called me "Lady Jane," thought I was an unreformably messy person—not really a value judgment, just an assessment on her part—and so left me reading) on the left side of the living room couch, legs drawn up and tucked left against the cushion, facing the piano and the banjo clock that hung above it, a position where I could look out the big front window if I cared to, or hear the kids outside through the front screen door if it were spring or summer or fall.

The Truth

School was at least not home. It was a wider world (not wide enough) but a bigger space, more options, more interactions, more different kinds of books to read. So when I went back into the public schools in college as a teacher in training, I felt a painful and compelling connection to many students I met there. They were me—some of them—kids of working-class parents, children of the unemployed wearing clothes too small or too tight, possessing the awkward manner of those who know they have been shortchanged, though pathetically eager nonetheless, immigrants so recent that they were bilingual (as my own parents were). I recognized myself in them. I knew, as if they were mine, their ungraceful movements, understood their unbounded desire to please. For their sakes, I wanted to be that other adult, the one who lived a richer, less constricted, more spacious, wilder, serendipitous life, someone whose stories (ones I got out of books since there had been nothing more expansive or exotic in my life at that time than a year spent at Penn State University in State College, and then three years at Rhode Island College, in Providence) made their eyes wide with delight, surprise, laughter.

This is not altogether the truth. No life, even a young one, can be entirely serene or typical, without alarming and instructional experiences. There was the summer on Martha's Vineyard, living in a seaside house. My boyfriend and I had been hired (through an intermediary) as caretakers to pick up the mail and clean up after the occasional visitors, family members, and friends who would fly in for weekends. The house, it turned out, was owned by an affluent African-American family who operated a chain of supermarkets in New York City, information we did not know nor care to know. We never inquired. It would not have altered our decision even if we had.

In July, three teenage sons, aged seventeen, sixteen, and thirteen, were sent by their father to the Vineyard in order to stay out of trouble in the city. That summer there were only teenagers in the house. Trouble was not something that could be left behind. The trouble had traveled with us: a white couple, both just eighteen, and three black brothers. Over the ownership of a frozen steak (we shared the single refrigerator), a fistfight and broken glass confrontation erupted one day between two of the boys, one black, one white. They circled the kitchen table with clenched fists and dirty language in their mouths until they ran out of insults.

Later, on a party night, the deep-seated anger and unresolved animosity exploded. The black kids with too much to drink could not contain their anger (which they were entitled to, for which there were reasons enough in the world, if not the reasons we gave them—like turning off the power after midnight since we were afraid that, if the police arrived, we'd get busted along with them). We heard them beneath us on our side of the house, the servants' quarters over the kitchen. Pulling open the little door to the twisty stairs, they shouted obscene curses upward, then climbed the narrow staircase painted a ghastly green color and pushed easily through the unfastened door to our rooms. Finding them empty, they ransacked them, ripping up clothes, pulling the pages from our books, and laughing uproariously because they knew we were completely terrified of them, the wicked, scary others. We had fled at the first sounds of their gathering in the kitchen below. Opening the second story window of an upstairs room, we had crawled out on the porch roof, shimmied down the supporting pilaster, and jumped the last five feet into the soft sand of the yard below. In the dark, we ran hard and stupidly away, down the middle of the road. The irony of what had happened was not lost on us. It wasn't the end, but rather the beginning of my education about race and class in a bigoted America.

The Ticket Out

After a year at Penn State, satisfied with the solid *A*s that appeared on my transcript each quarter (the ticket out), I decided to transfer, northeast somewhere. By spring, I was more often than not in Rhode Island on the weekends (unknown to my parents with whom I communicated by sending the occasional letter; we never called each other). Signing up on the ride boards in the student union, answering the ads—"Can take riders to New Haven, Providence, Boston"—it was a right-angled trip, east on I-80, north on I-95, straight into Providence, and up the hill where I would be dropped outside the gates of the university at dawn, the guard having given up long ago or no longer willing to bother with early risers—to visit my boyfriend attending Brown.

Once all the arrangements were in place, I announced to my parents that I would be transferring to Rhode Island College, a small, undistinguished, state teachers college in Providence, on the wrong side of the tracks, my side of course, about six miles or so from the hill where Brown and its artsy sister, Rhode Island School of Design, elegantly occupied the high ground (literally), an escarpment that rose steeply and massively up from the river that wound its way underneath downtown Providence. On hearing the news, believing that I had lost a good education and sacrificed my freedom to boot, my mother cried.

CHAPTER FOUR

SELVES AT THE BOUNDARIES

Two Stories of Becoming

Though she had felt this way for a long time before writing her thesis, Elizabeth had never tried to explain why she believed that language and self were intertwined. The introduction included selected autobiographical details along with her reflections on the meaning and repercussion of these events. Her journal was pivotal: "Without the notebook, I felt as though I wasn't real, that the grief defining my reality was not real. By translating my feelings into words and putting them in the journal, though, they became real—and so did I."

We all believe we have selves, but it is impossible to describe in any definitive way *who those selves are* because identities are fluid, constantly being made, unmade, remade. Identities are not concrete or identifiable even though language, the words used to name and define, makes them appear so. Identities are the result of processes. Nevertheless, amidst this fluidity, we experience our identities individually, calling this internal, private phenomena self, the reality of "I" Elizabeth refers to. Although we acknowledge that selves change—"I'm not the person I was three years ago"—we manage through various modes (for instance, in having a body) to feel the boundaries of a recognizable "I" clearly enough to say "that's me" or "that's not me." So while realizing our selves to be in process, in constant motion of change and evolution, we also hold fast to the idea of a recognizable or identifiable self— the "I" in relation to all others.

The dichotomies that arise in theoretical discussions of identity development such as ones I've been using throughout this book, including self/identity, inner/outer, given/constructed, public/private, create a tangled but interesting conundrum that would take some time to sort out. However, while acknowledging and respecting the valuable thorniness of theory, I will expend no efforts in this direction. Instead I insist and rely on the pragmatic. Students arrive in my classroom as individuals (empirical selves) who want to be teachers. Thus in practice, in the world, identities develop. The enduring question of this book concerns how identities come about. But since I can draw on limited information and experience, I am concerned with a considerably narrowed question connected to a local place and time: How do these students engage in the work of becoming teachers?

This chapter focuses on two students, Elizabeth and Rick, and tells their stories in more depth to demonstrate how variable identity processes are. In examining this synchronic slice of their lives, I attempt what I know to be impossible: to portray *who these students are* (not fundamentally but momentarily), and to delineate the forces, internal and external, that actively constitute their identities. My goal is to reveal—in specific contexts, in everyday events, in particular moments—the process of identities underway. How will I start? Where do I propose to look? On the liminal edges between body, place, and time since "identities are to be found and negotiated at their boundaries where the internal and the external meet" (Jenkins 1996, 24).

Elizabeth's Story

Inside Out

"Good writing comes from the inside out. This is at the heart of what writing should be," Elizabeth asserts very definitely, squinting into the sunlight as she speaks during an interview one afternoon in my fifth floor office. Incredible, an Expressivist, I think, feeling a little guilty for agreeing with and enjoying so much what she has to say. (Expressivism is a philosophy of teaching writing that came into prominence during the 1970s. Though not as popular a theory as it once was, having been superseded in the field by social-constructivist theories, it continues to exert tremendous influence on the practice of teaching writing and remains important because it describes what writers often feel to be intrinsically true about composing. Though I greatly oversimplify here and refer to originary claims [which have been modified and transformed in the ensuing decades], some of its basic tenet is that language always begins with the self. As it is directed outward, it undergoes a series of transformations from the private to the public. The goal of an Expressivist writing teacher is to help students gain access to their own unique ideas and to write using an "authentic voice.")

How did she come to this conclusion? I wonder. Was it Professor Langston's influence when Elizabeth took English 31 (Composition Theory and the Teaching of Writing)? Maybe. Partially. But it can't be the whole answer. Certainly students are sometimes affected by their classes but rarely converted or as knowledgeable about a specific approach to teaching writing. It makes me pay closer attention and to catalogue what I might already know about this young woman, and what I need yet to learn.

There are some objective facts. Like the others, Elizabeth became an English education major as a college junior. During spring semester of her junior year, she declared her intention to write a senior thesis and drafted a proposal. Her teaching practicum (fall of her senior year) occurred at a high school in a neighboring small town. In the spring of her senior year, Elizabeth wrote the thesis that included an analysis of her experiences as a student teacher. She completed her student teaching successfully, receiving strong, positive evaluations from her supervising teacher (university) and her cooperating teacher (high school). In the spring of senior year, Elizabeth defended her thesis, graduating with honors.

But this information mainly describes Elizabeth's overt acts. To know who she is (or was) during this time or anytime, we are compelled to make inferences: She intends to be a teacher and committed herself to that pursuit wholeheartedly during student teaching. Someone who writes an honors thesis is strongly motivated; recognition is important to that person. A student who manages to do anything else besides student teaching during that semester has reasons for working hard, for electing to take on extra work.

However, even these few inferences, ones that can be reasonably generated from the supporting details, only introduce uncertainty, hint at other possible images of Elizabeth's person: Who she is—her self, her identity—and how she developed. During the interviews, in conversations, and in her writing, Elizabeth repeatedly raised certain themes such as the primacy of writing to create knowledge, or the value of knowing what one really thinks. These themes were always contextualized; they emerged in relation to the time she was taking courses, while writing her thesis, during student teaching. In creating Elizabeth's "self" portrait, I have tried to be consistent with her ways of thinking. Her story reveals how internal and external factors are inseparable, coincident, and simultaneous partners in shaping identity. There are no single determining moments, incidents, predilections, or character traits. Thus, everything matters in some way or another—events have unpredictable effects, and there is very little that anyone can control. The lesson we learn as educators is to provide enough open ground for such dynamic free play to happen.

A Challenge

Halfway through her student teaching semester, Elizabeth's cooperating teacher, Mr. Collins, handed her an article and issued the following instructions: "Read this. I think you'll find it useful." Elizabeth had begun her practicum believing in whole language, an approach to teaching based on "integration and connectedness." Though common in elementary schools, whole language has not been widely implemented by high school teachers, partly because of the pronounced distinctions between disciplines in secondary education.

Written by E. D. Hirsch, the article was entitled "Reality's Revenge: Research and Ideology." In Elizabeth's mind, Mr. Collins's action was motivated by his desire to get her "back on track" since he believed that she had been "led astray by progressive or liberal ideologies such as whole language." After this exchange, Elizabeth's attitude toward her teaching changed dramatically. Instead of attempting lessons that mimicked Mr. Collins's style (lecturing, emphasizing historical background and close readings), Elizabeth sought out techniques for connecting students personally to the assigned literature. She taught the Romantic poets by asking students to play recordings of favorite songs or to recite poetry, and later by analyzing their choices according to Romantic themes such as unrequited love or the power of nature. On the morning of that particular lesson, Mr. Collins took one look at the CD player and circled desks and simply left the room.

A few months later, Elizabeth wrote the following about the episode beginning with the E. D. Hirsch article: "I did read it as promised that night, and probably five times since. What is so ironic is that the very article he thought would dismantle my idealistic beliefs, instead anchored them even deeper. Reading it allowed me to realize the tension between Mr. Collins and me was not the result of personality conflict, which greatly relieved me. It was unnerving at times to feel the tension between us and not know exactly why it was there. But by giving me that article, he was offering his educational manifesto, and it allowed me to see that we were operating from two opposing philosophies. Before I understood that Mr. Collins embraced a different philosophy to teaching, that of 'language as artifact,' I kept thinking he was not being a good process teacher. As soon as I understood that this was not his goal, I was able to appreciate his actions. Nevertheless, I knew I could not change my own philosophy any easier than I could change the events of my past."

This narrative reveals Elizabeth's commitment to internal standards; she speaks and acts with authority, an authority derived (as she insists) from self-conviction and internal authorization. During student teaching, when students are enormously pressured to conform to the practices of their cooperating teachers and the institutional norms, Elizabeth attempts first to accommodate but then she strategically resists. This transformation in her teaching is provoked by the discomfort of her situation. To eliminate the stress, she's forced to analyze what's going on and why. Once she is able to articulate the source of the difficulty between her and her mentor teacher as "a conflict in ideologies or a difference in goals," she is freed up to teach in ways she believes are appropriate. Furthermore, Elizabeth's actions are validated by her internal philosophy of teaching, which is nonnegotiable, feeling as permanent and real as the lived events of her past life.

But in Elizabeth's case (remember that I had only limited and partial contact with her in all these settings), there emerged four fields that seemed to affect her development as a teacher: her journal, classes at the university, the teaching practicum, and her honors thesis.

1. Journal: "A way of making sure I did not die." With little drama but with steadfast conviction, Elizabeth reported one day that she owed her very existence (and thus her imminent graduation from college) to the enterprise of journal writing. As a fourteen-year-old, faced with the unimaginable event of her mother's death, Elizabeth had one day shortly thereafter "grabbed a new, red Mead notebook, dated the page, and wrote, "I don't know why I am doing this."

Eight years later (and still writing a journal), Elizabeth describes that reason, one which she claimed to have known only instinctively before: "The journal was not only a chronicle of mother-loss and disconnection from family, but it was the *place* that I made sense and meaning out of life. It was how I learned to be critical and introspective—to find answers, reasons, and connections by thinking about thinking. The voice that I had created in the journal became my way of seeing and of being. It was my salvation and my way of making sure that I did not die along with my mother."

Writing saved her, she claimed, because it allowed her to create a voice, an actual, physical, external representation of the inner experience of being a person, an "I," one that felt tenuous, amorphous, and absolutely threatened. Since the book indisputably existed (she could see and hold it, turn the pages, read and reread it, always add more), and considering she had produced it, and it was hers alone, then by extension she must be real too. Or so she believed (and fortunately so) since "no one understood that my mother's death wasn't the unfortunate event that changed my life, but the condition that defined it."

The journal she described as a place, a context in which her self lives, but outside her embodied self. The journal allowed her to think, analyze, criticize, evaluate, see, to be, because of the dialectical movement between internal states and external representations. She was able to look at and examine the Elizabeth "out there" and compare it to the one she felt but could really only imagine inside, a process of identity making. She accounted for the effect this way: "Because Mom was not there to reaffirm my identity, to grant me acceptance or approval, I was forced to find my own way of doing it through writing." Elizabeth's reported experience suggests that identities are established through the affirmation of others who reflect approval and care back to us, which is undoubtedly true (our conversations are an example of this). But her case also demonstrates that when those important others are absent or few in number, that there are other avenues for creating identities. Elizabeth would say that writing a journal is one of them.

2. Classes: Occupying the "middle ground." During one of our first conversations, Elizabeth made her ambivalence clear: "At this point, where I'm in the transition of student and teacher, I don't know how all this stuff is going to translate when I'm really in teacher mode, because right now, I'm in this middle ground." For Elizabeth and her cohort, the middle ground of teacher education at Carolina from 1995–1997 consisted of a two-year sequence of undergraduate education courses that students took in conjunction with those required in their academic major. Thus, in practice, education students become "double" majors though they're not officially recognized as such. To major in education, students are required to formally apply at the end of their sophomore year to Education, a professional school distinct from the College of Arts and Sciences into which all entering students are first admitted. Because the certification program is relatively small, the competition for admission is steep; English majors have an average GPA of 3.2 after two years of general college.

Since the logistics of course offerings and other institutional configurations constrain students' schedules, they have relatively little exposure to the public schools before their student teaching semester. As part of a course, sometimes professors require students (as I do) to observe or tutor, but often these experiences are either limited to a few visits or else occur in elementary or middle schools, not high schools, which is where the secondary students intend to teach one day. Thus, the middle ground of teacher education, consisting mainly of self-contained academic courses, is fairly sterile territory unable to provide for students necessary information about the nature of schools or a sense of themselves as teachers in those schools.

But whatever their practical shortcomings and situational constraints, Elizabeth found her education courses valuable. They introduced her to new knowledge, especially to a philosophy of education she found convivial; they taught her ways of conceptualizing and understanding her discipline to order to teach it. In addition, she learned to plan lessons, to develop units of study based on themes or around rhetorical goals, and was introduced to array of approaches for reading and writing literary and nonliterary texts. Most important, however, were the connections Elizabeth perceived between her past practices and her university career: "As I began college, I also realized that the journal was directly related to my desire to become a teacher. What, though, does the role that writing played in my life have to do with the desire to teach? A lot." Elizabeth was surprised to discover that other people also had experienced writing as redemptive: "Throughout high school I thought my relationship with language was a special case, entirely personal and unrelated to academics. But then in college in the few courses in which I took root and felt at home, I discovered that my ideas about writing had a place in academics and applied to much more than my personal life." Recognizing the similarities between these two contexts—her journal and the classes at college where she "took root"—provoked Elizabeth into seriously imagining herself as a teacher. However, it was never the generic sort, but always that special variety she envisioned, a teacher committed to literature by way of writing, dedicated to instructional methods that originated with the personal.

• Good writing. One day when I ask Elizabeth to talk about the courses that influenced her thinking (belief system) at the university, she differentiates between assignments that led to "good writing" and those that call for a written product but where "you really are not writing." Elizabeth explains that her journal, where writing had meaning and purpose, is the standard against which she measured and judged other writing assignments as "good" or "useless." She explains that in her journal "the function of my writing took complete precedence over the form, and so I did what I needed to make it work for me." In contrast, Elizabeth recalls the literature course she took as a first-year student. The final project involved students in compiling a literature anthology. Elizabeth says, "I learned about the politics of making an anthology and what goes in and what doesn't. I was learning stuff but my opinion wasn't really important." And since her opinion didn't matter, the writing that resulted was form without substance.

In contrast, because of papers she wrote English 11 (basic composition) during her first semester on campus, Elizabeth became interested in majoring in education. It wasn't the topic necessarily that mattered but instead the process of researching and writing the paper that made it memorable. She was asked to interview a professor in any academic field and to discuss a problem in that field. Elizabeth was referred to a professor involved in the social foundations of education. She describes the research process this way: "I went and talked to him, and it was interesting because he talked about prenatal care. He didn't take one of those topics that are beat into the ground about the problems in education, all the things I had heard all along. It was a completely different aspect. I was intrigued by it."

When I asked why this assignment led to her brand of "good writing," Elizabeth replied that the research and writing involved figuring out not only the facts, or the opinions and beliefs of others, but led to discovering what she herself *thought*. Writing that's not real happens when the writer isn't personally invested, for instance, "when you do a research paper for the sake of doing research, like the seventeen page paper on Romanticism I wrote when I was a senior." "But," she counters, "those papers I wrote in English 11, I had learn all this stuff about prenatal care, and then about journalism, and one about the curriculum. I had to do research in order to support what I thought. And I had to really understand what they were saying because if I put something to paper that went against what I thought, that would suggest I was really stupid. So the research had an end."

In making judgments, decisions, and evaluations about her courses, Elizabeth returns repeatedly to the internal standards of her sense of self, weighing the degree to which her opinions mattered and how much she herself was engaged. This tendency to measure outer conditions against the solid weight of the inner seems to be a way of being for Elizabeth that transcends the specific situation of judging good courses; it is the criteria she uses to judge the value of all enterprises central to her self.

As Elizabeth advanced through the undergraduate program, taking more courses and making the decision to be an education major, her relationship to writing became more complicated. Her foundational belief in the primacy of the self remained solid: good writing depends on discovering and being true to what she herself thinks. But she became concerned with another more social, less individual dimension—the relationship of writer to readers. Writing must not only come from the inside, but it can no longer be only representational (the way her journal was); writing is good when it communicates what she thinks to others.

One favorite class was Rhetorical Theory and Teaching Writing. Elizabeth particularly enjoyed the task of writing a philosophy of composition. I know from experience that students often struggle with the concept of articulating a philosophy that is the process of laying out the underlying theory or rationale for classroom practices they're advocating as prospective writing teachers. Elizabeth remembers that "it didn't seem like so big of a deal, because you could put it together piece by piece. There was a response journal in that class too, so you were forming your ideas all along." However she does report one major problem. "And so the only thing hard about writing that paper was that there was something I wanted to say, and it was hard accomplishing it the way I wanted it to sound. So it was hard because I knew what I wanted to say, not because it was a difficult assignment."

In looking outward, by adding a new standard—"Am I communicating?"—to her long-standing insistence on representing her internal thoughts, Elizabeth stumbles on another problem that she conceives of initially as a writing problem. But fortunately the problem of making internal beliefs apparent in what you do turns out to be a useful one for a prospective teacher, for putting theory and practice together.

• Theory and practice. Arriving for her weekly conference, Elizabeth drops her bags, takes a seat and starts talking immediately about what she's written since our last meeting. Part of her thesis research strategy involves finding and rereading all the materials she's produced in previous classes, like her reading journals, papers, essay examinations, or projects. In a scheme like hers, in which she is writing about writing, the content or knowledge she learns forces her to reflect and think back about her own writing process.

She reports that after rereading some class notes, one idea popped out. What she found "most important was knowing there was a reason why people said and wrote things the way they did." Furthermore, being a good writing teacher meant you had to consider an individual's intentions: "If you don't start out with that reason and [compare it to] the way they did it, then, you're really not [going to be] successful" as a teacher.

Then she continues to discuss the process of her research: "The text that really made an impact was when we had to comment on the instructional models. I read what I had written, and that gave me a chance to express and figure out what I really thought about all that stuff." But suddenly it occurs to her that the idea she's mentioned a few minutes ago, "knowing the reasons behind what people write," is exactly the problem she's confronting at the moment. She wants "her reasons for teaching writing this way" to be evident in the way her thesis is written. This effect is extremely hard to achieve.

She was disappointed, she tells me, reading her draft late last night at the computer center. "It didn't work that well for me." She feels a gap between the thoughts inside and the way her reasons are represented outwardly in writing: "In some cases it did, but in a lot of ways I thought I really missed on making [the reasons] come through." But the experience is a valuable one, as Elizabeth understands now, firsthand, how tricky it is to connect theory and practice in the contained space of a text, let alone in a real classroom when she's teaching. She comments: "So that was important, realizing that it's not that easy to make it apparent in what you do." No kidding, I think. With that shared insight hanging in the air between us, she reaches toward me and hands over a sheaf of papers I'll read later. "See you next week," she says and swings out of the room.

• Legitimation. My first impressions of Elizabeth, whom I encountered as a student in my English grammar course, were very favorable. Observing how students behave in this class allows me to speculate about how they might turn out as teachers. About Elizabeth, I felt optimistic. In class she appeared confident, participating freely, joining in discussions, asking questions, and volunteering to put tree diagrams on the blackboard. (It is the rare student who willingly takes to the board in this circumstance!)

In the public space of the classroom, my actions and responses as the teacher conveyed approval and encouragement for any student willing to take chances and to be involved with the dreaded subject matter of English grammar. Although Elizabeth learned much about how English is structured, varieties of English, and the relationship of language form to language function ("it came in handy"), acquiring information was only one benefit.

Classrooms are social spaces, populated by peers and teachers, where students negotiate identities, presenting a public self through interactions with others. In talking about how she'd changed, Elizabeth described her teenage self as having a "very loud voice," one born out of loss and self-created through language. She regarded this voice as singular, internal, not connected to life outside, a unique perspective. College changed this perception, perhaps because Elizabeth predicated this self on knowing what she thought. And in college, thinking is academic currency. Many courses demanded her not only to think but to represent and support her positions and beliefs, not just in a private journal, but in class discussions, in papers she shared with writing groups, in class presentations and research papers.

Coincidentally, Elizabeth regards being clear about her own thinking as foundational to who she is. What Elizabeth discovered in the public dialogue of college was validation of her self from an external source. For instance, she remembered the assignment to write her philosophy of teaching writing as "a real big stepping stone." She continues, "It was the first time I felt that what I was thinking was *legitimate*." Her past experience counted too, magnifying the self-validation that resulted. "It sounds so simple and obvious but my philosophy of composition was the importance of thinking. I had the experiences of high school in writing classes where there was an absence of thinking and an absence of authority and ownership. So I had personal stories that illustrated what they were talking about in the articles." The match encouraged her, giving her, "the go-ahead to pursue it more."

Not that Elizabeth felt at this stage entirely secure in her position or in possession of authority that originated outside in the public arena. Paradoxically, the force of such congruence between her beliefs and those expressed by the authorities she's read in the discipline makes her hesitant: " Because I think it's so certain for me, I tend to doubt myself. Like, well, this must not be what they meant." Then she explains how it feels to want certainty and the authority that comes with it, but how difficult such development is in the academic community where students receive mixed messages such as "You're smart, but you're still only a student. You're not one of us, and if you'd like to be someday, you'll have to work hard, really hard. Can you really do it? You'll have to prove it." Elizabeth explained the anxiety this way: "You go along thinking you can never be an expert on anything, like you never could know what they really mean, it's just the whole atmosphere."

So becoming (an agent, an expert, something other than a student) depends on a delicate balancing act, comparing and adjusting inner states in relation to external cues, calculating the seriousness of negative signs and the value of positive approval (good grades, notice by professors, acceptance into the school of education, qualifying for honors). Nevertheless, this kind of grounded knowing (no matter how provisional, deceptive, or false) leads to agency. Elizabeth confidently visualizes herself as a teacher at precisely the point when she assumes the position of the knower: "I wasn't thinking in terms of this, but now, looking back on what I've written about the journals, I mean, that's exactly what it was—a situation where I didn't know really what was going on, and then the writing was a way to understand it. I can apply that in teaching. So that was the real key."

Elizabeth however continues to have reservations because her convictions have originated primarily in the realm of personal not academic knowledge. While she feels powerfully certain, in another way she also isn't sure after all. "Things that make you an expert have to be hard," she muses. In an academic setting she feels doubtful; in the personal world of her journal, she is absolutely convinced. The one thing that helps her to resolve these disparities is the "support or reinforcement I find in classes here or in texts." It is clear that Elizabeth doesn't want to give up on her deeply rooted beliefs but instead wants confirmation. She wants the outside world to function in part the way her inner world does. It has been an effort for her to reveal so much, to take the risk of being wrong. She guards against forces that might erode her inner beliefs. Receiving acknowledgment and positive reinforcement from outside sources would eliminate some of the anxiety she feels and make it easier for her to move forward.

I'm struck by Elizabeth's claims about how knowledge led to assuredness about teaching. So I ask, "Do you think this certainty is going to help you be a teacher?" Without hesitation, Elizabeth replies, "Yeah. It gives me a real reason to be there." She laughs. "I couldn't do it because I love English. I could go on and on with reasons why I couldn't do it. But if I didn't feel like I had a real reason to be there, then I wouldn't have ever majored in it." And what's a real reason? What counts as authentic motivation? It goes back to the transformative power of writing. About this, Elizabeth has a sudden premonition: "And so I don't know, it might make my job harder feeling this way and knowing what a real reason is."

• Experience. A few weeks before student teaching, I encourage Elizabeth through my questions to project herself into the future: "What about teaching," I ask, "Are there external things that reflect internal states?" "Sure," she replies. "The assignments, the nature of your class in general. The way you grade, the way you have class each day. Things like that. What you write about, the literature you read, everything in your class." Then she adds a qualifier, "But I don't know. I've never been in a situation where I can tell. So how would I know? I'm just imagining it." I counter by replying, "Of course you don't know, but you instinctively feel there are certain things you can do—" She interrupts, saying, "Yeah, that's all I have in mind, my *instincts* about it!" I add (too cheerfully), "Well, you have your experiences too." "Yeah, but I get so caught up in my experiences," Elizabeth retorts, a little agitated. She imagines her experiences are "pretty universal," and "go across the board" but then she comments: "Sometimes I wonder if I don't get caught up in my own narrow-mindedness just thinking that my experience is going to be everybody else's."

Although she can't envision being any other way, she worries about being different: "I wonder about other teachers. I wonder if I'm the exception." Her doubts arise ironically from the clarity of her image of the ideal teacher: "Is being a whole language teacher and really believing those things something that you can successfully attain from reading and studying, and going to classes and stuff? Or is it an experiential thing?" I assure her, "Experience matters, but it's not everything." I want to say, "Look at you! I'm convinced!" And I am. Besides, I also believe that she is right about the reasons for teaching writing as process, and justified (sadly) in questioning her goals (given the prevailing teaching methods in many high schools): "So when I get to be a teacher, is my mission going to be to get every student to discover themselves by writing? How's that going to translate into real concrete teaching, into the things that I'll be doing in the classroom?" Outwardly I'm calm. It is possible; she *is* right. While not the only mission, it is a really good one. But inside my mind races ahead worrying about what will happen when she tries to be a whole language teacher in a high school setting, let alone attempting this feat as a student teacher. But her situation sounds promising and I'm hopeful.

3. Student teaching: "Swimming upstream." Under the category "special needs" on the application form for the teaching practicum, Elizabeth requested placement with a mentor teacher who advocated a process approach to teaching writing. The "process approach" to teaching writing is fairly widespread in high school and college writing programs, partly because of the activism of the National Writing Project. (A process approach to teaching writing is based on the premise that writing is a process to be learned rather than a collection of sub-skills to be taught; that there is no one writing process, but a variety of recursive processes linked to a writer's purpose and the rhetorical situation; that writing is social and collaborative, not a solitary activity; that writers learn best from attempting whole texts rather than atomistic pieces, practicing small steps and subskills. Elizabeth's request, couched as the "process approach," made sense because some characteristics—being student-centered, emphasizing process over product—overlap with those associated with whole language philosophy and Expressivism in composition.)

It is unusual for a student to focus on writing not literature, on method instead of literary period, such as "American literature." Students more commonly might make a special case for a particular school or geographical area, or ask for a certain type student, such as advanced placement juniors. Nevertheless, a match was made. The head of the English department in a small town nearby was well-known in the district as an advocate of the process approach. He and two other teachers in the department constituted a working group, cooperating to design common syllabi and activities. Elizabeth and another student teacher, Linda, were assigned to this group, Linda to Mr. Streblinski, the department chair, and Elizabeth to Mr. Collins, another of the teachers. "Everything is collaborative, so when Linda and I create our unit, we have to do it together in cooperation with them because they're all going to teach it. They seem really three ideal teachers. I'm really lucky, and happy about where I am."

Though Elizabeth and Linda had met only the month prior to student teaching (Linda, three years older than Elizabeth, having recently moved to North Carolina from California, was in the graduate MAT program, which has little overlap with the undergraduate program), they ended up working closely together. Their relationship grew because of social, institutional, and physical factors: their mentor teachers met every day in adjacent classrooms in one wing of the building. This alliance also made for an atypical practicum situation, which is generally more self-enclosed, one mentor teacher and one intern, in a classroom full of students, with the door closed.

The teaching practicum is always complicated because of the relationship triangle between student, mentor teacher, and supervising teacher. In Elizabeth's case, the relationships multiplied into several connected networks. Not only did she interact daily with Linda and her mentor beside Mr. Collins, but I was also visiting the school periodically (a professional development initiative) and communicating with Elizabeth in person and by e-mail. Mr. Streblinski and Mr. Collins had a long-standing partnership, and Dr. Carson, her supervising teacher, and I were colleagues at the university. These relationships are important because interactions with authority figures powerfully affect who we become and how we think about ourselves.

Summarizing Elizabeth's experiences during her student teaching semester is nearly impossible. In lieu of telling a narrative, I present a scrapbook of quotations drawn from the interviews that represent Elizabeth's position and attitudes at different moments during this period. This approach will highlight the interplay of factors, experiences, discourses, and individuals that affected Elizabeth's developing sense of herself as a teacher. In being selective, I have left out a great deal. But my aim is not to present a complete or exhaustive picture of her teaching practicum, but to feature those moments Elizabeth herself accentuated.

Some background is relevant: Elizabeth was teaching primarily high school seniors, one section of AP students who were college bound, and three sections of standard senior English. Her first task was to teach *Hamlet*, both film and text, including a paper assignment. In addition, the NC curriculum guide specifies that all seniors write a research paper; this major project occupied about five weeks of Elizabeth's teaching experience working the standard seniors. For the AP seniors, Elizabeth taught units on eighteenth century and Romantic literature.

Early September 1996: First Impressions

- I walked in and saw this process-writing flow chart on the board, and I sighed with relief.
- Obviously it's reassuring to get somewhere and realize that everything you've *invested yourself in* for the past few years doesn't go completely down the toilet when you walk in.
- Even though Mr. Collins is the oldest of the three, you can tell he's coming from a slightly different perspective because he wasn't taught necessarily like this, but he's real open to it. Mr. Streblinski and Ms. Stevens (the other teacher in the group)—they've done it. They've got more that mind-set so they're kind of pulling him up.
- Some people go into a structure where they have to conform. You dread walking into a real structured hierarchy where "You learn what I do," and then "You do what I do." But they weren't looking at Linda and me as just "someone has got to come in." They wanted to get some things from us too.
- When I'm not in control of my own learning . . . I have the *motivation* of always wanting to do good, but that's not enough. So if I'm not in control then it doesn't come out as good as it should.

Mid-September to Early October 1996: Awakening

- The paper assignment for the *Canterbury Tales* was to take three characters from the prologue and compare and contrast them with three modern-day characters. Well Linda and I got this assignment at the same time. And between classes, we both ran out into the hall with the same ideas. She goes, "Did you see that paper assignment?!" I said, "Yeah, it's terrible."
- The day scheduled for "workshop" or "conferences" really puzzled me. There was no structure, workshop criteria, or mini-lessons. How was this process writing when they rarely talked about the writing to each other or to their teacher?

- I think Mr. Collins will be open to me doing different things but maybe not very approving of it, which concerns me because he evaluates me.
- I was talking to Linda about teaching *Hamlet*. And Mr. Streblinski overheard and said he really prefers they see the movie first and not read the whole text through first. I see that as valid; it's good to watch the movie first. But he confused me, he discouraged me.
- I went though the little packet they had created for the research unit and wrote down the things that were really horrible about it. The goals, objectives, were things like "Students will be able to synthesize or manage large chunks of information and rewrite it in their own words onto note cards." I mean what can I do with that? I can't throw out their note card system.
- I have a different impression of Mr. Collins. He seems a little bit more resistant. I think he pacifies Mr. Streblinski by agreeing to a certain amount, "Okay I'll let them do group work one day, but they're going to read this book, and they're going to know this other stuff."
- I can't do what Mr. Collins does. He knows so much; all he does is go in there and talk about what he knows. Intellectually I don't have that many facts stored in my brain. I can't go in there and teach them that stuff so I've got to make them *do* stuff together. I have this fear that he's going to walk in one day and see them talking to each other instead of listening to a teacher, and he's going to go bananas.
- I think in the end everything will work out. It might not be that I find my philosophical match in a mentor teacher but . . .
- The worst part, being in Mr. Collins's room, is that Mr. Streblinski designs all of this. Everything comes from his room to Mr. Collins's room. Everything. And Mr. Collins, this isn't his style, it's not how he teaches. So he doesn't explain it to the students. It just isn't his assignment. He has nothing invested in it.

Late October 1996: In the Thick of It
- The research paper is just another whole can of worms. It's scary [laughs]. "Synthesize information onto a notecard, blah, blah, blah." I asked Mr. Streblinski, "Just so I understand. Is the *purpose* of the research paper for the kids *to learn research skills*? Right?" And he said, "Yeah, that's it." Well, [agitated] that's a good purpose. That's real. That *is* motivational. That's really going to teach someone how to write? Anything would seem so much better [sighs].
- This is a mess. I really feel strongly that Mr. Collins would be so much better as a traditional lecturing teacher without this process stuff from Mr. Streblinski.

- Linda brings questions to Mr. Streblinski all the time and his standard response is "I've tried it and it doesn't work." And so you have a real doomed feeling.

- In some respects, Mr. Streblinski honestly believes it [process], but other factors are so powerful that when he gets into the classroom he just does whatever he can. But the point is that he hasn't completely disregarded it. He can go to people and say he's done this stuff. Students have some choice in the literature they read outside of class. They do a journal on it. They do two drafts for every paper. They have writing workshop before every final draft is turned in.

- I was writing about how, in my situation, theory was misplaced and misconstrued into a dangerous and destructive thing. I think sometimes I am too judgmental. I'm this wet-behind-the-ears undergraduate student and I shouldn't be making these kind of judgments. But I don't go in there with the idea of protesting! But I see these things and I just want to scream, "Stop! What are you doing!"

- I thought from Mr. Collins that he wanted me to do the text [*Hamlet*] then show the movie. I was gonna introduce the themes, have questions to organize the text around, but then I couldn't because you can't take the books home. I can't plan anything that doesn't involve taking the text home!

- I'm starting to actually like Mr. Collins a lot more than I did before. Because I'm able to sympathize with him because he has to deal with Mr. Streblinski dictating what goes on to an extent. So I can see why he does the things he does.

November 1996: Getting Her Bearings
- It's hard sometimes. I feel so much more allied with the students than with the teachers. One student in my class who had written his personal narrative about seven kinds of love didn't understand what Mr. Collins wrote on his paper. It had "Frag, Frag, Frag" written all over it. I said, "First I've got to explain this to you or you're never going to get a good grade." So we went through that.

- What he really wanted to know was how to be a better writer. He already understood the distinction [between being a writer and being able to fix surface errors] and so we just started talking. He said, "What should I do?" We talked about how to do an outline so your ideas aren't so confusing. We went through some things that aren't going to help him get better grades probably but just so he would feel better about what he was doing [as a writer]. But I did feel really torn. Should I just spend this whole time only explaining what sentence fragments and run-ons are or how to do this formula? It was so frustrating. It's frustrating all day.

- To change the research paper, the first thing was we did away with the "just choose a topic." They needed to have reasons for writing it. Linda and I thought that the whole idea of taking it from something that you feel passionately about, you're invested in, and having to defend your opinions— that's like the most basic reason to write. That was the first thing, to turn it into a position paper. Just that change was a huge thing for Mr. Streblinski and Mr. Collins to accept.

- It feels different when I walk in. I don't feel uneasy anymore. But a lot of other things have happened, like the day we had the discussion. They were saying things they wouldn't have said in front of another teacher. I said, "I realize I'm not much older than you, but please be careful what you say," because they were admitting a lot of things that they should not have been admitting to me. I think they were thinking that it would affiliate them with me, and so they said something about "What? You're not comfortable when you're with us?" I started talking about what it was like to be only three or four years older and teach them.

- They [the three standard senior sections] had a debate and then they wrote these discovery drafts. I took them home and read them this weekend, and wrote back what I thought of them. Not about what they'd said, but whether or not it was going to work as far as a research paper. It went really well this time. I think I could say the words *discovery draft* and not get a lot of backlash now. I don't think they feel like it's a horrible thing, or at least it's starting to be that way.

- I read Yvonne's paper, and it was just so good. One reason she acts up is because she knows what's going on. I made sure she got to say what she wanted that day in the debate about racism. She was having a real problem getting out what she was trying to say. I knew what she was getting at, so I expressed it the way I thought she meant it. I could see at that instant, all of a sudden, I was in a completely different light. Because I think she saw me as this prissy little white girl. Once she realized that maybe I agreed with what she was saying, it was a whole different story.

Late November 1996: Teaching Her Way

- Second period (AP) is a small class, only twenty-one people. He said to pick up with the eighteenth century. When I asked for advice, he'd rambled about Addison and Steele in the *Tattler* or some literary magazine and how wonderful it was. He was always saying go through [the literature] and have them paraphrase, find the allusions and the references to this and to that. And I would just nod and say okay and pray the next day at the beginning of second period he'd just leave. And usually he did. Because I didn't do that or I would have just bombed.

- Even if I knew what the literature meant, I wasn't to the point where I could explain it in any interesting way. I'd tell them, and they'd just kind of sit there. Instead, like when we were doing literary critiques, I asked them to write their own literary criticisms. That worked out really well. Some of them are really good. I typed them all up, called it "Literary Wisdom by Second Period." That was fun.

- He's such a critic. He thinks that literature should be dissected, taken apart, that kind of thing.

- Thank God for Linda. We were talking about Romantic literature and how it differed from the eighteenth century satire. It was didactic, supposed to be entertaining and educational; the Romantics were really individual. So I thought we would introduce Romantic poetry by asking them to bring in their favorite poems or song lyrics. It worked out. And when they did my evaluations they all said that this was their favorite thing.

- Today Linda said she's trying to find her philosophy. She doesn't know what she wants writing to be in her class. She's reading like three different books. She's kept on saying, "I don't know what I want it to be." And so we started talking about that, and everytime I talk about it, I find out more, what I think, so it's really good. I'm glad she's there right next door.

- One time before they had done some group work and it was time to share it. I felt like in such a small classroom we should get into a circle. But he always raises eyebrows at that. He really raised his eyebrows when he came back in that day.

- I'm gonna get in trouble one day. Somebody is going to hear me in the teacher lounge.

- Going back to the literature textbook was anticlimactic, to go from the circle activity—a good introduction, I got my point across—to "Elegy Written in a Country Churchyard!" Ugh! I felt like I was stabbing them in the back. "I'm sorry to do this." I kept apologizing for it. And that was bad. That was one of the things I shouldn't have done.

- Linda and I—we'll get something out of it but it's going to be a struggle. Talking it out with her helps me so much, just to get it out, to express it and be able to work with it.

- I like Blake's poetry. I spent a lot of time talking about his ideas of religion in life. They really enjoyed that and kept asking me questions that led to good discussions: Is God in nature, and this and that. We did "The Lamb" and "The Tyger" from Blake's *Songs of Innocence* and *Songs of Experience*. They were like, "Oh, the lamb is like childhood and the tiger is adulthood. And what about in between, what would we be?" So I said, "If you wrote a poem about being in the middle [being adolescents], what animal would you use?

This one guy says (laughs), "The Platypus because nobody knows what it is and nobody cares." One by one the light bulb goes off with the rest of them. Finally they said, "Ms. Tavey, what would you be?" I said to them, "A salmon! Because I'm always swimming upstream."

December 1996: Near the End

- Today was the ultimate test though. Mr. Collins is really undoing the changes we had made with the research paper, and he's undermining me and contradicting me in front of the class.

- The last week was good because I was really good at talking to the students during conferences. But I was really angry dealing with those research papers because I could have changed the assignment so it wasn't so difficult or malproductive for the students. We had time to make it better so that I wasn't revising ninety-something papers. The students are completely capable of reading a friends' writing and saying, "This doesn't make sense." It was just because Mr. Streblinski and Mr. Collins won't change.

- Mr. Collins just took over the research paper. From there it was just his show. And I was just a facilitator, you know?

- Some papers may look different just because of what they were writing about. That's at least one thing maybe we changed. There were a lot of papers on abortion and gun control, but also there were papers on things that previously students would not have considered a legitimate topic to write about, like the guy doing primary research on punk music.

- The students don't know what writing is. That sounds too basic to say, but teaching turned into giving them the formula. Because they weren't *writing* anything. They were just taking these suggestions or advice on the most surface level and trying to change things to make their paper better. They only understood writing when they didn't know they were writing. Does that make sense? Because I've read their discovery drafts. They understand *writing*. But, see, they didn't know that discovery drafting *was* writing. That's *not writing* in their definition.

- The students aren't situated inside of anything. They're just going through the motions. This research paper, nine weeks, is probably the extreme. It's killing them! Other kinds of writing, I think, they wouldn't be that removed, that clueless.

- It was so unnerving. I hated being in the classroom during the last weeks of the research paper. I hated it so much. Because they had nothing to do. They'd just sit there. I don't see how he tolerates that day in and day out. But there's no workshopping. They have no sense of where they need to be different on the second and third drafts.

- If I had to teach twelfth grade in North Carolina and do a research paper (Linda and I talked about it), I had originally envisioned it being something evolutionary that would span longer than nine weeks, but it wouldn't be something you worked on every day. It would be incorporated into something else you were doing. I envision it as something that's theirs, something they want to work on. We wouldn't spend three weeks in the library. I wouldn't call it a research paper even. Except for something like a personal narrative or creative writing, every paper is a research paper. As long as they use research then it should fulfill those requirements.

- Mr. Collins wants to discuss how my experience has been artificial because I had been involved in the research paper, not actual teaching. I don't feel it's been artificial. I feel like telling him if anything it's as close to reality as I can imagine. He said, "That's why I wanted you to take the second-period AP class who weren't doing the research paper so you could have some real experience with teaching." To me, second period was the most artificial part, after going through the hard times with third-, fourth-, and sixth-period seniors.

Late December 1996   Looking Backward

- It's those smart kids who get to do the things that make school fun. And it's the kids who aren't on the college path who do the horrible things that make it even harder. So they are trudging through this heinous research paper, and the AP kids are doing fun things.

- On the last day I said, "I hope I haven't cheated you out of the AP experience." And they were like, "No, it's so much better to be able to come in here and talk about something rather than to have to just listen."

- This whole concentration on doing college-level work in high school seems stupid. Mr. Collins would say things about the research paper like "Your college professor is not going to accept such-and-such." "Tell them, Ms. Tavey." I just wanted to say he's wrong, he's wrong. It's not like that.

- The reason to do well is good enough motivation for some kids, but in school there's no reason to learn and they're not. This is true moreso for the non–college prep kids. This sounds so silly but I want to make it fun. Because for the kids who hate school, if it's not fun, then forget it.

- If the third-, fourth-, and sixth-period classes did learn something unexpectedly from me, I think it was close to the beginning and that's so long ago. But with the other class [advanced placement], I just kept harping when they would write. I wanted to lessen the distinction between creative writing and real art and their writing. I think they picked up how I felt about writing, what I thought was real. I could see it when they would do free writing.

- Fun is not acceptable especially at the secondary level. It's not supposed to be like that. I felt almost like I didn't want anybody to walk by the door when I was sitting in a circle or playing music. And I don't even care. I'm not even part of that school.
- What I think about those theories, whole language, that hasn't changed. I don't look back think "I haven't done what Mr. Collins really wanted me to do." I don't look back on my theories and beliefs and go, "That's not reality, that's so idealistic."
- One time I was having a conversation with Linda and Mr. Streblinski about what avid readers they were as children. I was just listening. I really didn't read that much as a child. They asked "Do you read a lot now?" I said, "Yeah, I like to read." But I hadn't really started to like reading until I started to write. Somehow, in school that's not a legitimate way to love literature. You know? To want to write or to want to write about what you read.
- I'm not getting a chance to try things I really want to try. I think my first year of teaching now is going to be a lot more experimental than it would have if I had had a different situation.
- Linda and I were talking about student teaching, how it's good but it's bad (laughs). How it would be if student teaching could be without a critic teacher. So you have someone to evaluate and support you but not someone else's class to take over. You could just have a fresh group of students for ten weeks. That would be ideal student teaching. So I wouldn't be fitting into someone else's mode and struggling with already intact structures and ideas and curriculums, not that the struggling itself is not good!

Possibilities and Constraints

Elizabeth describes her teaching practicum as a struggle that requires her "to fit" into "already intact structures." She rejects this as less than ideal, insisting that it would be better for novice teachers to construct the classroom and its practices according to their personal beliefs and preferences. Thus, she privileges the autonomy of inner self over and above accommodating one's desires relative to external conditions as a better method for becoming a teacher. But such desire is really vain hope, something Elizabeth herself recognizes at another level. Removing one level of constraint in the form of the mentor teacher may give room for an individual personality to exert itself (or at least the illusion of freedom). However, as Elizabeth was well aware (given her analysis of Mr. Collins as "coerced" into cooperating with his team), there are many, many other sorts of inescapable constraints operating to construct individuals as teachers according to positions defined by the institution of school.

Although individuals have some degree of freedom in accepting or rejecting the identities available to them, they cannot construct identity positions themselves. A fixed number of identity positions exist within every institution. They are clearly defined, bounded, and are supported by networks of institutional practices. For teachers and other school personnel, categories like principals or school counselors are rigidly fixed. For the novice position of teaching intern, there is perhaps even less flexibility.

As part of the process adopting identity positions, novices must participate in the routines and practices that characterize and define a specific identity, other teachers in this case. In these tentative forays, in circumstances such as the teaching practicum which is a simulation, a mere characterization, the individual has the opportunity to experience the possibilities as well as limits associated with the identity position of interest.

Early in the practicum, Elizabeth is intent on searching the environment and analyzing her mentor teacher for traits congruent with or sympathetic toward her concern for the process approach to teaching writing that seems absolutely fundamental to her as a person. Thus, she is relieved to see the "process-writing flow chart" on the board during her first visit. She begins optimistically, a feeling that is short-lived since she sees in her mentor someone who is forced to live a double life, accepting the ideology mandated by his team while trying to teach according to his preferences and thus undermining the very approach Elizabeth is intent on developing. The case of Mr. Streblinski, a man who believes in process theory but cannot make it work in practice, is perhaps even more disillusioning to Elizabeth. She sees how hard it is to be different from mainstream, typical approaches or to exert even marginal control over the limited space of several classrooms. The school, the mandated curriculum, the teachers, the students are all barriers that Elizabeth must get past if she is to become a whole language teacher.

If "identities are to be found and negotiated at the boundaries where the internal and the external meet" (Jenkins 1996, 24), then in Elizabeth's case the negotiation falls apart. By the end of the practicum, she has experienced too many constraints and seen very few possibilities for a place in the institution of the public high school. The breaking point concerns the beliefs Elizabeth regards as most central to herself: "What I think about those theories . . . that hasn't changed." She will not compromise her internal standards developed through personal experience in the face of external conditions that will most likely require her to modify or perhaps relinquish such beliefs completely. The exchange with Mr. Collins concerning the E. D. Hirsch article certainly justifies Elizabeth's pessimism about surviving as the kind of teacher she wished to be. Also, there was the additional confusion Elizabeth had to sort out concerning Mr. Collins, who paid lip service to process-writing principles in public, with his colleagues, then undermined those practices every step of the way as he was teaching. Issues of identity aside, simply getting through the semester seemed challenging enough to Elizabeth given the circumstances: "I don't even care. I'm not even part of that school."

Why did Mr. Collins act that way? Why didn't he just live by his own lights as Elizabeth thought he should? In fact, there are rewards (in the form of resources, support, acclaim, recognition) for occupying positions in authorized, typical, or expected ways. Likewise, there are penalties for either rejecting, re-defining, or attempting to renegotiate these positions. Mr. Collins chooses to appear accommodating in public while resorting to subversive activities like de-claiming the writing assignments designed by Mr. Streblinski in the private space of his classroom. Elizabeth has some stake in taking exactly the opposite position. She has described herself to her students as "the salmon, always swimming upstream," against the current, an apt metaphor suggesting there is something she likes about resisting the status quo.

For Elizabeth, there are significant rewards in the form of students' reac-tions, such as "admitting things they should not have been," rating her exercise with song lyrics as their favorite event, and praising her for giving them oppor-tunities to speak instead of only listening. But she also believed these moments were unusual and in some sense unauthorized and transgressive. Certainly, Mr. Collins reacted as if they were—his raised eyebrows, his suggestions to lecture and to analyze the formal structures of the texts they read, his reclaiming of the research paper that Elizabeth and Linda had modified to be more meaningful for students.

These experiences made Elizabeth self-conscious about these institu-tional rewards and penalties connected to being a teacher. She both lived and witnessed, vis-à-vis Mr. Collins, the effects of resisting or renegotiating the given positions in the institution. She saw how Mr. Collins was manipulated by the structure, corralled into acting like he was a process teacher when he wasn't. While this insight allowed Elizabeth to feel sympathy, she also saw her men-tor's unhappiness and didn't want to suffer the same fate of being trapped in a position where she had to outwit or resist institutional norms. Ironically, resis-tance was the path she took as a novice during the practicum to preserve what was most important to her sense of self. But she concluded in the end that it was too hard to take on the establishment. Elizabeth could see that even in the best of circumstances, such as working with teachers known for their orienta-tion toward process writing, it was not easy as an individual to do what one wanted. Her personal beliefs about writing combined with a past that included survival through writing were more important positions to maintain than be-coming a high school English teacher, a way of living that would entail con-stant efforts with little support to teach her own way.

4. *Writing her thesis "Trying to become . . . and trying to know."* Elizabeth intro-duced her project this way: "This thesis is the product of the many ideas, expe-riences, conversations, realizations, and questions that go into trying to become a teacher, and into trying to know what you believe as a teacher. It is also about

how actually teaching and being part of a school changes, reinforces, widens, and deepens those beliefs."

Apart from a brief section describing the philosophy of whole language teaching, Elizabeth's thesis consists of four chapters, each a narrative set in the context of the high school, each focused on a single individual who played a significant role in her life as a student teacher. The first is about Elizabeth herself, followed by chapters on Mr. Streblinski, Mr. Collins, and Linda, her fellow intern. A short section entitled "Reflections" concludes it. "The process of writing this thesis," she writes, "led to three realizations.

"First, to be successful, teachers must decide what they wish to accomplish as teachers, what their goals are, and finally, they must determine how they are to teach. The method must stem from the underlying tenets of a teacher's inner self and be congruent with what he or she believes about the world and life. Otherwise, it will be just that, a method to be followed, not a creed to be lived.

"Second, E. D. Hirsch argues that in classrooms where skills are stressed instead of content, students do not receive the knowledge needed for higher order thinking skills. However, Hirsch seems to be missing the fact that when a teacher teaches skills for analyzing, organizing, creating, or communicating information, he or she has to include information. It is impossible to teach students how to think critically about history without teaching history. Emphasizing skills instead of knowledge does not mean teaching in a contentless classroom. That would be impossible. But what is possible is for conservative teachers to focus on content and teach in a processless classroom.

"Third, teachers who live by conservative ideologies are not fair judges of liberal teachers, and vice versa. In other words, teachers who believe that the goal of education is to give each student a 'bag of concrete facts,' cannot accurately judge teachers who believe that the goal is to teach students how to learn, think, and communicate."

What Elizabeth learned about herself, teachers, and teaching arose directly from the triage of relationships surrounding her. As involved participants in Elizabeth's situation, we played pivotal roles because we occupied such distinctive positions. Elizabeth moved among and between these positions, discovering her own place by charting her location in terms of how she was similar or different relative to each of us, idealized representations of friend, teacher, and mentor. Through such varied interactions, she clarified her own identity in very specific ways. As a professor and her unofficial intellectual mentor, I provided approval, representing the university environment where she felt comfortable and successful. Because she felt I demonstrated process teaching in my classes, I was also a strong role model, an example of what she aspired to.

The two teachers involved in her teaching practicum provided other images, ones Elizabeth ultimately defined herself against. Mr. Streblinski shared her beliefs but because of circumstance and personality and whatever else he was not able to live by them. For him, she felt empathy, though this emotion didn't prevent her ultimately from believing that internal conflicts made him ineffectual as a teacher. Toward her mentor teacher, Elizabeth's reactions were understandably complicated. She attributed some of his intensity and ideological fervor to a reaction against the institutional conditions that had "coerced" him into paying lip service to one set of beliefs he truly disagreed with. The fact that he did everything he could to subvert the practices linked to these beliefs had nothing very much to do with Elizabeth. This realization made their relationship less personal, providing the critical distance Elizabeth needed to complete her teaching assignment. He taught as he believed, but acted undercover. Elizabeth didn't want to disguise her beliefs; she saw by observing Mr. Collins how destructive that was. She couldn't say one thing and live another.

In a discussion after her practicum ended, Elizabeth reported that she did not respect much of the mandated work she had done as a teacher but valued the work she had done as a writer. Her appraisal was heightened by my highly positive attitude toward her writing and work generally over the course of the semester. Though I had also praised her instincts, beliefs, lesson plans, ideas, and performances as a teacher, the teaching practicum was not my official domain. Besides, no amount of positive praise from me could outweigh the failure and frustration she experienced while teaching at the high school. But, whether her reactions were positive or negative, the fact is that the judgments of all the significant actors proved formative and influential for Elizabeth. She didn't always accept other people's judgments, but she always *considered* them long and hard, from several angles. She appreciates critique and describes herself as a critical person: "I'm always apologizing for being judgmental but it doesn't stop me from being that way." Toward her thinking and teaching, Elizabeth experienced a fair amount of disapproval and encountered significant barriers. About her writing, the situation was far different. She is drawn in the direction of writer; this identity option becomes viable and attractive because she can see a path, a route, a way through.

Ultimately, the effect of writing her thesis was to clarify Elizabeth's future goals. "It was a process of elimination," she explained. The reflection entailed by writing distilled her thinking about what she wanted to do and who she wanted to be. A year later, sitting on the couch in her apartment, she commented, "I could see that there was no career-sustaining aspects of it for me, not like the consulting work I'm doing now for the textile school." After six months of thinking about it, Elizabeth enrolled in a master's program at a state university where four options, including a concentration in writing and rhetoric, were possible. Fortuitously, one of her professors who was involved in a new initiative regarding writing in the disciplines, recognized Elizabeth's interest in writing and knew about her background in teaching. Within weeks, she began working collaboratively with several faculty members to integrate writing into their teaching.

As she talks, she gestures, arms out, palms facing each other, and in a smooth chopping motion, moves her arms vertically parallel up and down, wide high up then closer together as she approaches her lap, "It was like a funnel," she says. "I was ruling out things I didn't want to do. Now I'm even more clear that I want to teach writing and be a writer." Without a doubt, practice teaching and thesis writing were both powerful, identity-forming experiences, but they generated in Elizabeth not the identity of teacher, but of writer. What Elizabeth found compelling wasn't the teaching itself but instead the act of writing about it. The attractions were formidable. Not only did she have confirmation from me, but she had inner certainty, satisfaction, and personal, experiential knowledge that was far stronger than any of the much less powerful experiences she had had as a student teacher. In this sense, identities as teacher and as writer conflicted. If she could have been a process teacher, if she thought that being that kind of teacher in a regular public high school was possible or feasible, she could have constructed both identities simultaneously. Instead, one ended up being much more attractive. Identities are not ours to bestow (no matter how powerful we are). They are something we can offer to others, but individuals must accept these visions of themselves before they can develop.

Nothing Final

Thinking about Elizabeth's experiences in several institutions, being a student at the university and a teacher intern in a public high school, we gain some insights about the development of individual and collective identities, about the potential overlap or discord between the two. Individuals have both private and public self-images that are created through the many daily encounters with others in everyday life. This identity making is reciprocal. Through the dynamic interplay between inside and out, between self and others, Elizabeth engages in creating not only her private self, individual identity, but also her public self, collective identity. As we've seen, identities are not ever accomplished by single persons: We need others as they need us. Mr. Collins, Linda, Dr. Carson, Mr. Streblinski, Elizabeth's students, and I (along with numerous others) all played a role in her identity development just as she contributed to sustaining, creating, changing the identities of everyone else she encountered. For instance, Mr. Collins, in trying to tutor Elizabeth in teaching techniques he valued, demonstrated behavior more vociferously than was perhaps usual for her benefit. Elizabeth's presence brought into stark relief the ideological differences between the two mentor teachers, effectively causing Mr. Collins to lose some of his cover as a "process teacher" and be more openly the "literary critic" kind of teacher he favored.

The institutional setting—that high school, those teachers and administrators, that particular small town, in the state of North Carolina—the specifics of that context, along with an assortment of ready-made identity positions and their associated routines and practices for fostering collective identity, is what brought the dramas of selfhood (for Elizabeth and the others) into being. Once Elizabeth entered the institution of school as an intern, she was subject to the forces that shape the collective identity of teacher. It is within institutions themselves that collective identities are resisted, deferred, accepted, adopted, or asserted. We know what happened with Elizabeth. In the university context especially, her individual identity as teacher flourished but, once in the high school, she rejected the collective identity of teacher proffered by the institution because it threatened beliefs, practices, and morals that she considered fundamental to her survival as a person.

However, there is nothing final or definite in this outcome. In another institution, in an alternative setting, in other circumstances, individuals may relate differently, be able to position themselves a new way relative to the social expectations and constraints that are present. In graduate school, working as a consultant for faculty in departments outside of English, Elizabeth reports feeling "even more clear that I want to teach writing and be a writer." Because she looks radiant, I am very pleased with the news. But I am also moved by her decision; I harbor a secret pleasure, a kind of pseudo-parental pride regarding her ambitions, emotions I try to express outwardly as enthusiasm not self-congratulation. After all, this conversation is about her, and not about me. But I have realized, with a jolt, the implications of what she has just said. Teaching writing and being a writer—that's me.

Rick's Story

Mr. Lambert, Room 122

His first period (eleventh grade literature, advanced) students file into the classroom. At 7:35 a.m. on the last day of March, eight months into Rick's first year as a high school teacher, it is already a sunny warm day, the air filled with the scent of blossoms from the dozen or so Bradford pear trees blooming outside the unshaded, six-foot-tall windows. From a seat in the furthest row of desks, I observe the entering students with my appraising teacher eye. For a moment I feel like I'm the teacher this morning, as if it is the first day and class of my term. The students look familiar—surprisingly like what I'm used to, young adults, not kids: the redhead in the purple sweater set, a woman, and the boy-man in sleeveless tee-shirt, his hat worn front to back, his posturing the only adolescent thing about him.

West Norriton County High, where Rick teaches, lies eight or ten miles south of Raleigh, in a borderland between suburban developments housing workers who commute to the city and farms and pasturelands where families (sometimes the same ones) over the last hundred years have been making a living. There is antagonism, Rick reports, between "what you'd call rednecks I guess" and the other teenagers from the developments. The student population is predominantly middle and lower middle class, racially mixed, a white majority, about a quarter African-American, a few percent Hispanic, a smattering of others (Indian, Native American, and Asian.).

"It's been hard since I look so young," Rick says, "Like one of my students asked me out," he adds, grinning, embarrassed. Though I see what he means, I had never thought he appeared any younger than his fellow undergraduates while he was a student at Carolina. Now, however, his hair is cropped short, almost shaved into a neat, tight cut that exposes his ears and forehead; his once-habitual earring is missing. His professional clothing consists of a white polo shirt, loose and comfortable, tucked into chino pants.

Rick opens class by discussing the upcoming research paper, seven to eleven pages, note cards, (there'll be lots of little grades on each step that add up to the final grade) on something that represents America. The students take notes. He moves the class to their journals, telling them they must produce at least ten lines to get full credit. They're reading Steinbeck's *Of Mice and Men*, and Rick asks them to consider the odd pairing of George and Lennie who are inseparable. "What brings them together?" he wants to know. "What are determining factors in your own personal relationships?" While they write, he returns papers, interacts individually with a few students, and purposely ignores the two male students sitting near me who talk and never write a word through the ten-minute exercise. Without any discussion, Rick moves to vocabulary words, presenting via the overhead an alphabetical list—enigma, ephemeral, enervate, equivocate—along with definitions that students copy into their notebooks. Rick reads each one and provides an illustrating sentence. They'll have a quiz on Friday.

Halfway into the fifty-minute period, Rick returns to Steinbeck's novel. He warms them up by reading passages he's selected about the characters and asking students to identify and discuss the qualities of character that Steinbeck so adeptly conveys. Students respond quickly: "It's Crooks," or "That's Curly's wife," "Slim." Without pause, he turns to page sixty-six and reads aloud, then stops, discusses a little, inviting student response, reads again. With his attention on passages from the book, I notice suddenly that Rick has become *comfortable*, expansive and relaxed, his talk comes more fluently, with more expression. Not that he was tense or uncertain before. The class has been with him the whole time, cooperative, attentive; it has been a very smooth and pleasant half-hour.

For the last six minutes Rick reads aloud from the text *Of Mice and Men*. The words, embodied by his voice, leap off the page. And the men, Lennie and Crooks (it's the scene where Lennie first approaches Crooks in his tiny barn corner) appear palpably in the classroom. There's real tension now—attentive listening and meaning making—as students (and I) tune into Rick's performance. We become conscious of the struggle going on between the two men to tease and test each other, to connect finally by successfully avoiding a physical confrontation. I haven't read Steinbeck in thirty years and the drama and intensity of his prose impresses me now in ways I don't remember feeling before. Then I realize it is not the writing but rather Rick's delivery that has got us all hooked. His abilities impress me. Though we are well acquainted (Rick has introduced me to his class saying, "She's no stranger"), I never knew, never had a clue, that he could *read* like that.

After lunch, I stay for fourth period. Rick has warned me in advance about this eleventh grade, standard, non–college prep class, about his students' rowdiness, their springy energy and exuberant, adolescent disobedience. So when the room is full of teenagers who simply can't be contained in a small space, muggy and congested without air-conditioning on a now hot, humid spring afternoon, I am in complete sympathy with Rick and his students who must somehow get through the next hour. Rick projects a firm, steadfast, and tolerant attitude as he walks forward and back up the rows to hand out papers, engage in banter, and assess just how difficult it is going to be today to teach anyone anything. With these students, Rick's teaching is very pragmatic yet filled with urgent purpose. He claims that literature is his most powerful teaching tool because it has the potential to enrich students' lives, to change them, and to open out the confining world (I hear him talking about himself here) they inhabit.

Since the majority of students in this period rarely complete homework, Rick can't count on their reading the text at home, even something as compelling as Richard Wright's *Black Boy*, their current book. His way of ensuring they read, he tells me with a trace of unnecessary apology, is to read aloud for at least thirty, sometimes up to forty-five, minutes of class time. The first twelve minutes of class resembles in form (though not feeling) the morning period, with a discussion of the imminent research paper, some journal writing and vocabulary words. Rick moves quickly, keeping the pace high and fast, allowing for noise, seat changing, cross-class exchanges shouted over the heads of neighbors, and for inattention. A few students simply stare into space. This flexible leniency is exactly how I would act as a teacher in his position. Despite everything, many students are involved and simply ignore the unavoidable distractions. Most seem happy and enjoying themselves. Their misbehavior is not overtly aggressive or disrespectful. They appear grateful for having been given some slack since they respond smartly at the transition point when Rick turns to *Black Boy*. He asks them some comprehension questions to focus their attention on the book. They show off, calling out loudly because I'm there and they know all the answers. He is pleased, and so are they.

Then he begins to read for a full twenty-five minutes. The magic of the morning is repeated as Rick's voice fills the room. His east Carolina accent, thick and resonant, the vowels open and mobile, uncannily befits Wright's narration of his little-boy self. Rick reads the scene when Wright complains to his grandmother about her method for wiping his rear end after a bath. Without strain or embarrassment, he lets Wright speak about things so personal that I wonder at Rick's courage as a teacher, wonder what students are thinking, wonder whether anyone has ever broached a topic like this one to them so openly and in such vivid and concrete details.

As he continues on to the scene when Wright goes to live with his mother at her more prosperous sister's house where food is plentiful and the cottage comfortable, I force myself out of the images of the book, out of the rhythm of Rick's speech, to observe the students. They are riveted. No one makes any noise or talks to anyone else. Two women in the back row who earlier in the period had an extended conversation about the Arkansas school shooting stare entranced. Their mobile faces change expression in relation to the story's action. The racist killing of Wright's uncle registers hard. Where else in their day, I think, will these students have the chance to think in any deep or eloquent way about how greed and hatred leads to bad things, that it is moral failure not skin color that makes someone bad, and that the evil that befalls us as children cannot fail to shape our moral characters as adults?

Driving home afterward, west on I-40, I realize that Rick has pursued a way to teach all his own. No education courses (as far as I know) promoted or even advocated that he captivate and educate students by dramatic reading. Perhaps there was a bit of reader's theater in his methods class, a demonstration or two at most. But I doubt Rick was ever informed that reading aloud for long periods might be the most effective way to connect students to literature. He may have taken Communications 60 and been exposed in that class to some performance techniques and felt himself at home there. But it was not anything he ever mentioned to me in all the hours we talked about teaching. Though I observed him frequently during his teaching practicum, I saw no similarities between the short bursts of nervous reading mixed in with more traditional lecture-discussion techniques he used as an intern and the skillful dramatic performance I had just witnessed less than a year later. He had definitely come into his own as a teacher. "How?" I wondered.

His performance was not simple though it appeared so. He read easily, beautifully, naturally, as if he inhabited the book and its characters. His talent lies in his ability to immerse himself like a good actor into the text. This identification may reflect his own attitudes and experiences with literature as compelling and transformative. He tells me during lunch break that he comes to school a lot of the time thinking not so much about his students but about the books he's teaching. When he is reading Wright, he personifies both author and the narrator so comfortably there is no discernible gap between the action in the book and the present, tangible experience of teaching in a close, crowded classroom.

One reason I think he is this effective is coincidental but nevertheless very significant. Students hear Wright's crafted literary language in an accent that, if not exactly like theirs, is North Carolinian, an accent the majority of them can identify with. This self-identification is critically important in terms of how much students learn, given the culture in this region of North Carolina where (as I've learned as an outsider) past and place are highly valued, where history and tradition live in the present moment, part of every social encounter, no matter how mundane.

He's one of them, a native son. When Rick reads, he opens a space for the students to fall into without effort; in this tactile, totalizing way, students participate in reading and know the literature. As he reads on and the story unfolds, his students are entranced, fascinated, spellbound. When he stops near the end of the period, everyone sags, released. The heat and tiredness comes flooding back, the bell rings, students gather their bags and books, and shuffle out into the crowded, buzzing hallway.

First-Year Teacher

Although seemingly without special requirements or large capitol investments, Rick's performative methods are still difficult for him to execute at his school. The institutional and curricular impediments to teaching well (as Rick defines it) are numerous and seemingly entrenched. For instance, he has requested to teach Toni Morrison's *Beloved* to two periods of his eleventh grade advanced classes. His request has been denied by the department head for purely bureaucratic reasons. This text has been approved by the curriculum committee only for eleventh grade advanced placement classes. However, he would be able to teach Morrison's *Song of Solomon* since it appeared on the list for the advanced classes. Though at best an arbitrary ruling, Rick agreed to the other text, believing that teaching Morrison is what matters. Then he discovered that the school owns only twenty-five copies of the book, enough

for only one section. This meant he would have to teach a different book to
the other advanced class, thus doubling his preparation time and enormously
complicating his teaching day. At these constraints, Rick is justifiably annoyed, not only at the multiple roadblocks he confronts, but because problems like insufficient copies of the text appear to have simple solutions. The
school could just buy more books! But the department is unlikely to do so;
somebody controls the too-small budget; and even if there were money, the
books wouldn't arrive in time.

These are the kind of institutional and procedural problems that first
year teachers have to face and find strategies for circumventing in addition to
deal with the more pressing issues of pedagogy, interpersonal relationships, and
their developing selves as teachers. Everything I observed suggested that Rick
was doing a very good job teaching and faring as well as any first-year teacher
could. Rick seemed to be fully immersed in becoming a teacher. From the perspective of the School of Education, he was one of our success stories since he
had sought out and accepted a position as a North Carolina public schoolteacher. Could our teacher education program take any of the credit I wondered? What practices helped him, and could other students in our program
profit from his experience? What were other sources, influences, events, and
persons that had fostered Rick in his goals? It is rare to have the opportunity
to remain in contact with our students once they have graduated, and I was
eager to hear what Rick had to say. He seemed equally interested in having
someone outside of his high school with whom he could talk about teaching.
The analysis that follows draws on a combination of interviews that occurred
over the next few months while he was teaching as well the ones happened
early on in the study.

As I tell Rick's story, the action will remain situated mostly in the time
I've just described—the spring of his first year of teaching, almost a year after
college graduation. However, at different points, in order to trace reasons and
motivations, the telling will take us back in time (via the interviews) to his life
as a student at Carolina, to family and personal history, to remembered events
and dreams of other possible futures. I begin with Rick's childhood experiences
with reading and literature, with what he regarded as his original motivation for
wanting to be a teacher. This analysis will be followed by a discussion of the
major topic—his decision to embark on a journey of "self-discovery"—Rick
raised during an interview that occurred midway through his first year of
teaching. Then I turn to Rick's attitudes about teaching and his success in the
classroom, which he attributes partly to another teacher who is both role model
and mentor. The chapter ends with Rick's sense of himself as engaged in an
unconstrined process of becoming. Being a teacher, he realizes, is only one dimension and not a decisive outcome.

1. Original vision. When I asked Rick (a college junior) in the initial interview the generic, open-ended questions designed for the study, he chose to talk extensively about his childhood. I had begun by inquiring about his decision to go into English education to begin with. He replied by describing learning to read in first grade, pulling readers off the shelf to discover new stories, hearing the teacher read poems by Shel Silverstein, being enthralled in sixth grade by fantasy novels like Tolkein's *The Hobbit.* "Fiction," he insists, "was always my big thing." Books, he believes, are indispensable: "The experience of reading and adventures was so powerful for me in childhood I've this magical belief that childhood is the key to everything we learn in life." About the language arts he makes this claim, "Literature is so tangible to life. There are so many connections. That's when I get excited." Considering his future students, Rick comments: "I don't know a single person who hasn't read a good book. And if there's some way I can find a happy medium between a good entertaining book and a book that has literary merit that can help them out in their future, that's what I want."

As a first-year student at Carolina, he reported finding conversations about books immediately compelling: "From probably the second or third day I was here, for the first time I was meeting friends who could talk to me about works I had read." Looking back, Rick regards the encounters with his friends "on road trips or sitting on the balcony at night" as most significant: "That's when I really feel, sitting there, teaching my roommate about the theme or what I believe this poem is about or a poem I've written or something, that's when I feel the greatest desire to be a teacher." Teaching will be fueled by these passions; he wants students to experience similar moments of transformation.

"Does this kind of teaching happen here at the university?" I inquire. "Sure," Rick says. "Dr. Donald Grove for Shakespeare, your classes. But it had to be provoked by the teacher. I'm pretty optimistic about a teacher's future if they can somehow get students talking like that. I don't expect everybody to want to jump in and relay what they believe. But there have been times in lots of my English classes where that has happened."

When my questions prompt Rick to describe the qualities of a good teacher, he invariably turns to the topic of literature, to the books he read, rather than the teachers themselves: "I took a class with professor Carl Rockwell called the Heroic Journey: *The Odyssey, The Iliad,* and *Sir Gawain* and the *Green Knight,* and finished up with Tolkein. I won't say I came out with the meaning of life, but I came out knowing why I read and what it does to me emotionally and absolutely."

However, when I redirect him to focus on people not books, Rick's criteria for a good English teacher has little to do with content knowledge and everything to do with personal involvement: "A lot of professors and high school teachers do not stress emotion as much as learning facts. When I come out of a class feeling really energized, it's because of emotions it brought out in me, not because of the facts I've learned." Rick's desire to be an emotional teacher surprises me. I wonder (and must use my imagination) about Rick's abilities in this venue: "Do you think the emotional comes easily to you?" "Uh ... it would with the people very close to me," Rick answers. "That's what I'm gonna have to work on. I don't think that's something you achieve the first year." In the context of his wishing to be an emotional teacher, to share transcendent experiences with his students, I now understand why Rick claims his life was changed by watching *Dead Poets Society*.

Looking back, after witnessing Rick's teaching, I see how certain experiences provided him with a vision of the teacher he was striving to become: his immediate identification with the teacher in the film, his emotional fulfillment in reading heroic literature, his fascination with books and the deep intellectual communion he felt talking with others about them. But at the time he was taking teacher education classes, when he was my student, I was unable to really imagine or even sense that this was the kind of teacher Rick was idealizing. Certainly, the few opportunities he'd had for microteaching or class presentations never clued me into the dramatic reader he eventually became as a first-year teacher. Perhaps these occasions had not been open or flexible enough, maybe he hadn't had the courage to display this preference, conceivably it was an insight about his teaching self that hadn't occurred to him yet, or perhaps the situations weren't real enough to make him feel like a teacher.

Now teaching, he feels successful when his students respect him and know he cares. He describes a good teacher as someone who is "not authoritative" but who speaks with "a voice that people will listen to and respect." He finds interchanges characterized by mutual respect and care that happen with his fourth-period class especially sweet. "We're not talking about a class you'd see in the movies, the inner city classroom where they bring guns and stuff. It's just your normal rowdy group of kids not going to college, happy with Cs and Ds, full of jocks, football players, and girls that are going to beauty-salon school." Though he prizes his ability to connect to these students, as he did reading *Black Boy* on the day I visited, he reports that these times "when I'm rolling come few and far between this first year of teaching." I sense frustration and also a kind of wistfulness in Rick's statement; it's the first inkling I have that he's struggling.

He continues: "Those are the days where you walk out and say 'Yeah, I can do this,' when you have a good class like that. It's when you've got the whole class laughing, when you're reading to them, because more than likely they're not going to take that book home and read it. But when you stop and explain it and they respond back, you really say, 'This could be a profession I could stick with' ." I never realized he had any doubts.

2. Self-discovery. In an interview after his first year in the teacher education program, the summer before the practicum, I ask Rick if he is a teacher. "I think I've felt like a teacher for a long time." He pauses. "Whenever I write a paper or something, I'm always a *prospective* teacher. But if I'm not trained now, I'm not going to learn it in the next month of my methods class!" Rick is fearful about the impending teaching internship but optimistic as well: "I've been so lucky in the School of Education and in college, in high school. I feel like if I do my best, everything works out." He continues, "At times you just have to put all your fears aside and say whatever happens, happens. And that's the frame of mind I'm in right now."

Almost two years later, in April, his first year teaching, Rick reports that people keep asking him a similar but forward-looking question: "So many teachers by this time of year ask you—they think you have had enough experience—they're like, is this something you want to do for the rest of your life? Do you see yourself doing this for the rest of your life? I tell them I have no idea." During the week of spring break, Rick arrives at my house on a Thursday afternoon: "I look forward to the interviews because I feel like I'm Tiger Woods or someone like that sitting over here giving up my life." About forty-five minutes into things, I ask him how he would describe himself to someone else. Rick says in a rush, as if he's anticipated the question, "Well, I'm going to be very blunt. I've got this big thing about discovering myself. It's caused me to end an eight-year relationship, and to really question where I want to be in three or four years."

"It's kind of the Jack Kerouac *On the Road* thing. I don't know if it's an excuse, or really is the core truth, but I can't be intimate with anybody until I'm intimate with myself. So right now I'm in this stage of trying to discover who I am, shape who I am, and really like who I am." His transition from college has changed more than just his status from student to teacher. "I've been alone more this past year, because my roommate travels in his job, and then with the breakup with Nancy and me. Subconsciously my family's strength in me and my profession has helped get me through it." Rick counts on going back to graduate school full time, but not while he's teaching.

"As far as my finding myself, they've been totally supportive, totally open to whatever I've wanted to try, always there to offer advice. With teaching, this goes beyond my parents and my sister, to my grandparents, and to my uncles, and my close cousins (my great uncle was principal of a really good high school, and my mother's brother is the principal of a middle school). It's like with Faulkner. We're all a part of the past. We never can escape our past, and so many times in novels that's a bad thing. You can't escape what your father and great-grandfather were like in Ibsen's play *Ghostwood*. But with my family, I don't even think about wanting to escape. They're there for me subconsciously and vicariously in my profession, and in surviving the tough times, and then when it comes to making decisions, they're there for support."

Rick believes he has agency, the ability to make life-altering decisions, and he feels convinced that now is the time to be open to different possibilities. He describes the immediate future as a "journey, whether it be psychological, or whether it be actually physically moving somewhere." The turn he's taken is one toward language. "I'm writing," he says, "or trying to write." He continues, speaking urgently: "I feel like I closed a door last May when I graduated, and I loved my experience at Chapel Hill, but I don't think I was defined as a person. I felt like I had to totally redefine myself. So I'm in that stage of my life. Everything I do—teaching, extracurricular activities, writing, reading, whatever, all focus in and *hone right down* to that aspect of discovering who I am."

In some ways, it seems that Rick is seeking radical change. His classroom, rather than a place where his self is located, seems more like a laboratory for his life experiments, given his declaration that everything connects to the self-discovery process. Revising his idea to be a teacher doesn't upset him. But I am surprised at his sanguine reaction to possibly abandoning teaching. His attachment to teaching seemed (from how he always described it) somehow more basic or constant. But I'm wrong about this. Although Rick finds satisfaction in what he's doing, there's nothing immutable in his decision to be a teacher. It is in the picture, but still very much up in the air: "When I come home, on a really good day, I sit back and say, well, maybe this is going to be a part of me. This teaching adolescents is going to be a part of who I am." He equivocates. Other, more general and encompassing questions of identity—who he is—are occupying his attention. His future, as far as he's concerned, is uncertain but limitless.

Though I don't ask the question out loud, I'm thinking about how he's so focused on himself. He was such a good teacher the day I observed. Silently, I protest, But what about your students? Don't they mean something to you?

3. Not the teacher I want to be. It is eight months into his first year as a high school English teacher. Though we've talked on the phone a few times in the past months about recommendations, credentialing, the lost phone number of a friend in common, we've hardly discussed his teaching. Rick simply asserted each time that everything was going fine, it was hard, but he liked it and had no complaints. Our conversations invariably ended with the promise to get together. One night we set a date to meet and decide to invite Elizabeth too.

Over a late supper on a school night in an almost empty restaurant, Rick blurts out, almost the first words he utters as we sit down, "I'm not the teacher I want to be." He reports doing a good job teaching, doing the best he can, especially for a first-year teacher, but he's not where he wants to be. But before I can ask what he means, he's off deep into a story about his first encounter ever with a threatening student. Elizabeth asks for the details. A rushing monologue pours out.

It is an interesting story but not one that sheds any light on what he meant by the self-critical comment he opened with. While he talks, I can't help thinking about his admission. What kind of teacher is he now? What makes him dissatisfied, uneasy, uncomfortable? I'm distracted, wondering, and hardly hear the story. But he's not at all conscious of my inattention. Leaning across the table, uncharacteristically anxious, his words come fast. He's turned inward, unaware of his audience or our reactions.

Several weeks later, during a subsequent interview, Rick returned to many of the topics he raised on the night of our dinner with Elizabeth. At one point, he says, "This first year teaching I'm so tired. Teaching can always be a continual learning process, but right now in school it feels like I'm going through the motions a lot—get papers from students, respond to their journal entries, read the five chapters that I am to teach this week. Maybe in two or three years when I've got those motions down, I can really start to learn more, and turn that learning over into teaching."

Then he adds, "I don't think I'll ever commit one hundred percent to teaching until I finish with *my* schooling. I love school so much, being in the classroom, doing projects, writing papers and especially the reading. It's a part of me that's absent right now, just the learning. It's so easy in high school to become complacent."

He attributes his discontent and restlessness to a reaction against his rigid life plan when he entered college: "I think it's backlash from how I was in high school. I wanted to find the love of my life when I hit high school. I was going to be a teacher. I was going to go to Carolina. For some reason I wanted to live in Maine; I had everything planned out, everything was black and white with me. But now I go with the flow, and let the flow shape me." Without prompting he continues: "Then that uneasy soul starts to pull at you—now hold up! You're twenty-three. There's a lot of things you want to see!"

He explains this yearning as a fundamental trait of his personality: "Both my parents would say the same thing—I'm always trying to find something different, something new to shape my own opinions. I guess it goes back to learning, to experiencing different things." While certainty and security appealed to him as a teenager, he categorically rejects it now: "I don't know if I'll ever—whether it be with a girl, or whether it be with my profession, or whether it be with my beliefs—be a stable anchor. And I like that. *I like that.*"

He goes on to confesses: "An aspect of me is bored right now. I'm intellectually healthy. I'm constantly learning. But I want teaching to be more than what's the best way to teach grammar." Chagrinned as these sentiments

yet resolute, he declares: "I feel like I'm somebody still with a completely
empty chalkboard in front of me, and I'm just going along with what I can
create with that."

In reply, I comment: "Teaching serves some of your needs. But there are
other things it obviously can't do, and never will. But if you continue on with it,
there's a way that the two things can feed each other." Rick understands my
point, but feels compelled to explain that his issues go deeper, are far more per-
vasive than I'm imagining. He counters, saying, "Oh they absolutely can, they
definitely can. But I just don't feel complete. Sometimes I feel like that causes
an inadequacy in the classroom, because I don't know enough about myself and
about the subject matter, enough to teach students. That's a void in my life, and
I really look forward to going back to school."

He aims for directness: "Look, I'm admitting doing as a teacher what I
didn't want to do when I graduated school. It's because of time. If I could be
blessed with the same eleventh grade curriculum next year, I would be such a
better teacher. Because this year I just have enough time to go home, do a little bit of grading, read the material that I'm going to have to do the next day,
come up with things to discuss, type up a worksheet that we can go over
together." The conversation swings, with a kind of doppelganger effect, between two poles—his teaching, commitments to students, a vision of changing their lives, and his concerns about himself, his quest for novel situations,
his desire to discover "who he really is." His attention vacillates between the
attractions that the real act of being in the classroom offers and the dissatisfied feeling that the teaching life as he knows it is not meaningful and does
not fulfill his needs. He turns repeatedly to other kinds of futures—writing,
traveling, and graduate school.

Well into the second hour of conversation, Rick returns to a much earlier
question about identity. Abruptly, he says, "I have an answer to what you asked
before. The word that keeps popping up in my mind—I don't know if my parents or students would ever come up with this—is *journeyman*. Because I'm always posing these questions to my students, or posing these ideas. And the first
thing after the question is—I don't have an answer. I would like to know
the answer, but I want you to start thinking about it." He grins, remembering
some recent incident at school, and continues: "Students see me as somebody
who's always testing boundaries, testing limits." But the "biggest key is open-
mindedness, whether it be controversial issues such as homosexuality, or racism,
or feminism, or whatever." In calling himself a journeyman, Rick invents his
own meaning, completely unlike the word's usual referent, an apprentice learning a craft or trade, though this concept would certainly be applicable to his position as a new teacher. Instead, he is referring to someone engaged in active
pursuit: "I'd like them to understand that part of learning is that maybe there

are not concrete answers to those questions. To ask the questions, and know the question is out there, and to know that discussing the questions is part of the journey, and maybe not finding the answer." This desire to have his students journey with him is perhaps the way Rick fuses the two worlds, his everyday life as a teacher and those private moments at home when his "uneasy soul" urges him toward "a hundred different things."

When he pauses for a breath, I test out my sense of things: "Your whole approach to teaching seems based on this aspect or quality of yourself, this journeyman." "I think it is," Rick assents. "And when it's not, I *make it* that way."

4. Experience . . . and a role model. By the time I pay my spring visit to Rick's classroom, he has had about eight months with his own students to test out and adjust the different methods he learned from Mrs. Altman, his former mentor teacher in the Seminar Program. While similar in size and demographics to the school where he completed his practicum, West Norriton County High School has no such alternative curriculum, and I'm curious to see what methods he has transferred, adopted, or revamped from one school to the other. Rick explains that he kept "coming in with lesson plans that I thought the students would be interested in," only to discover "so many times that, number one, they hadn't done anything that I had told them to do before. So I was going to have to just convey knowledge. Through the "those processes," repeated failures, Rick says he finally realized he had "to do something that at least plants the seed for them to be interested enough to go back and look at the material."

He hasn't figured this out all on his own. He's been lucky, "blessed" he calls it, to have found a friend and mentor, one of his colleagues in the English department. Sitting on the edge of his chair, he talks excitedly about Mr. Barton: "There's one male teacher who's been my savior. From the very first day somebody recommended him, said to ask him any question no matter how trivial, about being a first-year teacher. He's taught for twelve years at West Norriton High School." It couldn't be a better situation for Rick since Bill "coincidentally teaches eleventh grade English, the exact same, advanced and level two, like I do, which is the average." Knowing (from his many visits to my office while he was an undergraduate) how significant a mentor is to Rick, I appreciate the importance of what he's telling me: "From day one, just about every day of however many days I've taught, he has been a shoulder to cry on, or something that makes me laugh, or brings me back down to Earth. He's been wonderful."

Rick continues about what he's learned about teaching: "The big key with kids learning and enjoying is to get them to do the work, and prep for it. It's like Bill told me, 'You're going to have one percent of the students dislike a book that you've taught, if they've read it. It's the ones that say, 'I hate this book! I hate this damn book. I don't want to do this!' That's because they haven't read it!' So you say, 'What do you hate about it?', and they say, 'I don't know. I couldn't read it. It was too hard.' 'Well, what was difficult about it? 'I don't know, I put it up.' And you find out they haven't turned a page of it."

From Bill, Rick learns not only techniques but also field-based knowledge about how his students think and function, information he will acquire on his own only after many more years of teaching. Rick's admiration is unbounded: "I bought a Christmas card to give to him in December, and I had a hard time putting into words what he's done. He says that in ten years these students aren't going to remember the content but the idiosyncrasies about my teaching."

Rick elaborates: "If you can get them the day before to know a little— that's why in discussion just bring up a topic, everybody's got an opinion about everything. That doesn't mean their opinion's valid, or if this has any logic to it, but that's the way you can get people talking, get them interested, which obviously can be difficult." Rick looks pleased to be talking about what he's learned about approaching his students. He comments: "There's not a kid out there who's unintelligent. They know how to beat the system. They've either been pampered, they've been spoiled, they've been neglected, or they've been programmed. So you have to find out how they've been, in what way they have been molded, and try to in some way go with their flow." This sounds right to me, he's developing good instincts, and with Bill's help, he'll have a successful year, reinforcement that will motivate him to continue teaching. I realize that his earlier talk about his uncertain future is troubling me; I'm uneasy about where the conversation is going, a feeling which grows stronger as we talk.

The real crux of the problem surfaces as Rick shares more stories about why he likes and respects Bill Barton: "There are some wonderful teachers who scare me because their whole life revolves around teaching. That's not how I want to live." It's better for students, Rick says, "if you have a life outside of teaching. You're not just an English or History nerd; you bring in a lot of things off TV, or music, or movies. You're not just always having your nose in a book." Rick pauses, then adds about Bill: "This guy will be the first one to tell you that he believes his profession is geared more toward the students than toward *The Scarlet Letter* or *Huckleberry Finn*." Though this position seems to contradict Rick's own involvement with books and literature, he doesn't notice the conflict. He is intent on other things.

5. Becoming. At May graduation, Rick had been full of misgivings about surviving as a teacher; now, almost a year later, a sea change has occurred, caused by good experiences at West Norriton High and his relationship with his colleague Bill. Now that simple survival is no longer the issue, Rick finds himself thinking again about what it means to be a teacher over the long haul. About Bill, Rick says, "This man loves what he does. But it also doesn't control his life, and that's what sort of scared me." In revisiting his low feelings last year around graduation, Rick says, "It just seemed so dreary. I was so apprehensive because it seemed like if you were going to be a good teacher, you had to live it, it had to be your life, and I was like—Is this the profession I want to do that with? Do I love this profession that much?" He pauses, then slowly says, "I haven't decided personally yet." Pauses again. "But I can see that it can be done by watching Bill."

I follow up with a question about his plans for next year. He replies, "I'm going to shoot for four years teaching until I pay off my loan, and then go back to school." Hesitant suddenly worried about whether he may have betrayed me, his professor, or even a side of his former self, once so set on teaching, Rick hurriedly says, "This stuff about my own journey. You could look at that being very selfish, but. . . ." Interrupting him, wanting to forestall any apology, I say, "Look, I tend to think there are parts of yourself that come into play at different times in your life." Smiling, relieved that I seem to understand, Rick agrees, shaking his head: "Right, I couldn't operate daily if I felt like I was being selfish in the profession."

Without my prompting, he tries to explain his reasoning: "If I was giving one hundred percent of myself unselfishly to these kids and to West Norriton High School, I would feel like I was slighting myself. At the same time, if I was just doing teaching to make enough money to eat and survive, and I was completely blind to how I was affecting these hundred young adults that I see a year, then I couldn't sleep at night either. So I do work on two levels. That's what keeps me from believing that it's selfish." He speaks emphatically: "I do see teaching as a major process in my own shaping of myself. But at the same time I feel like I can balance my own motivations with helping other people." The truth of the matter is I am less anxious now, not so much about whether he'll give his life over to teaching, but about the effect his growing self-involvement may have on his teaching.

Cultivating Personal Theories of Action

Remembering the day I've observed him teach, how he merged his own pleasures of the literary texts with an approach to the books that involved his students, I believe he has achieved some part of this delicate balancing act. His identity, the teacher he wants to be, is complicated and maybe even contradictory. He can imagine teaching as a profession but it unnerves him to think of it as a life. Bill has demonstrated that one can still be a good teacher without it being all-consuming. However, there are other tensions to resolve—his quest for self-discovery that may turn him away from teaching, the increasing pressure to focus on students (as Bill says, teaching is about students not literature), the frustrations adhering to a mandated curriculum with limited resources, and finding ways to let the daily events of teaching provide meaning in his life. At this point, we cannot know whether or not he will reconcile himself to these circumstances and issues not how they will affect his teaching identity.

However, since identities are made in the dialectic between internal states and external contexts, there are several junctures that will surely be important. First, there is a fortuitous match between Rick's personal inclination to "embody" literature through dramatic reading and one reality of classroom life—that there are never enough books for students to take home, nor are students inclined to read in advance anyway. As a pedagogy, dramatic reading works for students who do not read on their own, whether owing to institutional impediments or to cultural factors that signal the non–college bound students that schoolwork is useless. Through trial and error, in conjunction with advice from his mentor Bill, Rick has discovered that a good solution for taking caring of a whole range of problems is to read aloud, something he already loves to do!

Second, whether because of his age, a young twenty-three, or in reaction to the conservative structure for his future—being a high school teacher and married to his high school sweetheart—he imposed as a teenager, or owing to the ties to family and community that bind him to North Carolina, the ultimate question for Rick (someone prone to asking questions that have no right answer) is who he will become. At this juncture, he is fascinated with investigating other possible forms his life could take. He searches openly and enjoys the idea that he doesn't know what will happen to him, declaring himself "ready to go with the flow and let the flow take me."

So far his journeys have all been metaphorical. Fortunately, the classroom is one context in which these journeys, investigating questions, are possible. As he said, he's "operating on two levels." Becoming a teacher, joining a profession, is one option he's exploring. It seems clear that discovering himself is what currently drives him. Teaching, he believes, is a helpful experience in this regard: as a process it "shapes him as a human being," it is a milieu that enables identity development in the broadest sense. However, Rick is not without a social conscience, and there is the additional dimension that he comes from a family dedicated to care and community. Teaching allows Rick to know he is positively "affecting these hundred young adults every year."

Rick's story is important to me as a teacher-educator because it reveals why we ought to help aspiring teachers to develop inner visions congruent with theories and ideas arising out of their idiosyncratic life experiences and that follow inclinations of the self. These personal theories of action can be cultivated in the protected context of the teacher-education program. With help from teachers and other mentors, these teaching visions can be projected into teaching situations, modified and further developed into effective and comfortable ways of being a teacher.

In this regard, Rick's orientation as a dramatic reader is a good example. His talent for the dramatic (an antipedagogy almost) went largely undiscovered and unremarked upon. It was certainly not actively fostered. Thus Rick's success as a teacher appears almost accidental. Fortunately, with a classroom of his own, given time, space, no explicit prohibitions against it, and a good friend and mentor, Rick does what compels him most. If this is true, then a pedagogy that provides open structures that students can use for whatever identity work is at hand should characterize the best teacher education curriculum.

Boundaries

The stories of Elizabeth and Rick demonstrate how selves are fluid and ever changing, labile and mutable, responsive to the forces of inner desires and outer conditions. Identities are momentary, almost ephemeral. Even referring, however metaphorically, to "boundaries of the self " presumes a stability that is nonexistent (if we trust the evidence presented in these two case studies). Events that proved to be impressive or profound (Rick's attachment to his fellow teacher Bill and Elizabeth's reaction to the E. D. Hirsch article) were unanticipated and not predictably significant. What mattered for their development as people was the variability, intensity, and richness of their experience, a flowing stream that brought Elizabeth and Rich into contact with other lives, other visions, other choices. Without worrying too much about uniformity or regulation, we as teacher educators can try to provide fertile, changeable, and challenging environments both in our classrooms at the university and in public school contexts that invite and engage students in the dynamic process of becoming teachers.

REFLECTIONS

Traveling

I am the subject of a photograph that I keep pinned to my office wall. In the photograph (snapped by my husband, an unusual event), I am cooking, stirring a large pot of tortellini for my children's supper. I smile straight into the camera as I stand behind the cooktop set into a wide, white, tiled counter. Behind me, the background is framed by two tall casement windows that look out onto a hillside of foot-high, bleached, yellow grass.

The family calls it the picture of greatest happiness: We're in Mendocino, at Sea Ranch, staying in a house that belongs to a friend of my husband, at the beach, though calling it that gives the wrong impression. A beach on the northern California coast means something else: great rocks and cliffs meet face-to-face with the pounding force of the sea, sand (when there is any) builds up and then disperses by the hour, the large dark brown rocks are covered with barnacles and sea kelp, dragged in by the tide. Pools form where sea urchins of delicate green, and starfish—Day-Glo orange, indigo purple, and several shades of coral and pink—by the thousands, inhabit the cracks between the rocks. The water is too cold for swimming, but it is so enticing, so alluring, that soon one is wet and shivering, feet and hands cut invariably getting in and then out of the water or when scrambling up the cliff face as the tide turns. When I glance at the photograph, I always see something that is not really there. I look past the forty-year-old woman cheerfully cooking dinner for her family, out the tall windows behind her, and into the wild and powerful landscape that lies out there, toward the western horizon. Without fail, it leads me to think about another time and turn in my life.

In the summer of 1974, I drove across the country in a midnight blue, soft-roof TR-6 convertible. The route we chose was a northern one, heading west across Pennsylvania and into Ohio, then shooting off, north by northwest, through the centerline of Michigan's Upper Peninsula. When the car's engine started sputtering, we checked the manual to locate the nearest Triumph dealership, which turned out to be in the Canadian town Sault Ste Marie. The trouble was only a cracked sparkplug, nothing more, and after a few hours, with a full new set of plugs, we were on our way; the engine sounded smooth and right again.

The route we renavigated (after the detour to the small isthmus that lies on the border between the United States and Canada) shunted us more north than west, around the Canadian perimeter of Lake Superior toward Thunder Bay. Eventually, we reentered the States at International Falls, Minnesota. Paradoxically (since we were heading for the West Coast) we commenced driving south with the Badlands in South Dakota on our minds. Spurning motels (and too poor to pay for them), we camped everywhere, using a telephone book–sized compendium of campgrounds that categorized and rated every possible location. This information allowed us to steer toward the most remote (and cheapest) sites, designated "primitive" by the guidebook. We carried everything we needed (tent, sleeping bags, a propane stove, cooking gear, deflatable water carrier, a change of clothes, toothbrushes, my journal, and very little else) in the tiny trunk of the car that we repacked and unpacked like a three-dimensional jigsaw puzzle every morning and night.

Driving through South Dakota, a corner of Wyoming, and across Montana and Idaho, we headed more or less west, aiming toward Washington state, anxious finally, after a month on the road, to see our first glimpse of the Pacific. The changing topography, the mountains, the wildlife (prairie dogs and buffalo, elk and longhorn sheep), National Parks, the small towns, and historic sites we visited—all these scenes I took in as a tourist, as an impressed but disinterested onlooker, remote from the actual settings, amazed at everything I was seeing, but fundamentally unmoved. Then something happened.

In all twenty-one years of my previous life, I had only known the gray, flat, dirty, dispirited Atlantic beaches of New Jersey as the ocean. My first encounter with the Pacific was off the Olympic peninsula, that arm of America that lies beyond Seattle, bordered on the east by Puget Sound and on the north by the Strait of Juan de Fuca. It was a world as exotic as the names I read off the map as we disembarked from the ferry and continued westward. (Eventually, after the events I'm about to narrate happened, we followed the ocean south, hugging the Oregon coast and entering the redwood groves and skimming the crumbling cliffs of Northern California.)

In the ranger station at Olympic National Park, we picked up backcountry permits to hike the coastal trail through the rainforest along the beach, parked the car, shouldered the packs, and started out. In a few short hours, no more than that, my mind was shattered during the first moments I beheld the white foaming sea, rocks blackened by water and whitened by birds nesting, immense stony islands looming like foundered ships, unscalable cliffs, fog—great billowing snowy sheets, and enormous evergreen trees growing right down to water's edge. The sea (no cliché) was full of life—sea lions, whales, fish we knew were there, and, in the pools we dug at our feet, clams, so many, that with a small pot and bottled water, dinner was done. With this shattering came not destruction but possibility. My mind opened to the wind and a world so different, so fantastically beautiful and wild, that I knew instantly nothing would ever be the same again, that I should not count on past experience as evidence of truth, reality, or knowledge. Concepts I thought I understood, deep down, had suddenly shifted, dissolved, evaporated, and been transformed by the simple act of walking down a trail in the state of Washington and out onto the hard-packed sand.

From then on (nearly two decades before the moment of the photograph), I have had no fear of going anyplace—real or otherwise. The experience left me only with an abiding desire to know everything and the realization that turning full force into the wind, open, wondering, and wanting, was how I was—now and hereafter—to live all the rest of my life.

A few years ago I read the novel *Cloud Chamber* by Michael Dorris who describes this type of metamorphosis perfectly. His character reports this insight: "And yet, I was altered. It's an odd thing how your life can change in the wisp of a breeze. A tinder may ignite or a fire blow out, but either way a boundary has been breached, a threshold irrevocably crossed, a key to the door."[1] It happened this way to me too—through a sudden conjunction, an alternative correspondence, an unaccountable coincidence, a moment of seeing something for the first time. It is a time and a place I can never forget (and always bring into the classroom with me).

CHAPTER FIVE

PRACTICING TEACHERS

Crossing Boundaries

It is the twenty-second of January, a mild, rainy day, and the beginning of a new semester at the university, Lauren's last as an undergraduate. Six weeks have passed since the final day of her teaching practicum. She arrives in my office animated and already talking, not pausing even for a second as she sits down since she sees by my position adjacent to the tape recorder that I'm prepared and listening. "So we're both concerned. I mean they're seniors in high school and most of them are college bound! And they are not going to do well unless they understand the writing process a lot better."

Yesterday Lauren returned to visit her students at Hillandale High because she "couldn't stop missing them." After we talk today, she intends to return again and regularly thereafter, having spontaneously arranged overnight "to be up there working *this* semester too, through teaching fellows." I need only to nod or make eye contact to manage my side of the conversation. Lauren sets the agenda: "And there's something else I want to talk to you about. We're talking about doing a group research paper with them. My teacher has never done this before and her colleagues are giving her a lot of flack about it, asking questions like—how are you going to work up accountability for that? But there is no way she can grade one hundred twenty research papers and give them the full attention that they need."

Lauren is concerned and upset about the students' abilities to produce a research paper—a statewide assignment for all high school seniors. About her conversation with Mrs. Jameson, she comments: "We talked about this a lot yesterday—how we can divide up the process, still have everybody work, and hold everyone accountable so they can really learn revisions. Give them a week to revise after the rough draft is responded to and given back."

"Right," I encourage her. "They need some time in class with you showing them the revision process." Then I continue, "What *I* would do is take a sample paper. . . ." And automatically, naturally, without thinking (but picking up on Lauren's cues) I quickly sketch out a workshop on revising. And for the next ten minutes we carry on that familiar and necessary kind of conversation teachers everywhere engage in, swapping stories of what works and what doesn't.

In this interaction—Lauren and I—we are teachers. No matter that Lauren is in my office on campus by appointment, ostensibly the student coming to see the professor. She engages me as a fellow teacher by discussing a writing assignment; she remakes the situation from an interview into a collaborative help session, two teachers working together. In referring to the outcome of her visit yesterday with Mrs. Jameson, it is not relevant that she be on the school district's payroll. She appropriates (and rightly so) the collective pronoun, "how *we* can divide up the process," to signify it's not only her own sense of this truth. Her language also represents Lauren's feeling that Mrs. Jameson's acquiesces to her status as partner and peer, as teacher. By taking Mrs. Jameson's side against some teachers who are critical of the group assignment, she asserts her insider position by assuming that her support and opinion will matter to Mrs. Jameson and the other teachers.

This chapter focuses on the development of collective identity, in this case, Lauren's newly formed perception of herself as an insider—a teacher— and the solidification of this identity through the reactions of other teachers (who treat Lauren as a teacher). Collective identities arise, like individual identities, through social interactions but particularly when those interactions occur in or around institutions (the public high school, the university) and with group insiders (cooperating teachers, university supervisors, and school administrators). Social categorization experiences (instances when other people recognize you as a member of a group or not) are especially relevant in constructing professional identities.

For persons who are developing teacher identities, collective identity work (being recognized and accepted as a teacher by other teachers, and by students, administrators, other school personnel) transpires most intensely during the practicum semester. Students and program faculty alike view the teaching practicum as difficult, stressful, a true test of their as yet untried abilities as teachers, and unequivocally the most potent identity-shaping component of the program. This occasion is the first time in our teacher education program that individuals go public as teachers, although not as full-fledged ones. In their respective school placements under the guidance of a certified teacher, they're referred to as student teachers, novice teachers, or (as we have recently adopted in our program) teacher interns. Defined as such, teacher interns straddle the social group boundary between several collective identities. Each day, even moment to moment, they are negotiating that boundary, crossing over, then back again, being a teacher, then not, feeling like a student, but addressed as a teacher.

The teaching practicum is supposed to help the student cross over the border forever, to live inside and join the collectivity of teachers. Sometimes it happens and sometimes not. In her work with prospective teachers, Deborah Britzman critiques what she calls "the myth that experience makes the teacher, and hence that experience is telling in and of itself." Such a perspective is problematic because it "valorizes student teaching as the authentic moment in teacher education and the real ground of knowledge production" (1991, 7).

Although powerful, the teaching practicum is simply one influence among many, and students' experiences and responses during student teaching vary dramatically from their attitude toward their placement, the personality of their cooperating teachers, and their actual success or failure teaching the students and subject matter associated with their situation. In fact, it is not experience itself that makes us who we are; rather it is the act of naming as well as the ways we talk about and represent the experience that constructs identities. In discussing their experiences in the interviews, the students chose things that were significant to them; in speaking, they invented themselves as narrators—the "I" of the story, and as persons—the self who speaks.

For Donna, Lauren, Elizabeth, Rick, Michaela, and Howard, what processes, events, acts, persons, contexts, institutions, seemed influential? How did they regard, describe, think about or explain their experiences? What topics, ideas, or events did they remember as significant and why? Answers to these questions will be drawn from several interviews during which students reflected about the thirteen weeks they spent teaching in a high school and about their sense of themselves as teachers just prior to college graduation.

It is important to me as a theorist to use the analytic method of focusing on interactions at the edges, the borders of things, because that's where identities come into being. They are "socially constructed at and across the boundaries which they share with other identities, and upon the process of recruitment" by others (Jenkins 1996, 102). This idea is not only theoretical. The pressures of the practicum are such that students must perform differently and develop new relationships with teachers and students. In their high school classrooms, they must project themselves as teachers although they know they are not (at least, not yet). Thus it's during the teaching practicum that students most keenly feel themselves crossing boundaries.

Affiliation and Collective Identity

Collective identity—being recognized by others as a teacher—develops primarily through interactions between interns and mentor teachers in an actual school context. My students' individual identities have been under construction as they have taken classes and participated in activities required by the teacher education program at the university. But in order for them to assume a public collective identity, they must be involved with professional teachers, members of the group they aspire to join. Also they must be in a real institution—a public high school—a setting congruent with the one they will one day inhabit themselves as teachers. Collective identities, then, are contingent on two things: first, that the intern is involved in actual teaching situation with a professional teacher, and second, that affiliation between intern and mentor occurs.

A word about affiliation. I use the term to refer to a relationship between individuals that suggests some form of association, alliance, union, or connection. Among other things, affiliations can have negative or positive valences, may exist when power differentials are slight or imbalanced, and can range from weak to strong. While "affiliation" is an inert concept, the processes by which individuals affiliate with one another are not. It is in the acts of affiliation that collective identities are constructed. To demonstrate this phenomenon, I will present several types of affiliation patterns as illustrated by the experiences of the participants in this study. These strategies are neither exclusive (they do happen to others) nor are they definitive (they are not the only means by which affiliation occurs). Consequently, such variation suggests that affiliation between interns and mentor teachers takes many forms and follows no set routes. Affiliation processes are influenced by a host of specific features including personality combinations, situational conditions such as the location of the high school in an urban or small town setting, school policies related to curriculum or behavioral protocol, the position occupied by the mentor teacher in the school's social milieu, and the school population itself such as the students' racial, ethnic, or economic characteristics.

Affiliation can be used not only to refer to relations between individuals but also to relations between institutions and individuals. Through participation in an institutional organization, individuals live out and publicize their collective identities. Organizations such as "the public schools" or, more circumscribed organizations such "the Chapel Hill Public Schools," or more narrowly still such as "East Chapel Hill High" have norms, standards, procedures, policies, practices, activities by which members of those organizations are known. Thus, the teacher intern must negotiate and forge a relationship not only with individuals but also with the institution itself. Such relationships are harder to actually see or identify though we are certainly aware of their power and influence in shaping who we are and how we behave. (It's what we mean in everyday conversation when we use the shadowy referent "the government" to account for some bureaucratic policy affecting us personally that seems to have no animate origin.) However, despite their abstract disembodiment, institutions do affect the development of individuals' collective identity, as the stories in this chapter show.

1. Affiliation through identification. For the teacher intern, the long process of sorting through and acquiring features or practices that define those who are teachers and those who are not occurs over many weeks, months, even years of everyday interactions. The strongest sense of Lauren's being a teacher came at the practicum's conclusion when she was technically to return to the university as a student. But Lauren had so thoroughly identified with her cooperating teacher she discovered she could not break away. Instead, she sought to stay connected, constructing an internship where she was both ally and collaborator in relation to her mentor teacher. Lauren's affiliation was so strong, her empathy so deep, it was as if she experienced everything exactly as Mrs. Jameson did: both were disappointed about the research paper, eager to improve the assignment, and indignant at the other teachers' reactions to their ideas. Furthermore, she hoped the solidarity signified by her presence at the school would protect Mrs. Jameson against criticism.

Mrs. Jameson's reactions to Lauren's overtures consolidated this affiliation. When she welcomed Lauren as partner and confidant, she encouraged Lauren to act a substitute for herself. Soliciting Lauren's ideas and pledge to "come back on a regular basis" makes her feel effectual and necessary, not just a beginner or a novice. Through the affiliative process, Mrs. Jameson actively recruits Lauren into group membership. I am struck (during our two-hour conference just after her practicum's end) at how fully Lauren associates herself with her cooperating teacher. The language she uses is especially revealing, for instance, her choice of pronouns: "So *we're* both concerned," she says, about how students didn't revise their last papers. "*We* talked about this a lot yesterday." "How can *we* divide up the process?" "*We* were just kind of brainstorming on the board yesterday afternoon." "*We're* going to talk about it some more." This language echoes the forms Mrs. Jameson used with Lauren at the start of the practicum.

Lauren uses the occasion of our talk to solicit reactions that further affirm her alliance with Mrs. Jameson: "I knew that I would feel better if I talked to you about it because I knew you would like the stuff that we did and I couldn't believe that the other teachers didn't. Because what they are doing is obviously not working. They need to try something else." When I nod, she continues: "So my teacher is really concerned and we talked about how—when we had a project—you would give us the rubric and tell us what we were responsible for . . . I told her [about your system] because I thought it was horrible when she told me her colleagues were discouraging her. I said I think it is a wonderful idea." Mrs. Jameson had confided many of her personal views about teaching with Lauren. While she was disturbed by what Mrs. Jameson revealed, Lauren obviously valued and appreciated how much her mentor needed her, further validating Lauren's place as a teacher. She says, "I learned about frustration, I really did. it is discouraging that my own cooperating teacher, who is a wonderful teacher, wonderful with the kids, [would] say sometimes, 'This is getting ridiculous. If it continues, I'm not going to be here. I know I shouldn't say this in front of you, but I feel that you need to know all aspects and this is one of them.' "

During other visits, Lauren has always sat in the chair across from me as a student. Now, despite the fact of my tape-recorder, my habitual seat near the desk and by the door, my list of questions discretely on my lap, all obvious features signaling student status, Lauren ignores them. Instead, clearly feeling herself very much the teacher today, she remakes these situational characteristics into ones that support her collective identity as teacher. No longer professor or interviewer, I am cast as expert writing teacher, experienced with groups, revising strategies, paper assignments. She can pick my brain.

Besides, I'm also a sympathetic listener, someone interested in her, two things she's learned from our previous interactions. In the past, these features made her feel comfortable, good, smart about herself when as a concerned and anxious student she would arrive at office hours to discuss papers and projects. Now she capitalizes on these interactional givens, certain that I will attend to her conversation. But she asks not for affirmation the way she used to ("Am I a smart student?"), but for information about structuring the paper assignment. These transformations suggest how firmly she's now situated inside a teacher identity.

My behavior further corroborates Lauren's insider status. I am pleased she disregards my interviewer's persona so I fully cooperate, happy to see her shed the role of student-interviewee. My adaptability in allowing Lauren to re-structure the interaction further reinforces her sense we're on even footing. it is easy to move into the scene where two teachers exchange ideas. Making no effort to readjust, I automatically lean forward; the pad slips off my knee. Catching it and putting is aside, I spin out custom-designed strategies geared to her students because I know what she needs. (I've been out to observe her teaching and have seen first hand the fourth period class she calls her 'Punkers' and the sixth period class of underprepared seniors.)

Although "teaching" is not anything that guarantees "being a teacher," it helps. (How helpful depends on the person, the relation to cooperating teacher, the school context, the curriculum one is asked to teach, the students, the fellow teachers, and numerous other individual features.) Situational factors have had a huge impact on Lauren's ability to imagine and enact a teaching identity, i.e., living, thinking, acting, enacting, interacting as a teacher. Thus, collective identity develops through the process of identification with her mentor teacher—when Mrs. Jameson welcomes Lauren back into her classroom, reporting the latest obstacles—and by my confirming her position and relationship with Mrs. Jameson—when I respond as teacher not professor.

2. Affiliation through differentiation. Identity cannot be "conferred," but group members can facilitate the induction of aspiring members. Therefore, what matters most is the relationship between intern and mentor teacher, that person who represents the collective of "teacher." Both parties understand the purpose of the relationship: to assist the novice to become a full-fledged teacher. Although every pair accedes to this goal, the process by which collective identity is achieved depends on the nature of the affiliating relationship between them. Rick and Mrs. Altman, his mentor, built their relation around a shared desire to be "a good teacher" with the common understanding that being "good" meant many things. Though very different in style, manner, and inclination, each believed there were many possible methods that were effective for students and also personally satisfying. One could teach well *and* be happy, sustained, and functioning as a teacher. This relative freedom combined with the sense of a shared goal allowed Rick to work on his collective identity as teacher without feeling that he was jeopardizing, compromising or constraining his individual identity.

Mrs. Altman taught in an experimental and highly reputed interdisciplinary seminar program that operated quite differently from the standard curriculum at the high school. Although learning to function as a seminar teacher added an extra challenge to Rick's teaching internship, he was pleased to hear about his placement because of Mrs. Altman's excellent reputation. More than anything, Rick aspired to being good but what this meant exactly as he entered the practicum semester was amorphous and unformed. He expected to develop style, methods, practices, rapport, discipline, and knowledge as he went along, however he idealized and romanticized teaching itself. His love of books and literature complicated his vision of self as teacher; he had a complementary or possibly conflicting desire to be both writer and literary critic, if not during this early stage of his career, possibly later. Mrs. Altman was daunting as a mentor, not because of her strong, determined yet understated personality, but because she was very skilled and deeply invested in the seminar program. The program demanded teaching skills like unit planning, integration across disciplines, nonpresentational teaching. It emphasized collaborative and cooperative methods, activities geared to account for individual differences, high expectations for students, and a teacher who facilitated, not lectured, and hence was highly structured and organized.

Rick was not. However, his singular talent, reading aloud, presentational performance, was something he was able to experiment with since Mrs. Altman was open to all methods, judging effectiveness on how well students learned or participated. Dramatic reading was not Mrs. Altman's style, which tended to be understated, firm, yet quiet and casual. Despite her accommodation and openness, Rick was anxious a lot about whether or not he could fill her shoes (very large ones); he worried that his students expected him to teach like her. To ease Rick's anxieties while at the same time promoting his development along the lines that suited him best, Mrs. Altman concentrated on providing constant and detailed feedback about his classroom performance. This strategy worked exceptionally well because both accepted and respected each other's positions as expert and apprentice. Though their relationship was clearly hierarchical— Mrs. Altman was the authority and in control in the classroom—it was also very generative and empowering for Rick. The structured environment supported him as a learner the same way it facilitated learning for the diverse students enrolled in the seminar program.

Because they shared a common goal and accepted their respective roles, the many differences between them (style, ideology, interests, etc.) never interfered with Rick's developing an identity as teacher unique to him. In fact, he believed Mrs. Altman was an excellent mentor, the best possible, someone who did everything perfectly. Under her tutelage, Rick remained positive and continued to be interested in teaching though he evolved into a teacher with a style and persona very distinct from hers. Differentiation (rather than identification) was the outcome of their affiliating relationship. Thus, depending on the dynamic between mentor and intern, a hierarchical relationship can foster a teaching identity without overpowering the individual's own preferences or inclinations. Notwithstanding the differences between them, Rick constructed himself as a teacher because his talents and preferences were appreciated and maintained by his mentor teacher. In turn, Mrs. Altman used her considerable power to further Rick's goals.

3. Performing the role in a substantive manner. What matters in establishing a collective identity are the *patterns* of interaction and their *repercussions* between members and nonmembers. The way that local and specific social interactions play out the actions and decisions made by individuals either promotes or prevents collective identity development. Consequently, identity arises from performing the role in a substantive and deep manner, for instance, when the experience of being a "student teacher" is less like a student and more a teacher. To adopt any identity, individuals must be enabled to act *as if* they are insiders. Furthermore, teacher interns can perform more like teachers when they have some power to define success in their own terms relative to the situation at hand. Because of her lateral relationship with Mrs. Jameson, Lauren assumed the position of co-teacher almost immediately upon entering the classroom. This immersion allowed Lauren to feel responsible and in charge, and freed her to pursue her primary interest—to connect with and care for students.

In fact, Lauren's teaching self depended largely on her having students. The faster she became "their" teacher, the more she thrived. This was manifested during a postpracticum interview during which Lauren rarely spoke about herself. Instead, after twenty minutes about Mrs. Jameson's predicament, she concentrated almost exclusively on her students. This contrasts with prior interviews where she spent much time airing her anxieties about how she would perform in the classroom. But four months of actual teaching seems to have relieved Lauren's worst anxieties, allowing her to devote full attention to her students. Entering into caring relations with students (akin to Nel Noddings's conceptions of "caring") is a teaching life she has previously aspired to, but, miraculously, now has accomplished: she has made an appreciable difference in their lives.

What enabled Lauren's deep involvement? There is no one circumstance; rather the particular conditions and qualities of the entire situation interacted to provide an amenable environment for Lauren's development. Mrs. Jameson admirably fulfilled her role as mentor by providing the bottom line (establishing content and process goals, requiring a certain number of grades, and asking for daily lesson plans) then setting Lauren free. The students (most of whom had little economic or cultural capital) needed her and she was thrilled to feel necessary. Although all the interns reported growing attached to their students, none bonded with students more than Lauren did. Her compunction to return to her students, I believe, was rooted in how they made her feel. It was only in relation to them was she able to occupy the identity of teacher. Once Lauren stepped outside these daily interactions with students, her teacher identity began to erode. Now, in her current life as a teacher in a sprawling high school near a major city in central North Carolina, Lauren attributes her confidence to the obvious support of her colleagues as well as the responsiveness of her students. Despite the school's dismal and discouraging statistics on achievement, attendance, crime, poverty, and drug use, obligation to students helps Lauren to persist and enjoy teaching.

4. Joint problem solving in a local context. Lauren's case indicates that patterns of interactions and their repercussions in local and specific social contexts seem most effectual in fabricating identities. Although the relationships and circumstances of persons and places are substantially different, a similar process involving personal networks is clearly evident in Donna's situation as well. Donna and her mentor, Ms. Kearns, are similar in many respects. Both are women in their twenties, neither is married, both are determined visionaries. But these features were relatively insignificant compared to their shared ideology—a singular, focused interest on disadvantaged teenagers and in the best methods for teaching them.

Donna was motivated to become a teacher because of her religious commitment to serve a higher power. In concrete terms, she envisioned her mission as working with disadvantaged and troubled teenagers. As requested, Donna was assigned to a twenty-five-year-old mentor teacher who systematically elected to teach the classes full of kids nobody else wanted. Ms. Kearns, or Emily, as Donna called her, recognized their commonality immediately and it was on these grounds that she worked to recruit Donna into the collective. The two bonded over a mutual philosophy revolving around "respect and self-control," with attentiveness to "fairness," "discipline," and "having a vision of what's possible for students with so many special needs."

A month into the term, Emily became sick and so Donna took over for the week or so her mentor was gone. As she put it, "I got stuck teaching without being prepared," her biggest lack being strategies for disciplining students, not the class subject matter, American Literature, for which she was well prepared. After Emily returned and they began analyzing what had happened, both agreed that firm discipline was critical to enable learning for students most in danger of failing. Emily immediately tuned into Donna's needs and they invented tailor-made discipline plans for each class. Her sensitivity and precise focus was key. Instead of offering generic advice, Emily invited Donna to work collaboratively on solutions linked to her personal convictions—that "my students see discipline as a form of care"—and customized to each class— "extreme constraint worked for fourth period." She "designed individual contracts for troublemakers in fifth period."

The specificity of these everyday interactions between mentor and intern powerfully shaped Donna in the area where she felt most vulnerable and uncertain. It was not simply a similar outlook that united them; rather Ms. Kearns seized on one feature in spite of other similarities that were possible points of connection. Thus some traits are more consequential to the individual whose identity is at stake. When both mentor and intern regard the same commonality as important, the door to group membership is more readily opened than if no significant common ground evolves. A strong identification can often help both individuals (teachers and aspiring teachers) to ignore or downplay what might be radical differences in other areas of their lives—such as different cultural and philosophical attitudes toward the subject matter, distinctive political ideologies, or distinguishing social class backgrounds.

5. *Oppositional affiliation.* Most teacher educators believe that working with a mentor teacher powerfully influences both collective and individual identity. The dynamic of identifying with one's mentor teacher can be either positive or negative; both forms are equally powerful. Thus, some identities will be created through dissimilarity and difference, in opposition to person and positions. In a congruent match, like Lauren's, the novice identifies positively with the person and profession of the mentor. In the opposite case, like Elizabeth's, her

identification was negative and the relationship with her mentor revolved around difference.

Elizabeth's situation was complicated by several prior conditions. She began her practicum ambivalent about the enterprise of teaching but certain of her individual identity as writer. She felt centered in her conviction that writing was key to adolescents' emotional, intellectual, and cognitive development. "I didn't love books," Elizabeth reported, "until I loved writing." These ideas on "whole language theory 'took' because I had had these experiences personally with writing." Furthermore, she experienced my courses as living demonstrations "of bringing practice and theory together." "It's what *you* do," she exclaimed during an early interview. Because she was simultaneously teaching and writing her college honor's thesis, Elizabeth was more intensely involved than the other interns in a continuous stream of action and reflection, a cycle of planning, teaching, and writing that heightened and made obvious the identity development she was undergoing.

One of Elizabeth's main goals was "for non–college bound kids not to hate school . . . School is pointless if learning isn't motivated." Her perspective was bolstered by the success she encountered with her methods. As part of writing essays, she introduced students to the technique of writing discovery drafts. Though at first students complained, when they caught on to its advantages, Elizabeth reports, "they were disgruntled when they ran out of time to write in class." But the conversion of one particular student crystallized Elizabeth's faith in herself. Yvonne, a class leader, a young black woman, typically ignored the teacher, disrupted class, and routinely refused to do class assignments. Yvonne was bored with school and books like *Hamlet*, but she found her own life and the world around her fascinating. Elizabeth introduced writing techniques that gave Yvonne "time, space, and voice," and it proved to be dynamite. When she caught on to Elizabeth's agenda, Yvonne became a co-teacher in the class, a strong peer who advocated on Elizabeth's behalf to her classmates, but also a live demonstration of how a teacher could turn a person on to learning.

Although Elizabeth was heartened and encouraged by the students' responsiveness, she remained conflicted about herself since Mr. Collins did not believe that student reaction was an index of success. His challenging discussions, though unsettling, became opportunities for Elizabeth to think through and refine her own position. In the end, such clear and diametric opposition sharpened Elizabeth's individual identity and made her keenly aware she possessed one. But because she defined herself in difference rather than likeness, Elizabeth felt like an outsider, unlike the teachers in the collective community of her school. Thus while resistance was a powerful agent of self-construction, she had little sense of group identity, of being a teacher among other teachers.

6. *Disharmony between individual and group identity.* Constructing an individual and collective identity is a complicated and continuous process. No matter how potent the shared connections between recruit and group member might be, the characteristics of the collective identity or its position vis-à-vis other social identities, for example, may prevent a person from accepting a group membership. Positive matches between intern and mentor in and of themselves cannot guarantee the construction of a collective identity.

Michaela's case demonstrates how the process of individual identity formation interacts with that of group identity. Just prior to graduation, I asked Michaela about applying for teaching jobs. "I have this love-hate relationship with it," she says. "I love the teaching part, taking a literature trip, but there's this seamy underworld to teaching, things that pit you against children. But the distilled essence of teaching I love and don't know if I can give up. it is a drug that way." In her practicum, Michaela was partnered with a high-powered and dedicated teacher, committed to the art of literature and its pursuits. Mostly, Michaela taught advanced upper-division English courses that she described as "a college class scaled down."

Given her own academic orientation and desire to be a writer, Michaela and Ms. Long were well disposed to work together. Though the work and preparation were constant and highly demanding, by midsemester Michaela felt that "something clicked," she had passed Miriam's tests, and their relationship solidified. From this point onward, Michaela was in a position to learn many strategies and approaches for teaching literature from her mentor. She taught Michaela a method of reading and conceptualizing themes that made teaching easier: "I've got confidence *knowing* what I want to talk about—religion, morality, whatever." Both mentor and intern believed that teaching literature was critical because books—their themes, characters, ideas, morals, and purposes—have the power to instruct their readers.

By the end of the practicum, Michaela knows she is a teacher. At one point during our last interview she shouts, *"I am Ms. Morris!"* Nevertheless, she finds herself profoundly ambivalent about teaching and is unable to settle into a teaching identity. The difficulties stem not from personal performance in the classroom, but from the institution of school itself, the social status of teaching as a profession, and the economic realities of a teacher's life. "It's a hard job to be parent, teacher, and therapist for $20,000 a year," she tells me frankly. As a teacher myself, I know the other "jobs" she's talking about. These other roles, for instance, teacher as therapist, are part of collective definition of who teachers are or can be or should be. Michaela finds it difficult to align herself with the group since she rejects or cannot be comfortable with many features characteristic of the category "teacher." At one point during her last interview she asserts, "I want to be an unreasonable teacher," one whose dreams and ideals are not compromised by economic or institutional limitations. Non–group members who are being recruited into a collective identity, like the teacher interns, have little power to intervene in terms of how their individual selves will be known, defined, or created by the collective membership. Sometimes the disparities cannot be overcome.

7. *Institutions act upon identities.* Institutions influence people's identities; conversely, institutions are altered through by the people who participation in them. "Institutions are organized and organizing with respect to social identity and behavior" (Jenkins 1996, 124). Different institutional contexts and organizational configurations, depending on how the social structures interact with the individual (and vice versa), influence identities but in unpredictable and variable ways.

The School of Education, and particularly the secondary-teacher education program, is one institution that figures substantively in identity development among my students. But the more significant institution for their collective identity is that of "the public schools" as represented by each intern's high school. Overall, the university has a relatively weak effect given the material conditions: as students they take required courses like "Adolescent Development" and complete assignments like creating unit plans for teaching. In the public schools, however, interns function as proto-teachers with actual students, under vastly different conditions. But whether the effect is intense or diluted, both institutions influence identity when individuals participate in established practices and in the myriad interactions between members.

On the other hand, institutions are not all powerful. While they affect identity development, they do not altogether determine it. Individuals have agency and can behave in any number of ways relative to the institutional situations in which they find themselves. Thus individual and collective identity depends on how people behave within the institution as well as how the institution influences action. Howard's reactions during the teaching practicum, at times respecting or on occasion rejecting institutional norms, demonstrates this reciprocal process.

Howard regarded his practicum situation as nearly ideal, certainly more congenial than he had dared hope. Located in a rural county with an expanding economic base and suburban growth, Howard's school was new enough to have decent facilities yet old enough to have established a good reputation. After some initial contact, Howard reported (with apparent relief) that his cooperating teacher appeared pleasant and more than competent; most important, the students were respectful and exhibited no major discipline problems. His primary concerns, though, were personal ones: How would he fit in? Would he like teaching? Would he be able to do what he wished? How much would he have to adjust? Would he have to change? Howard was facing a boundary problem. Neither college student nor yet teacher, his self was palpably undergoing construction as he tried to find a position to occupy in a new institutional setting.

As he began teaching, Howard was interested in exploring philosophical and existential foundations: What does becoming a teacher mean and what will it mean to *me*? Do you have to take on the job of teacher as "public servant" the way the culture defines it, and the way the institution is designed to promote it? Or can you try to shape the conventional role "teacher" into something more tailored to meet personal preferences or needs? Howard grappled with both these alternatives—institutional vs. personal agency—all throughout what was unquestionably a successful teaching practicum. In the end, he negotiated and accommodated to institutional forces in ways that preserved several strong personal predispositions.

For Howard, successful teaching depended on a few basic qualities, some of which he admitted to lacking. Structure was necessary on account of the institution itself, of the nature of public schools, their size and number of students. This quality he acceded to as essential and tried assiduously to develop it. In discussing how he learned to chunk his fifty-minute class into three activities, twenty, twenty, and ten minutes apiece, he comments: "I had to keep it structured and yet I'm not really a structure person (laughs). That's been the challenge. I knew going into student teaching that I would have to get more structure and more organized. I know those are things that teachers are supposed to be but I never bothered to learn those traits along the way." A few other conditions, like testing, he grudgingly accepted simply because they were mandated. "I had no test in the unit for your class. That wasn't an option this time [laughs]. Had to have grades. I'd rather not have a test. I'd rather have sort of a cumulative portfolio but I'm in someone else's system." Whereas other regulations like the standard curriculum, which may have seemed equally nonnegotiable and the rules "in someone else's system," Howard regarded as malleable or able to be circumvented.

The English curriculum is limited by the state to a small and canonical collection of texts; there are no resources to provide alternative books not reprinted in the adopted textbook. His frustration with teaching world literature is a good example. For African literature, the textbook contains only an excerpt by Doris Lessing, a writer "who was actually British and happened to live in Rhodesia," so, in Howard's mind, not an African writer. To compensate, Howard photocopied some African folk tales for his students, paying for the photocopies himself and ignoring the copyright regulations he discovered in his faculty mailbox that very day. Thus Howard's interests in literature were not very well served by the high school teacher's position. It seems that when an individual's stronger desires or orientations can't be matched up with dominant features in the identity under development, the individual looks elsewhere for another possible choice. In the end, Howard applied to graduate school in English, believing he could merge his main drives—teaching, but with an available and wide variety of literature.

Maintaining control in the classroom is another area where Howard imposed his own standards despite their obvious variation from the status quo. He describes himself as having "good rapport" with the students. They like him because he's "energetic and get-going." When Howard had full teaching responsibility, he aimed for classes to be interactive and talkative although his mentor teacher disagrees. After being away for a few days, "she was talking about how much noisier they were than normal. It was just because I was making jokes. Her style is much more structured. Her method is much different than mine." He knows he's successful if students are talking and feels guilty knowing that once he leaves they'll have to return to sedate lessons. "When I'm teaching," Howard says, "there is a really different attitude, and I'm not sure if it's because I'm more willing to let them get away with it or I'm younger or what. But there is a very different atmosphere when she's in the room and I'm teaching, or when she's teaching. Either one. When she leaves, they can see me sort of change and it picks them up a little bit too."

Howard believes his attempts at humor signal to students that there's a relationship between life and art. During the time they reading *Romeo and Juliet*, for instance, he thumbs his nose at the class, a gesture taken from the play. Though he tries to temper his behavior in front of his mentor teacher, to maintain his image in front of the students he purposely does not suppress his irreverent impulses altogether—"She did see me today stick my tongue out at students." In these areas of resistance, there seems to be a personal trait or disposition essential to Howard's sense of himself that conflicted with the institutional requirement. At these crossroads, Howard found methods to assert himself and be the teacher he aspired to be rather than the one (according to Ms. Stone, the public schools, or the university) he ought to become.

8. Identities develop concurrently. My students' individual and collective identities evolved concurrently and through parallel processes. Individually they ascribed to be teachers and at the same time were classified as such by others such as university faculty or teacher mentors. This self-attribution and categorization by others occurred in a variety of contexts: while they were education majors and taking courses in the secondary education program, as teaching fellows on scholarship (like Michaela and Lauren), as Sunday school teachers (like Donna), as children of teachers (like Howard). It happened during their internship in the public schools, when they were addressed as Ms. Tavey, as they were called upon to break up fights, when they were planning for and teaching five sections of English literature (anything from *Beowolf* to *The Invisible Man*), while they were attending school staff meetings, and as they assigned quarterly grades to their 120 or so students.

But no matter how strong their individual convictions as teachers, my students instinctively desired some other outside organizational, institutional recognition of their status as teachers. Their individual identities would be more secure, tougher, less subject to doubt or disintegration if there were a reinforcing match between private persona and public membership. For this reason, all my students expected their collective identities would be bolstered and more firmly established once they were in a school teaching during their practicum.

Indeed, this is Lauren's story. Among the many factors important to becoming a teacher, there were innumerable cooperative, positive, reinforcing and generative interactions: receiving a scholarship to attend the university as a teaching fellow; the organizational benefits of teaching fellows, including contact with the public schools; being an Education major and categorized as such by faculty members and fellow students; having had inspirational teachers, one in particular; discovering her passion was not for literature per se but for how she might teach it to students; a mentor teacher who viewed Lauren as a partner. This is not an exhaustive list. Not surprisingly, by the time of graduation in terms of any measure, including self-assessment, the evaluations of her university supervisor, mentor teacher, and students, according to the University Records Office and the state of North Carolina, Lauren was recognizably a teacher.

But as anyone who works in teacher education knows, there are no procedures to guarantee this process. As a committed teacher, I do what I can to be involved and interactive. And though students and faculty alike hope that the teaching practicum (as one of the more powerful forces) will result in the mutual reinforcement of individual and collective identity, this is not always the outcome. Of the six, Elizabeth had the most serious concerns about whether she "fit" as a teacher, and thus was anxious for some kind of public, institutional recognition of suitability as a member. In her case, multiple identity-forming processes were at work: Elizabeth had powerful transforming experiences with journal writing as an adolescent. She idealized my teaching and encountered ideas in books that harmonized with her own. In response, I acknowledged, recognized, and named her as an emerging teacher. However, once out in the public schools (a danger she anticipated), it became apparent that Elizabeth's beliefs were antithetical to the majority's. She developed no feeling of collective membership as a high school teacher, nor did she, after college graduation, apply for any teaching positions.

After six months of holding down a series of unsatisfying jobs, Elizabeth resolved her ambivalence toward teaching. On a return visit to campus, she discussed feeling committed to education, certainly to the field of writing, but also believed it to be a calling lived out in a different context where her particular individual identity would be welcomed. She wished to belong to a group where her orientation was relevant, primary. I advised graduate school, a master's program in the discipline of rhetoric and composition, writing theory and practice, hoping that Elizabeth might find herself an ideological home.

Unpredictable

Identities, whether individual or collective, are fluid compositions that arise out of a dialectic among individuals who participate in a variety of organizations and institutions. The dialectic process involves the interactions between self and others, the interplay between group members and aspiring members, all who have variable degrees of power, influence, or importance. The stories of my students in this chapter confirm the evolving nature of collective identity formation, demonstrating how such identities are "flexible, situational and negotiable" (Jenkins 1996, 102).

For Howard, Michaela, and Elizabeth, collective identities never coalesce. They decline the invitation of membership (in the end, they cannot see themselves being known as high school English teachers) partly because of certain conditions they can't live with or tolerate, abide, or accept. What these issues are varies from case to case. Alternately, Lauren, Rick, and Donna discover techniques to make a place for themselves in this identity position. They are certainly not unaware of the drawbacks, but rather imagine methods to "work around" the difficulties, circumvent the negative stereotypes, or otherwise to create a world in classrooms they can control. Adopting a collective identity means being willing to accept, modify, or compromise certain standards because they believe it is the only means to achieving other nonnegotiable goals fundamental to self-identity. This accommodation is what happens to students who accept "the call" to teach (Hansen 1995).

My students all felt drawn to teaching, but in the end some decided against it, which is not altogether a bad thing. Certainly it is no shortcoming or failure on the part of the program, mentor teachers, or the interns. The practicum affords a close approximation of life as a teacher and it is precisely the time to discover whether a particular identity could become central to one's life or existence. Those who end up teaching do so because they believe they can adjust to circumstances, tolerate sometimes dismal conditions, and still achieve something essential.

REFLECTIONS

The Seventies

A teenager in the early seventies, thinking of civic duty, of my political obliga-
tions as a working class liberal, and excited by the revolutionary possibilities
that public education afforded (my own experience of schools—miserable,
cramped, unenlightening, and downright boring), in college I majored in education, imagining myself an elementary school teacher. I had visions of free
schools, and schools without walls, one-room schools, and schools where curriculum was not a huge list published in a government binder, but an integrated
pursuit of living—students and teachers going through the day engaged in producing and making culture, ready to learn, investigating mathematics and science in the context of nature hikes and building bridges over creeks to extend
the hiking trails in their neighborhood. I was a twenty-year-old idealist, in love
with the idea of a utopian life of collective and productive work, and with the
vague idea that maybe sometime, somewhere, school could be like that.

Of the grim realities of school, I was well aware. The students I taught
during my teaching practicum lived on the fringe of a decaying urban center,
where jobs were lost more often than found, where the immigrant and minority populations were on the rise while whites fled to the suburbs, where housing and living conditions were downright dismal only two blocks from where I
lived as a college senior on a charming street full of carefully restored and lov-
ingly tended Federalist houses dating from the 1700s.

In 1973, the fall of my senior year, I was assigned to do my student
teaching at Fox Point School, an elementary school in a rundown slum adjacent
to the shabby and reduced gentility of the neighborhood just east of Brown
University in Providence, Rhode Island. My students were children of first-
and second-generation Portuguese immigrants, drawn to the area because of
the bay, the fishing industry, the work available in maritime shipping. I was
drawn to these children for other reasons—perhaps a curiosity about the exotic,
a sense of social responsibility, a belief in service in those times of political lib-
eralism. With my fourth-graders, I spent my days making maps of the neighborhood and translating into meaningful contexts the stories from the basal
reader about American families, tales of customs and places that to them may
have well been about life on Mars.

I adored the children and the dreamy way we spent our time together, but
I disliked intensely the institution of school, the routines, the oppressive rules,
the lock-step curriculum, and even the other teachers—not that they were bad
people—but because they weren't like me, with the life in my head more real

than the one I lived daily, with a book always in my hands. I couldn't imagine spending the next twenty years with them, sharing our stories about Carlos or Angela in the teachers' lounge.

Something Unformed, New, and Open

Later I went to graduate school, leaving New England and moving to California, trying to escape the fate of being a schoolteacher, abandoning the familiar and predictable landscape of childhood in the hope of finding something unformed, new, and open. I imagined having a Ph.D. would mean doing research, thinking about schools and the problem of schools. I gave no thought to being a teacher or a writer. I prevented myself from knowing (sheer denial) that that's what you become with a Ph.D.—a teacher and a writer (where my bookworm tendencies would in the end prove to be invaluable). There I was, a year prior to graduation, intending to use my doctorate in the field of literacy to apply for a job at a college or university. I had had no college teaching experience.

In this anxious condition, I apprenticed myself to the person directing the remedial composition program for students entering the University of California at Berkeley. I watched him teach his classes to prepare myself for teaching the following quarter. I was given a perch at one of the desks in the program office—two large rooms, ten desks apiece. There I met and was taken in by other graduate students in the program, some new, other seasoned teachers, but all enthusiastic, committed teachers *and* intellectuals from a range of disciplines, the Law School, the English department, Foreign Languages, Sociology, and me, ironically, the first instructor from the School of Education.

I discovered shortly thereafter that I was very good at teaching writing to students who were having difficulties entering the academic mainstream. Perhaps I understood them so well because I myself wanted and needed the same things they did: an erudite style, language that would not give away a lowly pedigree, and a comfortable place in a highbrow institution. In this remedial program, there were many nonnative speakers, Asians and Hispanics, plus native speakers who were not fluent enough in written forms of English to survive the regular academic composition.

Though I had been in school most of my life, I became a teacher (acknowledged and recognized myself) the instant I walked into the classroom and looked at my first class of twenty students. It was as if I had donned a coat (the long-disused academic robes) that signaled "teacher." Simply being with my students was exhilarating. I found them fascinating. I needed to know who they were, what they thought, where they were going, and most important, where they had come from. My instincts led me to sit and talk with them, to begin discussions on their home turf, to ask for writing from any angle or edge on information they had, to use whatever facts they knew about language (the required subject matter) as ideas, to explain straightforwardly that language is political, a system, a process, a way of thinking, an art form, a path for transcendence, a ticket for admission to their other classes, and a formula for manufacturing power: These moves, ones I made blindly but surely, were absolutely the right ones for them—and for me.

CHAPTER SIX

A Pedagogy for Identity Development

The Second Paragraph Must Have Eight

One night on the phone Ellen (a student from the previous semester now three days into her teaching practicum) wails: "I know what I believe about teaching! I know the kind of teacher I want to be!" She continues, in a tone both accusatory and appreciative at the same time, "*You* made us think about things like that!" She starts to cry, explaining, "My cooperating teacher thinks I'm kind of a blank slate when it comes to being a teacher. But I am not. I have spent the last several years writing and thinking, very deeply, with a lot of energy and love, about the kind of teacher I want to be. I'm idealistic but not unrealistic."

Then Ellen proceeds to list the comments made by her mentor teacher that at the time made her "want to die." These included the teacher's assertion about curriculum, "I just pick random things I'm interested in reading to teach the students. I don't do any of that theme-based teaching or anything"; her opinion on evaluation, "You have to give them grades for everything or they won't do the work"; her prohibitions about assignments, "You can't assign any kind of writing except formal essays required for the end-of-course testing;" and her advice about handling the paper load, "You have to use this rubric (to count the number of sentences per paragraph, and the second paragraph must have eight) because the grade has to be based on something."

Ellen's distress stems partly from new-teacher nerves and the shock of facing real students but also from recognizing the deep, ideological differences between her and her mentor. She wonders aloud if she will survive. Her crisis runs deep because she feels that her very self, her identity as a teacher, has been called into question by recent events. For much of the conversation, we analyze a disturbing incident about a one-page personal letter that Ellen assigned her students but which her mentor teacher read and graded according to word count, not content. The mentor teacher's interference makes Ellen feel betrayed. Furthermore, she believes her students' privacy was violated.

What is the point, Ellen wants to know, of grading according to a system that purposely ignores all the meaningful elements? She knows she could have designed a scoring rubric that took into account both meaning and mechanics. She is horrified at her mentor's advice: "You've got to pick *something* to grade with. Then just stick with that—don't make it so complicated!" But Ellen wants that "something" to really matter; the choice can't be arbitrary. My role in the conversation is tricky. How can I support both intern and mentor? I begin by reassuring Ellen that no matter what will happen in the next three months she would still be a teacher because the current situation is not and can never be all determining. Next, I focus attention on her mentor's role—to induct Ellen into the teaching profession and to guarantee her immediate success in the classroom. Somewhat unfairly, I oversimplify and reduce the dilemma by asking Ellen to see that the conflict is less about "self" or "person," an identity issue, and more about something superficial like pragmatic methods. Though I don't really know the real reasons, I suggest that the teacher is not attacking Ellen's long-held desires but instead is trying to steer her toward using methods the teacher believes work with actual students. For my part, I'm trying to prevent her from quitting on the first day of teaching. My strategy is to insulate her (a single person and a novice) from the shock of plunging into a teaching world that will act upon her almost too forcefully. There is a danger that these events will shape her into a teacher who merely reproduces prevailing ideologies and practices (ones that Ellen herself objects to). Teacher-educator Deborah Britzman calls this moment of struggle between self and the institution of school and its members "the hidden work of learning to teach." We see how Ellen must negotiate among "conflicting visions, disparaging considerations and contesting interpretations about social practice *and* the teacher's identity" (1991, 3). No wonder Ellen experiences this process as invasive; she has approached teaching as someone with autonomy, the ability to make independent judgments, and agency, the power to affect her students and school. Thus far, this vision of herself has not been affirmed; to the contrary, Ellen feels threatened and doubtful.

By the end of the call, Ellen is calmer, assuring me that she will try to regard the situation differently, not as an ultimate challenge to her teaching self. In closing, she is apologetic and brisk. "OK," she says, "I can be open about methods." After we hang up, I feel conflicted and worried but also gratified. It's good that Ellen is less upset, though I wonder whether my advice is reasonable or has long-term benefits. On the other hand, Ellen's expressed self-knowledge is persuasive evidence of investment in a teaching identity, which leaves me feeling affirmed and even more convinced about my approach to teacher education. Her assertions are true—she does know the kind of teacher she wants to be, and she even feels at some level she already *is* that teacher. For Ellen to occupy this subject position, the way I teach and the kind of pedagogy I employ must be partly responsible.

Pedagogy

Although I have referred exclusively in this book to teaching identities, in an educational institution like the university, our shared goal as teachers should be to encourage individuals to develop "identities" generally, whatever they may be. College, famously, is a time for "identity crisis," for the transformative reimagining of the self. Students arrive wanting to learn "stuff," but they also want to become someone. As educators, we can help. My teaching is based on the assumption that it is possible and desirable to encourage identity development ("teacher" is just one category). I do what I can, recognizing the limits and wary of the power of such an undertaking, to create classroom environments where identity construction is possible and, indeed, almost inescapable.

This chapter proposes a set of principles that, taken together, constitute a pedagogy for making selves. Although this is a pedagogy that originated in my work with prospective teachers, it has broader applications. These principles can be used by any teacher in any discipline to develop practices that construct identities—whatever identities are at issue. However, those teachers involved in postsecondary education may find this pedagogy most useful since its origins lie in the college classroom. Furthermore, since developing identities or becoming persons who are active and effective agents is the real point of a college education, this pedagogy may have additional and broad appeal to college faculty in all disciplines.

By pedagogy, I mean the process of structuring of activities, interactions, events, and assignments in teaching according to ideas that are congruent with or grow out of theories of identity development. In this sense, pedagogy is powerful when it is responsive, dynamic, and flexible. I agree with Mariolina Salvatori's definition of pedagogy as *"reflexive praxis."* She claims that pedagogy must be reflexive, which means "that a teacher should be able and willing to interrogate the reasons" for adopting a theory and "to be alert to the possibility that a particular theory and the rigorous practice that enacts it might be ineffectual, or even counterproductive, at certain times or in certain contexts" (1996, 4). Thus pedagogy is most effective when teachers engage in reflexive cycles that involve theorizing, applying ideas to practice, and evaluating results in light of specific institutional contexts and student populations. However, these principles do not proscribe; instead they illustrate the ways we can teach to engender identity development. The principles derive from a variety of sources, some in education, some in philosophy, some in rhetoric and composition. To those who have written passionately about teaching, I am greatly indebted.[1] But the richest source has been my own teaching, combined with the chance to witness other good teachers in action. From those individuals, mentors and friends, who invited me into their classrooms to work side by side, who conversed often and intensely about teaching, I learned the ineffable—what good pedagogy looks and feels like when it is lived.[2]

But I also feel compelled, in designing pedagogy, by something not easily articulated; that is, by a kind of desire that projects forward and back in time and space: my imaginings of all those experiences I wished I could have had with my students (now that I've heard and thought about what they have said), and experiences with students yet to come. Though less obviously, but most critically, my pedagogy is ethically driven, motivated by my obligation to be a good teacher. I wish to do well by my students, to make them the best teachers ever because we desperately need many good ones; this effort politicizes my desire.

Discourse

All teachers know that nothing significant in education ever happens without a lot of talk. Regardless of the educational goal, language—and its manifestations as discourse—is fundamental. Bakhtin describes it this way: "As a living, socio-ideological concrete thing, as heteroglot opinion, language, for the individual consciousness, lies on the borderline between oneself and the other" (1994, 77).[3] Thus discourse is central not only in cases where we want students to learn content information (knowing), but also if our educational goal is the development of identities (being). Thus, in the broadest possible sense, discourse is the viscous medium in which and through which identities arise and evolve.

The term "discourse" has many meanings and is widely and differently used in a large number of disciplines, including, for example, linguistics, literary and cultural theory, anthropology and history.[4] However, two definitions are particularly relevant to my argument. Theoretically, discourse refers to all uses of utterances or texts. Discourse has an historical and social existence. In this sense, it refers to the condition that language is central to human culture. We constantly draw on its articulate riches, comply with its many demands, and profit from its powerful operations. Life would not be possible without language. Pragmatically, discourse means the actual words we speak or write. It describes particular linguistic acts such as this book I am writing or the words Ellen spoke on the phone that night.

In the realm of social theory, the term "discourse" refers to the condition that people use language constantly, in many forms (conversations, letters, thoughts, business memos, emails, talk shows), as a way of being in the world. As theory, discourse is a general category encompassing all utterances or texts that people produce. It does not refer to any single, identifiable occasion, but rather to all occasions and all forms. However, this major category or "collection of all occasions" can be subdivided into smaller coherent collections of utterances according to who uses them (members of communities) and in what contexts (institutions, communities, etc.). Individuals belong to a limitless number of discourse communities (e.g. being a lawyer, being a suburban property owner), and participate in a wide range of different language practices associated with each (e.g. writing legal briefs, speaking at a public meeting to regulate on-street parking).

Overall, I find Foucault's definition useful for the purposes of talking about how discourses and identities are related. He defines discourse "sometimes as the general domain of all statements, sometimes as an individualizable group of statements, and sometimes as a regulated practice that accounts for a number of statements" (1972, 80). Thus, we can identify and recognize that some statements belong and function together as a coherent unit, such as "the discourse of student teaching" or "the discourse of scientific inquiry." The idea that discourses have the power to affect and influence us is important to my argument about how identities are made: Not only do individuals construct identities through discursive acts, but also discourses themselves shape identities. An example of such a discourse might be all instances, collectively, of conversations between interns and their mentor teachers about teaching. These conversations represent one aspect of "the discourse of student teaching." Participating in this discourse, individuals, like Ellen, are socialized about teaching practices. The interactions between Elizabeth and her mentor teacher over the E. D. Hirsch article are indicative of this same discourse. The fact that both Ellen and Elizabeth react against "something," a set of attitudes, practices, or beliefs, that they feel is working to change or mold them into a certain way of being teachers, also demonstrates the reality and social function of such discourses. Elizabeth and Ellen are right. These discourses do have a regulating function, as Foucault calls it, to shape, control, and produce the individuals who participate in particular discourse communities.

In applied fields like linguistics, discourse refers to the concrete actions or the actual interpersonal activities that involve language. Linguists often use the word *discourse* to describe the language itself, the words and sentences used by people to make meaning or to communicate. In this sense, discourse refers to the actual instances of reading, writing, speaking, and performing. I adopt David Crystal's perspective that examples of discourse include "conversations, interviews, commentaries, and speeches" but also forms like "essays, notices, road signs and chapters." Discourse, he says, "can be used in a much broader sense to include all language units with a definable communicative function, whether spoken or written" (1987, 116 emphasis his). A good example is the essay Ellen wrote outlining her philosophy of teaching. The essay is a particular instance of discourse that we can think about and refer to. Because it is a written form, it has a physical presence, a text I can see, hold, and write on. On the other hand, Ellen's phone call to me, though an ephemeral text, is also an example of what I mean by a specific instance of language use or a discourse action. Our phone conversation is an identifiable act, a linguistic event that served particular functions and caused various effects.

To understand how students become teachers, or how any identity processes work, we have to analyze not only how discourses (in the larger, theoretical sense) function but also we need to examine particular acts of discourse (in the specific, linguistic sense) that people engage in every day. At the macroscopic level, discourses function in institutional contexts to structure social relations and to transmit or reproduce beliefs, values, and attitudes. They are interdependent and connected to one another so that one discourse is often identified in terms of other discourses. In other words, one discourse can be recognized only in relation to other discourses, sometimes defined in negative terms against another discourse. For example, we recognize that my conversation with Ellen is part of the "discourse of student teaching" because it doesn't have the characteristics of, say, the "discourse of female friendship."

In addition, discourses can be hierarchically related to one another. Individuals are involved in many discourses simultaneously; sometimes membership in one conflicts with or counteracts membership in another. For instance, Ellen participates in multiple discourse communities because she plays in an all-female band besides being a teaching intern. Since each discourse has distinct rules, individuals are constantly dealing with conflicting values and tricky situations that involve reconciling potentially disparate perspectives among multiple discourse communities. Certain behaviors or ways of speaking that make her great when she's performing as a musician onstage may not be appropriate or effective during her daylight hours as a high school English teacher. On the other hand, Ellen's students may regard her participation in the "discourse of rock musicians" very attractive, lending her credibility and respect in the classroom environment.

The relationships between discourse communities are complicated. Sometimes the disparities between identities grow so great that individuals must choose membership in one discourse community and lose their voice or place in another. For example, one teaching intern whose tongue was pierced was told by her university supervisor that she could not wear a tongue jewel while student teaching. She was, he claimed, a representative of the university and the School of Education, institutions that stood for values other than those suggested by the jewelry she wore. Thus, after intense debate with friends, family, and other university and public school faculty, the intern consented to her supervisor's request. Among her friends, piercing signified strength and sensuality; to the high school community, teachers and students, it had very different, negative connotations. Thus, some discourses convey greater social value and prestige to their participants than others. The value of discourse is not absolute, however, but depends on the context and participants (as demonstrated in the case of body piercing).

In effect, not only do individuals create discourses by engaging in those practices associated with them, but individuals are also constructed by the discourses in which they participate. Any time we are active in a social group, we learn the rules and operate accordingly, thus internalizing the values inherent in that particular discourse. The discourse of student teaching is a good example of this process. Student teachers feel compelled by the power awarded to the supervising teacher to imitate their teacher's style. Comments from cooperating teachers such as "Just do what I do," or the opposite injunction, "You must teach in a way that suits you," reveal the mundane power of discourse in the very consequential setting of the intern's classroom.

In essence, all social interaction can be described as discourse, which is the environment where identities develop, the method individuals use to make identities, and the process that acts upon individuals to shape identities. Since everything—social structure, institutions, communities, selves, social practices, identities, culture—is constituted by discourse, through discourse, and in discourse, then the issue becomes how to work deliberately and self-consciously within this universe of discourse to foster particular identities.[5] I am suggesting that one such location (site) involves the institution of the university, in particular, the secondary teacher education program. As teaching faculty, we can design and implement a pedagogy explicitly geared toward identity development (of teachers in this special case), taking into account the multilayered field of discourse where everything happens. Considering the centrality of discourse to my thinking, it is no accident that my courses are emblematic of the pedagogical principles that follow. A description of one course that epitomizes this process approach to teaching and learning follows.

The Literacy Course

Many of the illustrations for the pedagogical principles are drawn from "Teaching Literacy in the Content Areas," a required course for all secondary education majors, regardless of disciplinary field. Its purpose is to provide secondary teachers with knowledge about literacy (e.g., how reading and writing are learned) along with methods for teaching literacy (e.g., writing-to-learn across the curriculum, or the reading workshop). However, this content information cannot be transmitted in any kind of neat package to students. (Recall Dewey's admonition that ideas cannot be handed over to students like bricks.) For students to learn anything, the course must serve their needs, in this case, to become high school teachers in a specific discipline. Given these divergent goals, teaching the course poses various difficulties (which each faculty member has resolved differently). My version of the course has a dialectical design that alternates between but always includes two domains: questions of knowledge (What's jigsaw grouping?) and issues of identity (What kind of teacher will I be?). To accommodate both of these dimensions, the course is organized around several major projects that begin on the first day of class and end during the final examination period. My role is to set the class in motion, guide students toward relevant information, invite them to critique the topics and methods they are researching, form the class into a working community, maintain deadlines, offer expert advice when asked, and cultivate sharing and responding generally.

The course-design project spans the breadth of the course and subsumes many smaller but important minor assignments. Students are asked to invent from the ground up—the curriculum, goals, texts, plus methods of teaching and evaluating—a class they might reasonably teach (for half a year) as high school teachers. The first subassignment is a book evaluation project where students survey available textbooks in regard to the state-mandated curriculum, then choose whatever texts they plan to use for their own courses. They are free to make radical choices since what matters is that students become invested in the course they are planning. Another assignment asks students to write a philosophy of teaching, one that matches in theory, method, and approach the course they've designed for themselves. This philosophical essay undergoes many revisions (drafts are required) since students' ideas evolve during the semester, especially as they experiment with new methods and notice what their peers are doing.

A third component of the course design is to devise and articulate a month-long unit of study that demonstrates what students have learned about literacy and teaching. These units include process and content goals, daily lesson plans for twenty classes, and all the necessary supporting materials. As they construct their units, they are supposed to act as if they might very well be teaching their course the next week. Along the way, students work in their small groups to research and write a report on current theories and practices of literacy teaching. In addition, one class period is devoted to "centers day" when we experience learning centers (labs or stations set up around the classroom for active learning) designed by the groups.

Near the end of the semester, several class periods are set aside for individual short (about six minute) performances. On this occasion, students create and perform an event that represents themselves as teachers. The performances have included dramatic readings, a staged demonstration, and games involving the audience. But no matter what they plan, students take seriously this opportunity to invent themselves as teachers. The results are sometimes astonishing and always moving. In addition, a final portfolio is required and includes the course design project (and its components) as well as a letter of self-evaluation regarding their project and progress in the course generally. Many of these projects will be referred to in more detail as I discuss the principles that follow.

Principles of Pedagogy

My proposal includes ten principles, some structural, such as dialogue, and some performative, such as agency. When taken into account by teachers as they plan and implement classroom activities, these principles constitute a pedagogy for identity development. (Obviously, I'm not alone or unique in my desire to promote a transformative pedagogy; my debts to the intellectual community, past and present, are many.) My proposal draws upon and owes its power to many pedagogical theorists who precede me, including John Dewey the pragmatist and Vygotsky the constructivist. I invoke Bakhtin with his emphasis on dialogue and Paulo Freire with his linked notions of literacy and liberation, and incorporate the postmodern sensibility of Michel Foucault, among others. No less influential have been alternative conceptualizations promoted by social and educational critics such as bell hooks, Henry Giroux, and Nel Noddings. Thus, the principles themselves are not original but are inspired and informed by many others; my contribution lies primarily in suggesting their aggregation.

There is a great deal of flexibility and power in the pedagogy I propose since it is based on a series of already robust components; I regard it as a kind of hyperpedagogy. On its own, each principle is theoretically and pragmatically significant; otherwise, the concept would not have survived, vital and intact, in our collective intellectual and historical memory. Teachers could adopt any one of the principles individually or integrate several (all ten work together). If, for example, a teacher chose the principle of deliberation (adapted from Dewey), then invented a series of related activities and practices, I have no doubt there would be significant ramifications for what students learn and how they experience the class.

Adopting these principles can transform how a person teaches, though how much things change will depend on personal philosophy, experience and inclination, plus the individual methods already in place. I would like to stress that these principles are entirely open-ended. They are focused on the process of teaching. I intend for the principles to guide the social structure of a course and the interactions among participants, not its academic content. Combining principles (e.g. dialogue and collaboration) enhances their power exponentially since their interaction reinforces and elaborates the effects of any one principle.

These principles are not methods; rather they are notions that ought to motivate, inspire, inform, and animate our practices. In my descriptions, I have tried to present the theoretical lens connected to each principle along with description precise enough for teachers to generate practices congruent with each. In my ongoing quest for teaching theories, I have encountered and been attracted as a teacher to many ideas that seemed intuitively right, on the mark, visionary, and ethically responsible, yet had no obvious practical consequence. One case in point is Henry Giroux's claim that "[c]ritical pedagogy suggests both confirming and legitimating the knowledge and experience through which students give meaning to their lives. Most obviously, this means replacing the authoritative discourse of imposition and recitation with a voice capable of speaking in one's own terms, a voice capable of listening, retelling, and challenging the very grounds of knowledge and power" (1988, 165). Yes, this is exactly what I want for my students and what they want for themselves; for example, there's Ellen who wishes for "a voice capable of speaking in [her] own terms." The kind of work that theorists like Giroux produce is absolutely necessary, indispensable, and useful. For instance, he lays out very clearly what is at stake in education—the potential loss of self, voice, agency—and he sets out a clear objective—for pedagogy to confirm and legitimate students' knowledge.[6] I agree wholeheartedly and he makes me eager to begin. But how? Where? His call to action gives practitioners no immediate ideas about how to alter their classroom practices to enable such challenges to authority.

My goal, therefore, is to activate the connections between theory and practice. All ten principles are illustrated with examples, activities, and experiences drawn from my own teaching. I hope to make these ideas for other teachers easily transferable from page to classroom. So rich are these principles that designing instruction congruent with any single principle would allow a teacher to foster the development of identities in their classrooms. While my own practices often fall short of the glorious dreams I fabricate ahead of time, these principles are the ones that have worked best with the students who have inhabited my classrooms. Each semester students have been generous in their feedback. Over the years they have offered articulate critique and perceptive evaluation. Thus this pedagogy is, in the most essential way, theirs.

Principles

The principles fall into two categories, structural and performative. Structural principles describe general properties that should characterize the curriculum, shape the classroom environment, and inform the teacher's approach to course design and methods. Principles related to structure include discourse richness and openness, dialogue and a dialogic curriculum, collaboration, deliberation, reflexivity. In contrast, performative principles concern what individuals do. Everyday actions are performances. These principles focus on persons as actors and on the drama of social interaction among them. Principles of performance include theorizing in practice, agency, recursive representation, authority, and enactment.

Structural Principles

1. Discourse richness and openness. Discourse constitutes self and experience. Through discourse—acts of language that communicate and connect with others—we make our identities and, reciprocally, they are made for us. In the essay "Experience," Joan Scott argues that the historical processes of discourse "position subjects and produce their experiences. It is not individuals who have experience, but subjects who are constituted through experience." (1992, 25–26). Our attempts to interpret and articulate experience make it real for us. Essentially, experience does not exist independently of language. The philosopher Hans Gadamer believes that telling is embedded in experiencing: "It is part of experience itself that it seeks and finds words to express it." (1975, 377).[7] Without a doubt, discourse occupies a singular and powerful role in postmodern theory: discourse is universally productive, creating selves, constituting experience, and, in essence, constructing reality. Therefore, a good pedagogy is one that recognizes the centrality of discourse and encourages its proliferation.

One model is the curriculum proposed in James Moffet's classic book *Teaching the Universe of Discourse* (1968). Although he was inventing an English curriculum, his model is relevant to a discussion of identity because it postulates the constructive nature of discourse as its foundation. Moffet proposes that learning subject matter knowledge (content or facts) is less important for students' growth and future life than learning how to (process) (3). He advocates a structural curriculum, one that involves creating discourses based on the *relations* between things, parts, elements, because relationships by nature are generative and active rather than static and finite. Learning is best achieved when we produce discourse, "any piece of verbalization," in the widest range of possible relationships. Moffet delineates it this way: "The elements of discourse are a first person, a second person, and a third person; a speaker, listener, and subject; informer, informed, and information; narrator, auditor, and story; transmitter, receiver, and message. The structure of discourse, and therefore the super-structure of English, is this set of relations among three persons" (10). In short, Moffet is advocating that students produce discourse as they occupy different roles or stand in different relationships relative to different elements, for example, the I-you or the I-it relation. Translated into a curriculum where the goal is to produce teachers, Moffet's triad of relationships suggests helpful parameters for ensuring that students produce discourses of all types, at different degrees of abstraction, of many varieties.

A pedagogy for learning how to be a teacher (and by extension for becoming a teacher) is characterized by discourse richness, situations that are structured to put into play all possible relations. To learn the most, students should explore the whole realm, switching among different roles. However, these structures must be open, allowing the students to conceive of, construct, and articulate the knowledge most important for themselves, relative to the topic under consideration. Open structures ought to stimulate inquiry, lead to the unexpected, and actively inhibit predictable or pro forma responses. Discourse structures should contain no specific intellectual or disciplinary content; that is, the content must be student-selected and not dictated. Discourse openness makes certain that students, through acts of writing and speaking, can direct (to some degree) the development of their teaching selves.

When the goal is discourse richness and openness, the point is to get students busy, in the thick of it, involved in many relationships with others, from widely different perspectives or roles. In general, language activities should be designed to maximize variety and change in terms of audience, purpose, form, mode, setting, and along any other dimension the teacher can imagine. For instance, language activities could alternate between forms—narrative or expository, modes—spoken or written, audience—peers or teacher, topic—conceptual or methodological, and so forth. Formal essays, class debates, small group conversations, informal written responses to prompts, and oral feedback are just a few of the options available. Changing the audience and participants to include variations such as student to student, individual to whole class, teacher to student, adds even more options.

Invariably, students must produce a variety of discourse modes if we require them to submit a portfolio, a collection of materials representative of their work during the semester. One standard assignment asks students to write a philosophy of teaching in their discipline. The assignment is made early in the course, during the second week, although it will not be due as a component of their portfolio until the last class. It always creates a stir. Students' initial reactions are mostly anxious and fearful partly because, at best, the term "philosophy" sounds unusual, and, at worst, abstract and hard to get right. (These are very good "students," used to knowing exactly how to proceed with any assignment their teachers hand out.) However, I use the term purposefully, not to heighten anxiety, but to signal that the assignment calls for something other than the standard drill of learning and repeating back the professor's lectures. Although formulating theories is a necessary aspect of becoming teachers, students have not been asked to seriously investigate their principles of teaching. They hesitate because a teaching philosophy is an intellectual and personal genre. It will entail theorizing and reflecting, reading thoughtfully, taking a position and arguing for it, and, even more threatening, it will require them to reveal their beliefs to others in the class, not just to the teacher.

The advantages to this assignment are many, not least of which are the numerous preparatory activities (ranging widely in form, audience, purpose) students complete during the semester as they are drafting the philosophy. Even the occasion of assigning the philosophy becomes an opportunity for class discussion and interpretation, an excellent activity in itself. On the day of the assignment (usually the third class period), I plan time for group processing. Without provocation beyond the written description, students begin asking good questions: What exactly is a philosophy? What goes into one? What do you write about? How do you write philosophically? Working through the assignment may take up the whole class period, but the time has been well spent: it has established the tone (high standards but plenty of support) and the methods for proceeding (working together through a series of steps).

The philosophy is completed in stages, including writing several short pieces due at timed intervals during the next month of the course. In each phase, students share their writing in draft workshops, giving and receiving peer feedback. During the preliminary activities, they confront many issues such as what constitutes a discipline, what are the assumptions in their discipline, what do they personally believe about the discipline, and how are their ideas different from or similar to mainstream perspectives. Other prompts along the way focus them on teaching: If teaching is more than method, whether teaching involves ideology, which approaches center on students or on content? Before the semester's end, students go through many cycles of writing, sharing, thinking, talking, listening, reacting in regard to their teaching philosophies that grow progressively more distinctive and comprehensive as the semester goes on.

Not only do students discover that they hold positions, they become aware of their classmates' thoughts and beliefs. The range is often wide; there are many diverging opinions (e.g. heterogeneous grouping is good/bad) based on different assumptions (e.g. because better students help the less skilled ones/the poor students prevent the better ones from learning quickly enough).

Students also sometimes get the first glimmer of understanding about the influence of cultural values in writing their philosophies. It occurs to them that similarities among the group may stem more from current trends in the profession rather than individual choice (e.g. performance is a good way to learn literature). But, most significantly, students begin to understand how personal traits such as gender, religion, or class, affect profoundly their ideas about teaching. Since the philosophy is being written over the whole semester, students have a chance to experience how this lengthier process deepens their thinking or even changes it.

In Elizabeth's case, doing the research and reading required to write the philosophy allowed her to discover other writers who shared what she had previously thought of as "personal and idiosyncratic" ideas about teaching. Writing her philosophy allowed her to feel "legitimate." On the other hand, she recognized how distinct her views were compared to those of her classmates, prompting her to dig into the material further to offer clear explanations and maybe even to persuade others to take her approach. If nothing else, Elizabeth's behavior—to pursue a topic wholeheartedly—served as a model of intellectual life for her classmates.

The philosophy assignment, in the broadest terms, has several functions—to clarify personal views of themselves as teachers and to articulate assumptions about why and how they would teach a particular subject, discipline, knowledge, or process. While these are the overall goals, each exercise along the way that contributed something to the final assignment had very specific, local, and sometimes different purposes than the final product, including projecting, analyzing, summarizing, interpreting, and reflecting. This diversity helped students to have a comprehensive view about their positions as teachers and a good understanding of their ideas relative to their classmates.

In regard to promoting students' identities, two meanings of the term discourse are relevant. As everyday practice, discourse refers to transactions between speaker and hearer such as the language activities in the classroom. As theory, discourse refers to sets of cultural practices associated with social and institutional contexts that organize social relations and transmit values such as the experience of student teaching. These regulating discourses— always multiple, some competing, some congruent, some complementary— work continually at shaping the identities of all who are members, or wish to become a member, of any discourse community.[8] Engaging in everyday acts of discourse leads students to perceive the presence and activity of these abstract, but powerful discourses of cultural construction. To engage both levels, teachers can design a structural curriculum that incorporates many long-term, process-based assignments (like the philosophy) in order to keep the discourses that inevitably structure learning as rich and open as possible.

These are the materials from which students construct themselves as subjects and as teachers.

2. Dialogue and a dialogic curriculum. Dialogue weaves together language and social interaction. An analogous form for dialogue is conversation—utterances exchanged between people to make meaning and communicate. Talking with others is the typical, social, human condition. Thus, the nature of human interaction is dialogic. Through dialogic exchange, social knowledge and selves are constructed. In this sense, dialogue is the essence of education. Mikhail Bakhtin provides the best explanation for how dialogue works.[9] He considers all uses of language to be inherently dialogic: "Life is dialogical by its very nature. To live means to engage in dialogue, to question, to listen, to answer, to agree" (Todorov 1984, 97). The most significant aspect of dialogue for Bakhtin is the form and nature of the exchange that occurs between participants. The dialogic form consists of two parts—utterance and answer. One speaker calls and the other responds. As Bakhtin suggests, meaning is created at the point where two or more voices come into contact: "Utterances are not indifferent to one another and are not self-sufficient; they are aware of and mutually reflect one another" (1986, 91). Conversational partners alternate between being speakers and listeners; they are actors and respondents in repeating cycles. The power of the dialogic process is the shared meaning that partners create as they switch roles. As a discourse process, dialogue creates the self ("what I think"), generates knowledge or understanding (the content, ideas, shared meaning), and constitutes the other ("what she thinks"). Furthermore, dialogue is inherently dynamic; the alternation of turns sets up an active cycle in which the expectation of response is built in: we speak in order to get a reaction.

The dialogic process contains an ethical component, something Bakhtin calls "answerabililty." As participants in dialogue, we are responsible for the meanings we make. All statements are subject to the judgment and reactions of listeners, who hold speakers responsible. Because a reaction is always anticipated, every utterance is necessarily incomplete. Listeners may revise, reconstruct, challenge, evaluate, extend, question, and elaborate in reply to speakers' statements. Therefore, the social knowledge or experience that is created between speakers and listeners is always a collaborative, a mutual effort. And since language is never neutral but inflected with people's beliefs and values, then the dialogic process affects individuals' internal states and external social conditions as well. Dialogue, for Bakhtin, is necessary for ethical and socially responsible communities to thrive. Through dialogue, meaning is negotiated jointly, every voice is "animated" by other voices, and individual experience is collectively interpreted through a shared body of cultural assumptions.

As a structure, form, and practice of language, dialogue depends on give and take, comparing and contrasting positions, and articulating beliefs and countering challenges. These qualities of dialogue foster identities construction. Gregory Clark articulates this process well: "We communicate not to others but with them" or, in other words, "the act of communicating is more a cooperative interaction than an assertion of self" (1990, 2). In dialogue, the identities of self and others are equally promoted.

Although Bakhtin would claim that all teaching situations are inherently dialogic, we can design activities for our students that explicitly bring the positive qualities of dialogue to the forefront.[10] To take full advantage of dialogue's creative power, assignments must be structured as real interactions between two or more individuals. The activity's purpose should encourage dialogic exchange of ideas and ideologies among groups and discourse communities to promote identities.

Writing letters is one activity I've used with prospective teachers.[11] Though perhaps not a typical genre to find in a college course, letters are quintessentially and transparently dialogic. Paired mostly with peers, but sometimes with the teacher, students write two letters weekly: the first addressed to their partner, the second in response to their partner's letter. Although I have experimented with electronic forms, these proved less satisfying so I opt for the old-fashioned kind, those written on paper. As physical objects, they carry more weight and are taken more seriously. Students deliver the letters to their partners when they arrive for class. While the content, style, and voice is left open to the writer, students are invited to use the letters as an alternative to journals, focusing on issues and ideas related to teaching, drawn from the readings, discussions, and experiences in the course.

Letter writing has many benefits; students reported enjoying them for their intellectual and social value. Lauren wrote that she was "proud of these letters because I actually got past my doubts, and in letters eight, nine, and ten, I formed ideas about how I want to teach." These ideas were generated because of the conditions of letter writing: a writing partner initiates a relationship with social responsibilities, and the letters are written to a live audience and with the expectation of receiving a response. Because letters are personal, students chose issues that were meaningful to them as prospective teachers. To Bethany, Lauren wrote about the method of teaching "language as expression": "It sounds like a really good idea, but I am not sure that I could ever do it." From their writing partners, students receive information and attention (Bethany confided similar fears in her reply), but they also challenge and validate one another.

Rick, who had long been interested in issues of racism and educational opportunity, used the letters as a venue to explore problems such as how institutions unofficially "segregated" white from black students. When his peers discovered his concerns, they raised the topic more regularly in class and asked questions about instruction so that teaching African-American students became a public part of the course curriculum. In a letter to Rick, Holly asked whether students who use "black English" ought to be corrected. While Rick was able to offer her pertinent information about grammar "BEV (Black English Vernacular) does have distinct and solid structural rules," he also extended her inquiry to include ethics when he replied with the following question: "By allowing dialectal differences in students' writing, am I hurting them?" With the entire class participating in these weekly exchanges, the dialogic effects are amplified. The letters transform my classes into a community faster than any other activity I've tried perhaps because the letters are real artifacts, visible representations of the dialogue that is ongoing.

In reflecting about writing letters to her classmates, one of my students wrote this: "I look back at the letters I got from Amy, and those I sent to her, and I wish that I could have written to her all semester. She called me on every mistake in my logic, including my attitude problem, and her ideas were so different from mine. We both could have developed our ideas a lot better by arguing with each other more, but then I remember that we probably would have killed each other after more than one week of being partners." The benefits of writing letters for this student are obvious. However, this exercise, because it is open, can be problematic. We should evaluate, analyze, and reflect on the nature and effects of any dialogic activity that can be affected by factors like the relationships of the participants, their relative power, the possibility of a dominating voice (and that individual's ideology). Other issues include questions of knowledge or prior assumptions informing the exchange, individual beliefs and commitments, and the rhetorical strategies used by the participants. Despite possible drawbacks, we remain obligated as teachers to create assignments and contexts that promote more rather than less dialogue. As an interaction mode, dialogue can be a democratic, egalitarian, inclusionary, and open-ended process. The challenge for us as teachers is to develop assignments or classroom practices that can foster equal partnerships in dialogue.

To capitalize on the dialogic properties Bakhtin believes are inherent in all human interaction, the curriculum itself (not just single activities) can be conceived of as a dialogical structure. Paulo Friere's liberatory pedagogy (1987) demonstrates how the whole educational enterprise can be opened out to include the voices and perspectives of all participants, regardless of their status. Inclusion of all voices and perspectives would expose the submerged assumptions about language, knowledge, and power that drive the traditional curriculum.

Freire claims that one of the powerful effects of dialogue is that it is "in itself creative and re-creative." In describing how he and Ira Shor composed the book *A Pedagogy for Liberation*, Freire notes: "We are each other's reader as we talk. We stimulate the other to think, and to re-think the former's thought" (1987, 3). The intricacies of Freire's approach are too complicated to present in this brief account. However, I wish to reiterate several of his ideas that are applicable to the teacher education curriculum and speculate about how things might change.

Students and teachers would not be subject to the standard curriculum, but would be empowered to create knowledge rather than to accept "official" knowledge. Freire states that "liberatory dialogue is a democratic communication which disconfirms domination and illuminates while affirming the freedom of the participants to re-make their culture. Traditional discourse confirms the dominant mass culture and the inherited, official shape of knowledge." The hierarchical relationship that now exits between faculty and students (as prospective teachers) would be transformed into an egalitarian one if everyone works jointly to understand conceptual knowledge. Teachers would no longer be experts who possessed knowledge, but partners exploring knowledge with students. Friere explains how the learning situation differs from traditional relationships: "The object to be known is put on the table between two subjects of knowing. . . . Instead of transferring the knowledge statistically as a fixed possession of the teacher, dialogue demands a dynamic approximation towards the object" (100). Through dialogic practices, the whole community—education students and faculty—would be engaged in the project of learning to teach and in becoming teachers.

Although dialogue is an open structure, it occurs in a specific social context comprised of values, beliefs, and cultural practices. Participants in a dialogical situation have to be respectful and disciplined. Friere says: "Dialogue does not exist in a political vacuum. It is not a 'free space' where you can do what you want. . . . To achieve the goals of transformation, dialogue involves responsibility, directiveness, determination, discipline, objectives" (102). As pedagogy, dialogue does not involve any kind of strict or delineated form or method. Rather, it is a structure that is plastic, malleable, and responsive to situational features. A dialogic curriculum would mirror the same qualities that characterize conversation—multiple agendas and voices, interdependence and a recognition of contingencies, and memories of histories.

3. Collaboration. As a theory and a practice, collaboration implies joint effort, shared goals, collective responsibility, and commonly held social values. In classroom settings, collaborative learning is a method whereby students work together in small peer groups to accomplish tasks set by the teacher. Ken Bruffee (whose work on this topic changed the way writing is taught in college classrooms) defines collaboration simply as "social engagement in intellectual pursuits" (1984, 412). The idea appears deceptively simple—instead of one large group of students who listen to the teacher, students are organized into small groups whose work is guided by the teacher. The implications of moving away from a teacher-centered, lecture-style format toward a conversational, peer-centered arrangement are extensive and unexpected. Collaborative learning creates a social context that helps students negotiate entry into the academic discourse community and acquire disciplinary knowledge. But, at the same time, their joint efforts will produce new knowledge, and eventually lead to a critique of accepted knowledge, conditions, and theories, as well as of the institutions that produce knowledge.

Because collaborative learning alters the nature of social interaction, identities (which are constructed in social interaction) are affected as well. When individuals are working together, the collective, public, social aspects of identities are reinforced. But group effectiveness depends on individual participation; therefore, as students converse, their own ideas and selves are developed. To put it another way, identities are manifested in the individual, but they exist as social categories. For instance, in saying "I am a teacher," I assert a teaching identity in two dimensions. First of all, the emphasis on "I," as in "*I* am a teacher," means that, individually and personally, I see myself as a teacher. The statement denotes my individual identity. Second, in stressing "teacher," as in "I am a *teacher*," I declare a collective identity, membership in a group of professionals who are teachers. In this context, "teacher" refers to a social category. Thus, being a teacher, in the most robust sense, entails developing both an individual and a collective identity. Collaborative practice encourages both dimensions of identity to evolve.

Teacher education courses can be structured as collaborative environments where students' individual and collective identities are fostered simultaneously. As members of a working group, individuals are called upon to express their thoughts and opinions, listen and respond to the ideas others offer, take account of prevailing ideas, and negotiate new positions. This process cultivates students' selves as teachers and also makes them invested in the group. If groups are the mainstay of daily classroom instruction (where the real work is accomplished), then students will begin to identify themselves as group members. As a social unit, any group has multiple agendas and social functions; in a particular course, the curricular and content goals will determine the group's character. In my literacy course, it is knowledge about literacy and teaching that gets produced, sanctioned, interpreted, and absorbed according to the norms or ideologies developed in the group over time. In a teacher education class, because the teacher introduces disciplinary knowledge and theories, these group norms will reflect in some way (but indirectly and incompletely) those of the discipline and of the professional world of teachers and teaching. Students become acculturated as teachers through identifying with a collective; for prospective teachers, this process can begin through small group membership in their education courses.

Collaborative learning works best when it is carefully planned and structured. Teachers must pay attention to how groups are formed and they must provide intellectual tasks that can best be accomplished as a group. To achieve good results, the spirit of collaboration has to permeate the classroom culture. In my classes, collaboration begins on the first day; students spend time writing and sharing with a partner, asking questions about teaching and learning during whole-class discussion, debating answers in small groups, and reporting on group discussions. By the end of the first class meeting, the room looks different. We have shifted our chairs, rearranged furniture into clusters, and accommodated physically the collaborative processes we have just begun. When students come to class the next time (and every other class period), they know to arrange the chairs and to sit with their group, already a microcommunity.

A month into the semester, Lauren hurries into class a few minutes late; she slips into place, the last chair vacant in her group's circle. Interrupting, she says, "Sorry I'm late but I was at the library," she explains, "and copied two really good articles." The group carries on, sharing what they've each discovered about "writing-to-learn" strategies. One project in the literacy course asks students to research current professional journals for teaching methods that provide an alternative to lecturing but deal with the same subject matter. Because resources on the topic are plentiful, students each bring different research articles to the group where it is discussed and evaluated. (Lauren had brought one article about journal writing and another about clustering.) Eventually, students will design a lesson plan incorporating one of the strategies. But as a group, they will have had a chance to work through the theory behind writing-to-learn, assessed the qualities of a dozen or more strategies, designed a preliminary lesson, argued about what constituted an authentic activity, then received feedback (support and critique) from their group about their choices. My role as the teacher during each class period is to set goals for the groups (e.g. pool information), to suggest a plan of action (e.g. each person verbally outline the strategies), and to facilitate group dynamics, checking by observation or consulting groups when necessary.

When it comes to making knowledge or creating identities, the real benefits of collaboration lie in the energetic and unpredictable nature of the group process itself. Neither the way people work together, nor what happens when they do, can be controlled or dominated. Collaborative environments are open-ended, contingent, flexible, negotiable, conditional, and responsive, thus allowing the groups to engage with issues related to its members' individual and collective identities. Identifying with a collective (whether teachers as a whole or as members of a working group in a classroom) is what matters, especially when exchange and exploration in the group are valued over efficiency, closure, or truth.[12]

In trying to become teachers, students must develop an internal, personal sense of themselves as teachers. But in order to thrive as teachers once they leave our classrooms, they must develop an external, public, collective identity as a teacher. This involves learning how to participate in the discourse community of education, becoming members of the teaching profession, and seeing themselves and being seen by others as teachers. Students can begin this identity process in a collaborative classroom that functions as a community. To help our students survive as new teachers, we are obligated in teacher education programs to foster their sense of belonging to a teaching community before they are actually teaching. This point is well illustrated by the story of three young teachers I happened to meet one evening through a colleague in the School of Education.

Cheryl told me said she was "born knowing she wanted to be a teacher," but her first year of teaching was "so bad" that she quit in June and took a job with an insurance company. Two other first-year teachers at the same school (in a rural county) stuck it out through the second year but were miserable. Cheryl missed teaching; she had moved away but stayed in touch with Linda and Susan, who were both seriously considering other jobs. In desperation, Cheryl made a proposal, asking the other two teachers to move to a larger town near a university where they would share an apartment and apply for new teaching jobs. They agreed. When I met them, all three were teaching. "It's because we have each other," Cheryl said, "We talk, and laugh, and cry together." All three claimed they would not be teaching now if it hadn't been for Cheryl and her insistence that they try one last time — together. The group was particularly effective in counteracting the isolation and loneliness of their first few years out. Their mutual support was also an antidote to the horrible self-doubt and low self-esteem they had felt as new teachers. Their first year was the worst, they reported. They remembered feeling especially successful and competent fresh out of college. But after a few months of teaching, they were depressed; by spring they felt like failures. "If Cheryl hadn't pulled us together, we wouldn't be here," they said.

Cheryl's intervention was crucial, but each of the three also had other resources to draw upon. Besides their strong desires to be teachers as motivation, each had developed a "provisional" identity as a teacher (derived from good experiences in their teacher education program). Identities can be more or less integrated; first-year teachers are just beginning to assemble their identities,

which are malleable constructions, sensitive to contextual forces, shaped by interactions with people, institutions, discourse of all kinds. Even though these
three teachers left the teacher education program with emergent identities,
their sense of self and individual mission was not powerful enough to stave off
the onslaught of persons, problems, and institutional pressures they felt during
their first year as teachers. Group solidarity was also needed to prevent the
complete dismantling or disintegration of their teaching selves.

Our teacher education programs should foster teacher identity development to the degree it is possible. We can make students self-conscious about
what is happening to them (becoming teachers) and raise their awareness about
the strategies (like "deliberating," "writing philosophies," "working as a team")
used in our teaching that promoted their identities. Once these strategies are
internalized, new teachers can rely on them to advance their development.
When teachers collaborate, using these strategies to work toward becoming the
teachers they each envision, their power to resist the negative institutional
forces that threaten to overwhelm is greatly enhanced. For these three teachers,
working as a group and functioning as a community with shared values provided strength, energy, and direction, making it possible for them to remain in
the classroom. Their story proves the value of teaching with collaborative
methods that locate knowledge, authority, and power in small, working, peer
groups. Our students will succeed if teacher education programs provide them
with the experience of learning in a collaborative environment, one they can
recreate in their future lives as teachers.

4. Deliberation. "Deliberation," Dewey pronounced, "is . . . an imaginative rehearsal of various courses of conduct" (1922, 135).[13] Dewey believed that
teachers had to find a way to create a curriculum that students would find useful, would see as a means to an end, and would make personally meaningful.
Deliberation, a process by which "we give way, in our mind, to some impulse;
we try, in our mind, some plan," was a strategy Dewey devised for bringing
students and the curriculum to life: "Deliberation is dramatic and active, not
mathematical and impersonal; and hence it has the intuitive, the direct factor
in it" (135).

The intuitive, the direct, the personal—these are qualities of the individual that Dewey felt must be activated in order for learning to have "consequence—or meaning or import." A curriculum that stimulates personal and
invested thinking is especially important for educating teachers. Our goal is to
cultivate good teachers who are not only knowledgeable in their fields but who
will also create drama and activity in their future classrooms, who are also dedicated to helping students develop into people capable of using their knowledge and skills to benefit themselves and others. Good teaching is, in this sense,

a moral craft, one that could be learned by asking students to be deliberate about their teaching practices and to deliberate about their theoretical beliefs.[14] Deliberation, then, could be considered as a conceptual framework and a method for conducting a teacher education course. Because deliberative acts are both safe and real, they have tremendous potential for developing students' teaching identities.

Dewey believed that effective education or preparation for life outside of school depended on the nature and quality of interactions between students and the curriculum. Learning, for Dewey, was not a passive process, but depended on students' active engagement with the ideas, skills, and values being taught. Deliberation is a useful concept in this regard because he regards it as "an experiment in finding out what the various lines of possible action are really like. [Deliberation] is an experiment in making various combinations of selected elements of habits and impulses, to see what the resultant action would be like if it were entered upon. But the trial is in the imagination, not in overt fact. The experiment is carried on by tentative rehearsals in thought, which do not affect the physical facts outside the body. Thought runs ahead and foresees outcomes, and thereby avoids having to await the instruction of actual failure and disaster. An act overtly tried out is irrevocable, its consequences cannot be blotted out. An act tried out in imagination is not final or fatal. It is retrievable" (Human 1922, 190). Thus, deliberation is a productive, real act but one without permanent repercussions, an exercise ideal for identity development.

Deliberation, though only a single component, is representative of Dewey's general ideas about education. Student interests and curriculum should be integrated; furthermore, students ought to be actively engaged in the curriculum. Learning and development is not limited to students' cognitive skills but depends on certain moral traits of character as well (being open-minded, for instance). Individuals grow and learn best in the context of a functioning cooperative community and when their interests are aroused. Dewey believed that when students find reasons for using the curriculum, it becomes a means to an end; motivation is both internal (to serve the self) and external (to serve the community).

All students in education courses have an end in sight—to become teachers in a specific discipline. The literacy course is designed as one huge exercise in deliberation. I set them to work on designing a course and fleshing out a unit, essentially inventing a curriculum and setting goals, describing teaching methods, and constructing a classroom environment. This simulation is as near an approximation to the complexities of real teaching as I can invent. Because of the limits of a university classroom, their immediate goal is to represent themselves as teachers on paper but in ways that are indicative of their future selves. In the absence of real high school students or an actual high school, this

assignment requires profound acts of imagination, projection, and vision. However, before presenting the final version in their portfolio, students will have
had many opportunities in class, among peers, to experiment, for "finding out
what the various lines of possible action are really like." The classroom then becomes a place in which to conduct experiments. Steve Fishman and Lucille
McCarthy (two Deweyian practitioners) report that Dewey advocated learning
through experimentation or "indirect instruction, work laced with drama and
tension of discovery; desires aroused, problems clarified, and hurdles coopera-
tively overcome" (1998, 54). This latter point about cooperation is important
since Dewey believed in some natural inclination toward connecting with others. We are committed in everyday life "to give out, to do, and to serve" (55).

One formal occasion on which we attempt to live up to such magnificent
criteria is on "Centers Day," several class periods during which students rotate
through one another's learning centers (a concept unfortunately limited mostly
to elementary schools, but one that I've seen very effectively used in high school
settings). Centers are designed and operated by small groups; the point is to
create a center that engages another visiting group in an activity where students
learn content by doing. No direct instruction is allowed. Groups collectively
choose content (e.g. Thoreau and Transcendentalism, the Beat Poets), generate
ideas and materials, test out different activities beforehand, then run the center
during one class period. Afterward, centers are evaluated by peers, revised, and
submitted as part of the written portfolio, but students learn the most by observing how their centers function.

What is difficult to capture in this description of Centers Day is how
students invest all dimensions of themselves in their creations. One student
who worked on the Thoreau center is an environmental activist and hoped
through the activities to cultivate students' abilities to contemplate and appreciate nature, a driving passion in his life. Dewey believed that moral traits of
character were as critical for individuals to develop as cognitive skills. In the
person, mental and moral were interdependent parts; the process of education
should involve both. But in university classrooms we are often hesitant to invoke the moral. This reluctance is costly. I have discovered that students' moral
commitments are often what have brought them to teaching and compel them
to try, despite the unfavorable conditions. However, Dewey's deliberative practice gives us a way to acknowledge and include the moral sphere: "Moral deliberation differs from other forms not as a process of forming a judgment and
arriving at knowledge but in the kind of value which is thought about. . . . Precisely the same object will have a moral value when it is thought of as making
a difference in the *self*, as determining what one will *be*, instead of merely what
one will *have*" (1922, 134–35; italics his). Consequently, deliberative practice
encourages the students to be drawn into the curriculum, to become "aroused"

(in Dewey's terms) when the everyday work of the classroom focuses on how one will be a teacher, an investment of self, rather than on emphasizing only knowledge, technique, method.

There are many ways to invite students to articulate personal commitments and individual goals as part of the process of learning subject matter and teaching methods. We can better guide our students if we understand their orientations. In her teaching philosophy, Lauren wrote that one high school teacher showed her that "a student can learn more from a teacher than just the required subject matter. This teacher told me on many occasions that he understood why I was having difficulty with some of the other students, but he never allowed me to question whether or not I needed to strive to understand them." His profound influence made Lauren feel she "could make a difference" for students even as she was teaching English: "Students should leave my class every day (or most days) feeling they learned something that will help them later in life. Reading literature and discussing it with their peers will help them understand human thoughts and feelings." Lauren's lessons were geared toward increasing empathy and connection among students (in fact, one of Dewey's major concerns).

Donna had different but equally strong reasons for wanting to be a teacher. Perhaps because she was forbidden by state law to openly express her strongest conviction, "serving God wholeheartedly," she searched more directly and self-consciously than other students for ways to make her lessons "opportunities for initiating students' exploration of the spiritual realms." These convictions undergirded all Donna's lesson planning so that every activity, even "learning vocabulary words to increase precision," achieved multiple purposes, "to increase students' ability to communicate spiritual verity." As a result, though "God" or spirituality were never overtly mentioned, Donna's activities were infused with vitality; they were inventive, tempting, novel, coherent, pragmatic, and always inviting. Her ability to engage with students through action proved to be an invaluable asset for Donna, especially given her desire to work with disadvantaged teenagers. Our students appreciate and benefit from our efforts to involve them. In a letter of self-assessment to me, Donna wrote: "If your goal has been to facilitate the development of writing teacher skills in a provocative and experiential way, you have accomplished it." Thus, in allowing students' moral investments to influence their course designs and imagined future classrooms, we can positively facilitate the development of prospective teachers.

5. Reflexivity. Reflexivity is the act of self-conscious consideration. While deliberation moves toward the future, reflexivity entails thinking that turns back on itself, a reexamination or revisiting of a project or an activity, and a questioning of motives, frameworks, assumptions, working strategies, con-clusions, beliefs, and actions. The social theorist Anthony Giddens describes reflexivity as "not merely 'self-consciousness' but as the monitored charac-ter of the ongoing flow of social life" (1984, 3). Individuals are reflexive not only in regard to their internal, psychological, or mental states but also when they consistently consider the conditions and persons of the outer, social world. Giddens explains: "In circumstances of interaction—encounters and episodes—the reflexive monitoring of action typically, and again routinely, incorporates the monitoring of the setting of such interaction" (4). This prac-tice of reviewing and reconsidering leads a person to new knowledge, the kind that is potentially transformative. Consequently, reflexivity or intensive reconsideration can lead people to a deepened understanding of themselves and others, not in the abstract, but in relation to specific social environments. In addition to increased self-knowledge, reflexivity fosters a more profound awareness of situation, a better sense of how social contexts influence who people are and how they behave.

Because of the interdependence between writing and thinking, some composition teachers use reflexivity as the philosophical foundation for their methods of teaching writing. In *Turns of Thought: Teaching Composition as Reflexive Inquiry* (1997), Donna Qualley advocates and describes a reflexive pedagogy as one "that uses reading and writing as vehicles for constructing, deepening, and challenging students' and teachers' understandings of their subjects and themselves" (137). She asserts that using language to be reflex-ive can make, change, question, revise how one understands one's self in rela-tion to other individuals in a particular and local situation. As a result, reflexivity is never solipsistic because being reflexive about the self always means looking outward to reconsider one's relation to other people, events, texts, or circumstances.

It is important to distinguish reflexive thinking from reflection, a re-lated process (but one less potent for identity development). We could de-scribe reflection as the experience of contemplation, moments of quiet thinking that have no inherent critical function. The act of reflecting may be a satisfying practice in and of itself. In these terms, reflection is a process analogous to meditation. On the other hand, reflexivity is instrumental, an intentional means to an end. It involves a person's active analysis of past sit-uations, events, products, with the inherent goals of critique and revision for the explicit purpose of achieving an understanding that can lead to change in thought or behavior.

One instance of reflexive thinking is Elizabeth's attempt to articulate a philosophy of teaching writing, an assignment she found both intriguing and baffling at first. She approached the task initially by reviewing three years of college notes and journals. Elizabeth reports that it was the activity of looking backward while in pursuit of a future self that made the difference: "It was the process of having to go through and read those [notes] and decide, out of the whole of what we had already done, which ones really said what you thought was important. [It was] having to distinguish fine shades of meaning. And if there was something you really thought and it wasn't there, then you could go and look for it. That's when I went to *Community of Writers* looking for something. It was the first time I had even seen the phrase 'whole language' and I had no idea what it meant." Reflexive analysis ended up generating a real and urgent question for Elizabeth about the theory of whole language, the answer to which eventually shaped her fundamental approach to teaching.

Reflexive practice changes the way a person understands those things and thus how that person acts, thinks, lives. Qualley describes it this way: "Reflexivity involves a commitment to both attending to what we believe and examining how we came to hold those beliefs while we are engaged in trying to make sense of an other" (5). Reflexivity is valuable for identity development because it entails a dialectical process, reviewing the self while taking into consideration the other. In fact, Qualley claims that reflexivity is "a response triggered by a dialectical engagement with the other," especially when that engagement "is ongoing and recursive as opposed to a single, momentary encounter" (11). It is in the process of trying to understand "an other" that our own beliefs and assumptions are disclosed. Once uncovered, our assumptions themselves can become objects of examination and critique.

Elizabeth's experience with Mr. Streblinski (Linda Lenoir's mentor teacher) during her teaching internship demonstrates how this dialectical process works. Reflexive inquiry was already something Elizabeth understood given how she had approached writing her teaching philosophy and the resulting clarification of an ideological position. When it came time to write her senior thesis (about trying to be a whole language teacher) while also student teaching, Elizabeth automatically fell into the reflexive practice that already seemed an integral part of her writing process. It was a way of thinking that fit the situation: she was planning and teaching every day at a local high school, then returning to the university for weekly conferences about her thesis.

Because of her topic, Elizabeth found herself writing about several teachers at the high school. Though Joe Streblinski was not her mentor, he played a central role in Elizabeth's teaching life because he teamed with Mr. Collins. Early on, Mr. Streblinksi had seemed to Elizabeth a likely role model and a possible ally. But there were tensions and political differences between the two teachers, and Mr. Streblinski's teaching approach conflicted with his professed theories. Although initially disheartened and constrained by the situation, Elizabeth gradually she gained confidence and authority, both as teacher and a writer. Reflexive thinking enabled these changes.

Reflexivity, Qualley suggests, is stimulated through "a dialectical engagement with the other—an other idea, theory, person, culture, text, or even another part of one's self, e.g. a past life" (11). Of these possible encounters, the ones we have with people who are most different from ourselves (or who have the greatest dialectical distance between them) lead to the most learning. Qualley calls this phenomenon "the stranger experience." Its value lies in how students "discover that their customary ways of making sense may not be sufficient for understanding their subjects or themselves" (139). As a result, students are forced to readjust, reinvent, and revise current positions or understandings as a result of confronting the strange other, the role Mr. Streblinski played for Elizabeth.

One day in conference, working on a thesis chapter, Elizabeth sized him up this way: "Joe thinks he's really grounded. His room is just covered in Nancie Atwell" [a well-known proponent of whole language teaching]. Honestly, I don't know if he believes it, but it's just that those other factors are so powerful that when he gets into the classroom he just does whatever. On the other hand, he hasn't completely disregarded it [whole language theory]. They have two drafts for every paper, writing workshops before every final draft." But because it was necessary to find a way to work with him, Elizabeth analyzed Mr. Streblinksi's contradictions. As she wrote and sorted through her notes and memories, she realized not only how bad such contradictions were for students, but also how advantageous such behavior was for Joe—a way of saving face, accumulating moral capital, accruing political power, and exhibiting expertise. In the context of the high school, these were not inconsequential gains. Repeated analysis over the course of the year led to many insights both personal and philosophical. Over time, reflexive thinking increased Elizabeth's self-understanding but also heightened her appreciation and sympathy for Mr. Streblinski, a point of view that reduced frustration and made the internship semester productive.

Qualley argues that the primary value of being reflexive with language is the way it deepens our understanding. Elizabeth's case is certainly good evidence. But we could make the further argument (which lies implicit in Qualley's work) that the dialectical process and resulting apprehension is identity-constructing. Being reflexive allows students to reinvent themselves by returning to certain experiences or understandings (concepts) and rethinking them, and in the process creating selves that take into account new ideas or experiences. Identities are produced by this reflexive process, as prior assumptions about self and other are recognized and evaluated in light of social conditions. But revisions of assumptions and beliefs are always provisional and therefore subject to reconsideration during other cycles of reflexive inquiry.

Performative Principles

6. *Theorizing in practice.* To teach is to theorize. My goal is for students to understand this relationship and to embrace it when they are practicing teachers. Theory, I tell them, is everything that isn't action. It can be something homespun, personal, familiar. At first, when I bring up the word *theory*, students imagine I'm talking about Piaget or Erikson and their theories of learning and development. This sort of high theory, a set of principles or a broad framework for interpreting facts, students see as something abstract and foreign, as knowledge that exists outside of them and is unrelated to the practice of teaching.

But, by theory, I'm referring in the context of educating teachers to something else, to grounded theorizing, or theories that individuals create out of their practices, as they practice. In other words, theory is the account that action gives of itself. It is the reasons we might offer prior to action for setting out to do something in this way rather than that. Thus, if theory is an accounting for action, then every act of teaching is embodied theory. Therefore, action, or practice, never stands outside of theory but resides inside of or exists as a result of theory, and vice versa, theory always enables or informs practice.

Gail McCutcheon defines such knowing practice as personal theories of action, "sets of beliefs, images, and constructions about such matters as what constitutes an educated person, the nature of knowledge, the society and psychology of student learning, motivation and discipline" (1992, 193). Without coherent, broad, and flexible theories in which they are invested to guide their teaching plans and actions, novice teachers will be stuck with blind experimentation. For instance, some students may remember a particular strategy or technique from a methods class, but when applied to a novel situation in a real school, it may turn out to be completely useless without an underlying rationale. In generating personal theories, students will discover that knowledge about Vygotsky and Dewey and their learning theories, for example, is important but as a resource to draw on, not as a substitute for their own theorizing. Teaching entails invention and adaptation; nothing can be transferred directly from one social context to another.

The following story illustrates the usefulness of personal theories of action and shows why we must make sure our students leave the teacher education program with the ability to theorize in practice. In September, four months after receiving her MAT degree, just beginning of her first year of teaching, Linda Lenoir (Elizabeth's friend, Mr. Streblinski's teaching intern) comes to my house to borrow books about teaching reading. Linda was hired at

Waterview High School, a nearby urban school, as an "English resource" teacher, not a regular classroom teacher. Her classes are an odd and challenging combination: one is study skills, two are reading for learning-disabled students. Many of the sixteen and seventeen-year-olds she's teaching cannot read at all.

As I'm handing over the books in the hallway, she says, "When you're in school (referring to the teacher education program), they tell you—there's a big difference between theory and practice—and you kinda know that— yeah, yeah. But as I was saying to my husband the other morning, there's a *big* difference between theory and practice, a *real* big difference, and you *really* need that theory. I absolutely need those theoretical ideas to hold on to. I need to know what I believe because, once you get out there, everybody is telling you what to do, what to think! They say stuff like—just give them dictionary work, have them look up words, that'll keep them busy, and quiet." Linda continues without pause as I pass over the books from my arms into hers. "So it's hard to know what to do, how to sort things out. Theory helps you do that. But in the face of what's going on minute to minute at school, it's so hard to remember the theory, to hold on to it, to know what *you* think is the right thing to do. Because when you're a beginning teacher, there is no one asking, 'How are you doing?' or 'Let's sit here and talk about your classes.' No. They just tell you a lot of stuff to do. And they even tell you to *forget* theory. It's just . . . overwhelming."

From what I can assess at this moment, Linda will succeed as a teacher (at the very least she will make it through the first stressful year of teaching) because she sees herself as a theorizer capable of solving the educational problems of her students. Techniques, she understands quite clearly, are useless unless she has some way of deciding which techniques might be useful for each student and why. Linda has asked me for books that reveal how the reading process works, that outline the sorts of difficulties students have reading, that provide an array of methods for teaching reading. What's critical is that Linda's theories are dependable and useful because she has created them out of academic knowledge and experience. They have utility because they are her theories of how things work, joint articulations of the personal and the theoretical.

Aspiring teachers can become adept at theorizing by making them account for or explain the rationale behind every activity or lesson plan they invent while they're taking education courses, before they're out in the field even as teaching interns. The process of linking theory to practice can be built into the experiences students have in their courses whenever they are designing content units in their discipline for teaching. For instance, one part of the course design project in the literacy class is to develop a four-week unit with twenty lesson plans. A teaching philosophy that draws upon disciplinary knowledge, learning theory, and educational research accompanies the unit plan. Both the philosophy and the unit are developed simultaneously during the entire semester. It is while students are drafting pieces of these projects and sharing in class that the process of theorizing in practice can be taught and encouraged.

Many students are motivated to become teachers because of a passion for the subject matter they plan to teach. This was true for the six in this study, although they were attached to different aspects of the discipline. Howard had cultivated an American Studies perspective and was interested in stereotypes and myths of the "American West." Michaela was keenly interested in twentieth century literature, particularly drama (including African-American writers in that genre). Rick had no favorite period, but loved reading and literature for its own sake—as art and as life. Donna believed that through teaching literature (the great lessons of character and life) she could (indirectly) bring students to Christ. For Lauren, literature was another language, one that could enrich students' lives. Elizabeth loved writing; for her, it was potentially a more powerful activity than reading literature.

But when it comes to translating these attachments in teaching performances or even into a rationale of how they might teach, students are often at a loss. However, by asking them to work on small pieces and later connecting them, I have discovered that the process of knitting together theory and practice becomes possible and easier as the course nears its end. For instance, students must choose a topic and appropriate texts as the center of their units of study. In small groups, students have to explain their choices, providing reasons for their selections. With the help of feedback questions I have provided, students help each other to evaluate and improve their choices. Similarly, on a day when students have designed an activity to teach one of their texts, they are asked to explain the activity structure or sequence. Group members are guided to propose alternatives, such as what might happen if writing were incorporated or if students worked in pairs. This kind of analysis, feedback, and sharing in peer groups makes it easier to see how to put theoretical ideas into practice. If students ought to be active participants, then it makes sense to plan for them to write in response to an open-ended question before discussion. If collaboration benefits learning, then students should work as partners rather than individually to interpret dense passages from the novel being studied.

I can further support students' efforts to make practice and theory inform each other by modeling the analytic process on the spot using their examples during class. One student might present a lesson plan that we critique as a class, bringing to bear theoretical knowledge (for example, Vygotsky's concept of scaffolding), to justify a sequence of steps in the proposed activity. Sometimes, we might investigate my teaching, discussing the structure of the class period that day or unpacking one of the larger project assignments. Once it is clear there should be a theoretical rationale behind every choice or design, students begin to inquire into their own lesson plans without prompting. They also get experience with the alternative process—beginning with a theoretical idea such as scaffolding and attempting to invent an activity that demonstrates the principal.

I attempt to make students self-conscious about their own theorizing partly by asking them to write a description (included in the final portfolio) of how their course design projects evolved. Howard described the project as an opportunity "to organize my thoughts about educational planning . . . I found that many concepts I had 'grown up with' in my own classes could work for me as a teacher just as they worked for me as a student." He responded to the assignment as an opportunity to theorize about curriculum, to essentially evaluate the university curriculum he'd just completed to discover how he might teach the same subject matter. He recalls a history course (taken as a college freshman): "We began the course reading Frederick Jackson Turner's hypothesis about the American frontier. We then considered the ever-moving frontier concept as a definition of American culture. I then began to formulate my own hypothesis, one that defined American literature along this same ever-moving line of the frontier. I decided that this would be a new and different way to examine American literature." His goal was "to focus on debunking myths and scraping away layers of legend to find the 'actual' truths behind events and people. This is problematic, for I have to be careful what I choose. I need to watch the biases of the authors I select—those who are rewriting the West might be as wrong in their angle as those who built it up."

Howard is theorizing his relationship to his intended discipline, and, in the process, defining his view of that discipline. Establishing such concrete understanding before he was teaching proved to be invaluable groundwork. When confronted with the mandated curriculum as a student intern, his prior convictions were something to hold on to. They helped relieve some measure of the frustration so many new teachers experience at facing such limited choice in available literature. Rather than succumbing to the system and feeling bad about losing his principles, Howard was able to retain some autonomy and looked for strategies to work with and around the mandated curriculum. This negotiating would have been impossible without his prior insights about how to teach an American literature course to begin with. It is the theoretical ideas that are transferable, flexible, and applicable to many different situations. Specific practices can't be imported wholesale or conducted the same way in two different contexts, or even on two occasions with the same class. Good teachers adjust to the contingencies of the moment. Without theory, there isn't anything to guide or drive those split-second decisions. Theory is transmutable, and leads to creative, realistic practice. Being able to theorize is what enables teachers to improvise and adapt, to make every teaching moment memorable.

7. *Agency*. Agency is (as the philosopher Michael Oakeshott defines it) "the starting place of doing" (1975, 32). Agency is the quality of an individual that makes doing possible; it means believing that one's self is capable of action. This view of agency is particularly central to the practice of teaching. If teachers are to survive, they must not only feel empowered but also must possess efficacy. This is no easy matter; developing agency is akin to cultivating a form of will. In light of this purpose, this discussion will not be a sociological analysis of where agency is found or located; instead, I assume that agency exists, and that it can and should be fostered in prospective teachers.

Agency can be defined as the power or freedom or will to act, to make decisions, to exert pressure, to participate . . . or to be strategically silent. Although agency can't be externally fixed or even identified, we can recognize it in ourselves. We experience agency as an internal, embodied feeling, a self-consciousness, or a will to act. In Oakeshott's view, an agent is someone "who is recognized to have an understanding of himself in terms of his wants and his powers and an understanding of the components of the world he inhabits" (32). Consequently, actions result from knowing agents: "Action is recognized as an illustrative exhibition of this understanding" (32). Therefore, if we want to cultivate teachers as agents who act, then our classrooms must be environments that cultivate perception and knowledge of the self, because agency depends "on a state of reflective consciousness, namely, the agent's own understanding of his situation, what it means to him" (37).

Why is agency important for teacher education? The belief in doing, or in performing action, fuels my efforts as a teacher (of teachers). When I question my own situation, inquire what it means, I invariably conclude that my efforts are worthwhile. Quite simply, I think my teaching affects students' identities as teachers. By extension, I think the same is true of my students. They need to feel capable of action as teachers, first and foremost, as motivation, to keep them invested in teaching when outside factors—social conditions of school, poverty, troubled students, low wages, a mandated curriculum—cause them to question their sanity in choosing a profession as a teacher. The difference between us is that I know (through personal comments, course evaluations, visits from returning students) that I'm influential, effective, to a certain degree. My students, prior to the realm of experience, don't yet know their actions matter, but to have such influence is what they each hope for. Agency is what my students are referring to when they insist "they want to make a difference" in schools, or in the way English is taught. Michaela explains: "I care about my subject and I care about what I'm doing. I hope that will communicate itself to my students so they'll care about what they are producing and creating in my class." Lauren writes: "Part of the reason I want to become a teacher is that I went through high school thinking, 'I can do this better!'" Howard believes he can reveal "the negative power of controlling language, with inherent biases" by teaching literature that has created damaging stereotypes written about oppressed groups (Native Americans, in his case). Regarding their various issues, my job is to convince them that their instincts are right. Language does have the power to injure people. High school teachers can better care for students. So even if we consider agency a fantasy narrative, a positive fiction, to believe that one has agency and to act as if it's true is something I *want* to cultivate through pedagogy.

Identity and agency are linked in a reciprocal manner. This chapter opened with Ellen's identity crisis, triggered by her transition from the environment of the university to the public school classroom. Her story is useful because it demonstrates that agency, a will and confidence to act, along with the means and methods to be an English teacher were jointly fostered in her teacher education courses. This forceful combination of self and subject-matter knowledge makes her feel able and eager to act. She fully believes she can positively affect her students. Her readiness to act and the power she feels in knowing what to do reinforce her feeling of identity. In turn, the more Ellen identifies herself as a teacher, the stronger her feeling that she is a positive subject, an agent with the power to act. While this effect is exactly what we ought to aim for, her sense of identity and agency was fostered in the limited domain of the university classroom. However, now there are other aspects of the situation (her mentor teacher, the public school itself, the culture of public education, the needs of students) to consider. These latest conditions greatly limit Ellen's ability to act according to her desires, hence the conflict and distress she experiences trying to negotiate this new setting without sacrificing her sense of self. But Ellen's strong convictions are a good thing, preventing her from being overwhelmed as she accommodates her ideal vision to one reality of teaching.

Agency is always a possibility. We are agents when we experience ourselves as such, not because we have been granted any special position or power. In everyday life, we live and breathe as active agents. For instance, I write this book because it could potentially change people, introduce new ideas, affect institutions, modify teacher education programs, make better teachers. (I hesitate in asking exactly how a book will do this. Nor can I be certain how or even if any of these things will come to pass as a result. But as I struggle to write and to find a reason for writing, the answer I discover is one of agency: this act, my book, will go into the mix, somehow, somewhere.)

These ideas reflect my interest in and sympathy with those philosophers and writers who are considered pragmatists (for example, John Dewey, Charles Peirce, Michael Oakeshott, and Hans Joas).[15] Their notions about agency and action counteract a prevalent postmodern view that individual action is nonexistent because every action is overdetermined purely by external, social, political, and ideological factors. In proposing a modified theory of agency, current pragmatist theories of action grant agency to the individual, but a person who is a fabricated, contingent self, not the autonomous self posited by the modernists. Instead, the pragmatists conceive the individual as a social self, living in a world that includes other people, social arrangements and institutions, and the physical environment.[16] Thus, agency is interactive, with no one factor any more controlling than another. We see that while Ellen is capable of action, her intentions and actions are inextricably tangled up in the dynamic of a situation that includes her mentor-teacher, students, the immediate context of the school, the institution of public schools in general. Such a complex web means that for any individual and in any one moment, there are many possibilities for action and response.[17] For Ellen, there is no one right thing to do; there is only the realization (and its accompanying urge) that she can and ought to do something. She feels neither powerless nor passive. Her recognition that she can alter the situation by some action of her own is what is significant. This is agency.[18]

How can we cultivate agency in the classroom? More than anything else, encouraging agency depends primarily on the attitudes and expectations we project as teachers throughout all interactions with students rather than with any particular method or assignment. My efforts are concentrated on creating an environment (physical and conceptual) in which I expect them to act and to care. However, I'm not just standing on the sidelines outside of this space. My self is fully invested in teaching and in caring. In this content, I use the term "caring" to signify a reciprocal relation between people, a definition promoted by the educational philosopher Nell Noddings: "Caring is a way of being in relation, not a set of specific behaviors" (1992, 17). She describes "a caring relation" as "a connection or encounter between two human beings—a carer and a recipient of care, or cared for" (15). Furthermore, caring relations "cannot be achieved by formula" but follow unique paths forged by the individuals involved in the encounter in response to each other and the social setting. Noddings claims that "caring requires address and response; it requires different behaviors from situation to situation and person to person" (xi–xii). Since it involves a relation, caring is not one-sided. It is not the sole responsibility of the teacher to care, but those who are the recipients must signal that care has been received, thus completing the cycle. Furthermore, Noddings insists that teachers must not only establish caring relations, but "they also have a responsibility to help their students develop the capacity to care" (19). This kind of relational caring requires two things from the teacher: sustained attention and simple persistence. My approach is to be vigilantly mindful: I attend to students, watching and listening for those details that reveal the individual student's particular concerns, interests, or inclinations.

Over time, I learn to know (apprehend, perceive, appreciate, recognize) my students, and I encourage students to know one another in this robust fashion. "Being known" by peers and teacher makes a significant impact on students' sense of themselves as instrumental and effective persons. We discover one another through various means and over time, throughout the span of the semester, or build on our relationships from one semester to another. (In a small teacher education program like ours, students take the same classes together and often take several classes from a single professor). However, acknowledgment doesn't happen by simple proximity; the interactions in the classroom have to permit sustained and substantive exchange among peers and between student and teacher. For instance, students do not come to know one another in the sense I'm talking about just because they have taken several lecture classes together. A case in point is Donna's disclosure to Lauren (in a peer-letter exchange): "In our four classes together I have been able to watch you interact with other students, observe your mannerisms, expressions, and style of communicating. Now I will have the pleasure of knowing you through your writing—I am anxious to receive your letter!" At best in a lecture style classroom, students may develop a social relationship, although even this more limited knowing may not occur even though students sit side by side for fourteen weeks. For acknowledgment or recognition of people to happen, something else is needed.

It is essential for the time spent together in the classroom to be experience, no different in quality, intensity, or possibility from other experiences. Students have reported that these kinds of activities were useful in this respect: writing personally about teachers who mattered to them, engaging the whole class in discussions of different teaching methods (e.g. collaborative vs. presentational), providing rationales for lesson designs, writing weekly letters, and having microteaching opportunities. In all instances, students receive response or feedback from me and from their classmates so they are never left wondering or worrying about what others might think of their individual ideas or intentions. In addition, I notice and comment on each person's progressive development, sometimes through comments on written projects or during periodic individual conferences. In fact, the six students in the study all remarked that, apart from student teaching, the interviews (though lengthy and time-consuming) were a better pedagogical experience than anything else in the teacher education program. Although long interviews would be impossible, brief interviews of fifteen or twenty minutes several times during the semester are manageable. Students could also conduct interviews with one another. Parker Palmer, an educator particularly concerned with supporting teachers' inner lives, advocates interviewing as an activity that benefits both parties: Interviews are "a way of looking into other people's behaviors and attitudes that opens our own lives to view" (1983, 62). Microinterviews are a simple but meaningful way of attending to students, and they confer the same benefits (e.g. putting students at the center, focusing on individual qualities) as do the longer interviews.

This interactional loop, made possible by including an opportunity for response and revision, is critical for building students' confidence to reveal more of themselves and to care more about others. Students report that such experiences matter. In fact, Donna (in an evaluation) described the course as "an experiential class." She believed the class was so influential on account of "the unusual circumstances of having such a small number of fellow students and, as a result, more attention from one another and you." But also she claimed that its effectiveness had to do with "freedom of exploration, frequent writing exercises, high levels of participation," plus "repeated practice, direct observation, and frequent interaction with peers." Donna understands this way of teaching from experience. If agency is the starting place of doing, which involves the will to act, then the first thing we need to cultivate in our students is belief in their abilities to act. But belief without evidence is frail and easily undone. To go forward, students must know through experience—feel it in their bones, see it in the faces of their peers, hear it in the words spoken back to them—that they are acting for real and that their actions have meaning and impact, now, in the present—and later, in the future.

8. Recursive representation. Identities are created through recursive representation, or the process of representing and successively rerepresenting the self to others in whatever various forms are available.[19] Though they would not have described their desires to achieve a teaching self in such abstract terms, nevertheless, my students knew at some intuitive level that identity-making occurs through a series of progressive tryouts. They arrived in my classes expecting that their education courses were going to make them more teacherlike: They were to think, act, reason, behave, move, talk, react more like teachers as they moved through the program. Essentially, we were to teach them (as in Goffman's famous term, "the presentation of self in everyday life," how to present themselves to the world as teachers. This process was to be achieved or enacted by creating and then trying out different representations, seeing reactions, and receiving feedback, revising, and representing images of themselves as teachers publicly but in the protected space of the college classroom before they are actually seen as teachers.

How are selves represented? Representations can exist in many forms, given the social circumstances, but, in school, language is primary. The most powerful function of language (if we are concerned with students' learning and becoming), is its ability to represent a person's thoughts, experiences, ideas, interpretations, through its many forms and genres, including spoken and written texts such as conversations, lesson plans, response papers, essays, debates (forms students regularly produce in my classes).[20] But representations may also take visual forms, for example, photographs, drawings, sculptures, or may be expressed through the body itself, through physical signs such as posture, gesture, physical attributes that are enhanced or highlighted (hair color or body piercing), or even by clothing. These representations can be actions, behaviors, or performances, simple or complicated, unitary or extended, happening in one form or in multilayered combinations of forms. Whatever their shape and venue, self-representations are not individual or isolated occurrences but are embedded in the flow of social interaction in specific contexts. Representation is a constant activity (not something we do part of the time) but some occasions encourage it, allow room for more possibilities.

Our classrooms can be one of these open sites, where students during every class have the chance to create multiple self-representations. Halfway through class one day, Michaela's voice catches my attention. She's passionately explaining to her four group members that African-American slave narratives and Native American myths *are* (she's emphatic) American literature, though these forms are not part of the accepted canon and are therefore not ever taught as such. "Why not?" one student asks, which provokes Michaela to puzzle through the reasons, working hard not only to understand why for herself but also to inform her peers. In this interaction, she presents herself as thinker (keeping out slave narratives means not admitting to slavery in our history), as knowledgeable reader (black theater was a rejection of white traditions), as social activist (I intend to teach these works to my students). Throughout the semester, Michaela had been working on developing a course of study appropriate for high school students. Her intention was "to show students how they figure into the picture of America—where women, men, blacks, whites, Asians, indigenous peoples—everybody—has been and where we are going." After careful consideration ("in doing this project I began to realize the pressure of trying to accomplish this while also teaching state requirements and literary tools and techniques"), she decided not to "include any works of the American literary canon" assuming "they'll find a way on their own into my curriculum." Her final product was a four-week unit on African-American drama, composed of twenty daily lesson plans, all representations of her teaching self, but ones that retain many of her other dimensions. For instance, in one plan, after a week spent reading and performing parts of *Raisin in the Sun*, her students will debate whether or not the play "represents black drama and culture or upholds white middle-class values and culture."[21] Michaela arrived at these decisions about curricular choice, content, approaches to teaching, projects, and evaluation, by a long process of provisional sketches that evolved (as she did) in response to feedback over the course of the semester. It is through these repeated acts to represent ourselves to others that we become who we are.

To develop identities, our classes should be designed to foster students' self-representations and subsequent revisions, something I try to achieve by teaching workshop style, and by structuring the course around integrated, long-term projects. In planning any course, I design the projects first (keeping curricular and content goals in mind), then go back and choose books to read or to map out what content will be the focus of any given day. Organizing the classroom as a workshop is a model I carried over from my academic training as a writing teacher.[22] The idea is to change the physical arrangement of persons and space, to redefine teacher and student roles, and to emphasize doing (producing products) in class.

The workshop environment shifts attention away from the teacher as someone who dispenses knowledge toward the students as participants who construct knowledge and meaning in the context of a social community. Unlike traditional whole class instruction, students are put into small, stable work groups, around which classroom activity is then arranged. These groups have multiple functions that range from critique, such as peer-response groups, to collaboration, such as teams that investigate joint problems. The role of the teacher is to structure time and interaction, to design activities, and to organize productive ways of sharing work in progress and receiving feedback from peers and teacher. The role of the students is to actively engage in the tasks at hand, ones they create for themselves, and to take responsibility for themselves and their peers to complete the work that needs to be done.

As a workshop, the classroom exists as a place where products (texts, performances) are made, where goals (understanding concepts, learning new knowledge) are accomplished, and practices (planning, sharing, questioning) are engaged in. In addition, the workshop environment, just like the historical apprenticeship relations in craft guilds, promotes the process by which a student novice moves toward becoming a teacher. Although students are producing individual work, they always belong to a group, and this group membership provides support and connects them to the community. A workshop classroom is characterized by a set of predictable activities or events that can be flexibly arranged into different yet familiar patterns. For instance, on a day when the topic concerns teaching to diverse groups of students, the class may open with focused freewriting, writing informally for several minutes in response to a prompt on inclusion and diversity, move to a whole group discussion based on selected student responses, change to a small group activity where students share drafts of lesson plans designed to incorporate diverse populations, then end with a report from groups to the class about the lesson that best accounted for student difference. Workshop teaching presents many opportunities for students to interact and complete tasks, thus encouraging them to create multiple self-representations in relation to different audiences even on a single day.

I'm advocating classroom contexts that encourage students to produce as many recursive representations of themselves under a variety of conditions as possible. Multiple and frequent opportunities are essential since any form of representation is momentary and partial; what a person says in one setting will always differ from what she might say on the next occasion. All representations are approximate; what a person writes or how a person behaves on any one occasion is only tangentially linked to what she intended. It's only one version relative to other possibilities. Furthermore, all representations reflect or retain some remnants of prior attempts. A representation that works, or is satisfying, has benefited from the less satisfying attempts, the failures. The key then to generating representations that more closely portray or communicate (to others) and develop (for the self) the identity under construction is the chance to revise and repeat acts of representation. Therefore, situations that call for recursive representations or rerepresentations are better for identity development. Integrated long-term projects (such as the course design project I've discussed elsewhere) are ideal because they establish specific dates when students will share their work in progress with others, offer feedback in response to others, and begin revising in preparation for the next due date to present their work. But until the final day of class, no project is ever complete or done; rather, it is merely at a later stage than the prior version. Only because the semester is finite, is there an arbitrary point at which product is considered finished, and the work is evaluated. Thus, no matter what identities are underway, the process of becoming who we are happens partly through our repeated attempts to represent our selves to others.

9. Authority. In a word, authority is power. As teachers, authority allows us to function: it affirms our sense of what we have achieved, and it enables us to carry out our role to educate students effectively. Having authority means having the power (as well as the freedom and the obligation) to act, judge, or command legitimately. Authority comes to us through various means; it may be delegated, awarded, earned, generated, but it is not a commodity. Like authority, power (as Foucault has famously claimed) "is exercised rather than possessed" (1979, 26). Therefore, power, and the authority that accompanies it, derives from the network of relations among individuals.[23] As authorities, we have the right to speak, we are regarded as legitimate sources of information, and we possess the ability to persuade or even force others to act in particular ways. Moreover, as authorities, we offer respected testimony and bear witness in special circumstances. Of all the qualities we may help prospective teachers to develop, authority carries the most weight, holds the most promise, yet is the most difficult to propagate. The proposition is tricky: to allow our students to exercise power, we must practice our authority as teachers.

As a professor, my authority in the classroom is signified by presence (a body with weight that occupies space) and by voice (a speaking self). Philosopher Charles Taylor explains this conjunction: "Our understanding itself is embodied. That is, our bodily know-how, and the way we act and move, can encode components of our understanding of self and world" thus shaping "my sense of myself, of the footing I am on with others" (309). Thus self, voice, and authority are interdependent; one is evidence of the other. Authority entails having a voice, the ability to speak, the safety to speak comfortably, the comfort of being listened to, and the power of being heard. Voice, though not easily definable, refers to inherent textual qualities: does the text have resonance, does it feel embodied as if a person produced it, does it have force or weight? Though an intangible feature, a text that is voiced is unmistakable.[24] Our goal in the classroom is to get our students speaking, to develop their voices, to act with authority.

The relationship between self and voice is complicated but worth pursuing. Just as there is no single self, individuals don't have a singular voice. "Voices" like "selves" are produced in the discursive practices of everyday life. In proposing a complementary theory of self and voice, Kathleen Yancey emphasizes their contingent and responsive natures: "For whatever kind of self we experience, it becomes within multiple contexts: the larger social structure, the local context, the personal. It relies on no single logic, but on a multilogic, expressed and created through a multivocality" (1994, 301). Both voice and self are multiple, situationally specific, and called into being during interaction. Furthermore, voice, like power, is generated through a network of relations. If we want our students to develop voices, then their speaking and writing must arise on account of their relations with others. In order for the words to have resonance, to be voiced, to have the weightiness of the body, the person, within them, the author has to be writing (or speaking) in relation to someone else. If this assertion is true, then the only remaining question is how to create such discursive relationships.

In a discussion of teachers and their authority, composition scholar Xin Liu Gale (1996) believes that we can make space for students to understand, participate in, and inevitably critique, the dominant cultural discourse by exercising our authority as teachers to reveal how language works in academic settings. Relying on Richard Rorty's (1979) notion of the "edifying philosopher" as one who is skeptical of foundational truth and critical of the power of reason, Gale proposes a parallel ideal in the form of the "edifying teacher." The edifying teacher understands that her authority can be ascribed to her institutional position and accompanying expertise in knowing and using dominant discourse (the language of the academy). Teachers can empower students by acknowledging the prestige dialect of academic work, but also by revealing to students how discourses function and are powerful.

The best contexts for uncovering discourses of power are classrooms that promote interaction and communication, and that accommodate various critical and even incompatible discourses. Gale advocates "teaching in such a way that the tension between the different, very often conflicting, discourses provides a space, or a context, for students to develop their own discourse" (124). By not presenting course content as if it were truth and by inviting students to inspect, judge, add to, and question the topics under discussion, teachers make room for students to participate. Furthermore, teachers and students ought to be "conversational partners." Conversation as a dialogic model of interaction keeps "spaces open for new voices." While Gale is interested primarily in how new voices in the conversation inevitably change or disrupt and challenge the status quo, there is an equally powerful effect on those who are speaking. As teachers, it's important to keep in mind that voices (and selves) come into being only in the practice of speaking, in the exercise of power.

In reality, many exercises are needed before students in a classroom setting experience authority and feel comfortable first entering and then holding their own in the conversation. Perhaps because it was such a sustained effort, Elizabeth's thesis turned out to be exceptionally productive in these terms. In the end, Elizabeth managed to turn the conflicts between what she had been taught, what she believed, and what the people and institution of the public school demanded of her, into a document she authored. But the project began in a jumble. Though Elizabeth had prepared a prospectus for her thesis the previous spring, everything changed once she began student teaching. Her thoughts and experiences clashed; all had authority or were valid, but their credibility came from different sources. Starting in the fall, Elizabeth arranged to meet with me weekly (the standard practice for thesis projects). Talking straight through our first meeting, Elizabeth complained of feeling caught as she described a series of contradictory events (for example, being asked to correct grammar errors in rough drafts, the opposite of what process teachers recommend, or having to explain the four pages of requirement to students for the research paper, supposedly an "open-ended" assignment. It was apparent that Elizabeth was virtually suspended in a web of competing discourses.

To these meetings, Elizabeth brought along what she had written. The meeting format was conversational, but structured, with the student speaking first, either reading or explaining her work. The teacher's role in this kind of conference is to keep the dialogue focused on the student's work, to "say back" the writer's ideas, language, reactions, or concerns.[25] She had always intended to focus on whole language,[26] but the form and to some degree the content of the thesis was largely undetermined. These elements—we both knew from experience—would evolve as the project and her life as a teaching intern unfolded.

As the months passed, Elizabeth struggled to analyze the situation, her teachers and students, the high school, public education in general, as well as her own thoughts and behaviors. Each week Elizabeth and I plunged together into this maelstrom of conflicting ideas, messages, ideologies, meanings, and experiences, hoping that by the end of an hour a writing plan for the upcoming week would emerge. My role as thesis director was to provide extensive response and feedback, by echoing her concerns as I heard them, asking questions, summarizing, offering interpretations when asked, and providing positive reinforcement and general support: "Keep going; you're on the right track." Elizabeth would read her drafts aloud, to which I would respond verbally, asking for clarification or pointing to places that struck me as significant. My final advice was to write more just like she had this week. For a writing teacher, trained in a process approach, well practiced in teacher-student conferences, and comfortable with response techniques that focus on writer and text, this was familiar ground.

The effects of extended conversations about academic issues, with time to work through the conflicts, in the service of writing a document that Elizabeth felt was representative and truthful, were impressive. Gale's theory that teaching by using "the tension between different, very often conflicting, discourses provides a space, or a context, for students to develop their own discourse" was born out in Elizabeth's work. Eight months later at her thesis defense, one committee member described the thesis as "a page turner," by turns dramatic narrative then impassioned exposition. Its voice and grounded claims made it the best work by an undergraduate writer the professor had encountered to date at the university. She turned to me and inquired, "How do you do it?" This seemed an unfair question, given that it was Elizabeth's moment; the question hung unanswered between us.

Throughout the whole project, Elizabeth was intent on formulating what she thought and articulating a position in language she recognized as her own (not uniquely "hers" since all language as a communication system is shared, but words she could imagine using). This urgency was not something I instilled in Elizabeth, but I made every effort to validate it, make it real. For reasons I cannot discern, Elizabeth felt ready to speak and to be an authority; my job was to facilitate that process. The significance of this experience for me as a teacher and for Elizabeth as a novice teacher and emerging writer was the changes it wrought in her as a person, a thinker, a writer, and a teacher. Nonetheless, the bound thesis, defended before her professors and installed in the library, remains an expression of authority and the product of an exercise in power. With Elizabeth, I learned to look for moments when she spoke in a powerful way, language infused with voice. At the outset, this could have been any voice. But with practice and an increasing ability to repeat the experience of voice—of hearing and feeling one's self speak, confidence increases. Those who have achieved voice can cultivate authority; then it is only a matter of time.

10. Enactment. On a good day, I lose myself in the act of teaching. In its boldest sense, enactment entails a full investment of my self (person, mind, spirit) in the act of teaching and learning alongside my students. Enactment means embodying the principles I espouse in this book when I'm teaching so that students experience me simultaneously as theorist and participant. I embody my theories of action when I design a variety of structures, activities, and discourse opportunities for each class that we then do together. Thus the form my teaching takes *is* the theory. How I behave in the classroom and what I ask students to do are enactments of my beliefs and self (the teacher I am at that moment).

To make such commitment possible for me or any teacher, the curriculum must be reorganized to depend on cooperative and collaborative activities. Enacting this pedagogy requires moving away from monologue to dialogue as the primary mode of interaction in the classroom, drastically reducing the amount of teacher talk while increasing proportionally student-student and student-teacher exchange during class time. It involves designing activities to foster this shift in attitude and practice away from traditional teacher dominance. Furthermore, the daily class activities themselves must be implicated in and necessary for students to complete the major course projects. Students must feel that the class work (discussing, inventing, critiquing, arguing, discovering) advances their own individual projects while also realizing it benefits the class as a whole. Finally, to accommodate this collective structure and to value students' participation, teachers must design and use nontraditional evaluation and grading systems that provide feedback to accommodate individuals' needs and efforts.[27] Such constant, repeated, everyday interactions help them to know one another, to create obligation and to foster responsibility among the students, making them into a functioning collective. Much of this kind of working environment can be established through the development of substantive and long-term course projects or in the production of a course portfolio (a collection of student work).[28]

Major projects must take a central role in the course; they must be pragmatically obvious. In other words, students must be able to see the immediate benefits to them professionally and personally. Their value must derive from their potential usefulness to students in the future when they are practicing teachers. Value should not be measured in relation to the circumscribed idea of success in the course—getting good grades, but should be determined by transfer potential—could students use this knowledge or skill when they are teaching? In addition, projects (which have many subparts) should begin on the first day of class, be worked on, revised, added to, extended, enlarged, as the students move through the semester. Projects end on the last day of class, not because they are finished, but because the course is arbitrarily over. In fact, these projects if they are processes that become well-practiced, ingrained, continue to happen long after students finish the course. For instance, students learn to design an integrated unit and, out in the field, teaching by way of integrated units is simply good practice.[29]

I never can be sure if what I'm doing with aspiring teachers is right since a student has to spend several years as a teacher to really know what was helpful. But that kind of feedback rarely gets back to me. Mostly, I operate day to day with a great deal of hope and a certain amount of faith. But sometimes I get lucky. During a coffee break in a conference about culture and education held not long ago on our campus, a former student approached me with a smile, holding out her hand and reintroducing herself (though I remembered her perfectly well: Melinda Burns.) "I finished the master's program and now I'm teaching," she said, "and I just wanted to tell you that I'm using the unit project!" I did some quick calculations. It had to have been three years or more since she took my course. She must have read the look on my face as doubt (though it wasn't what I intended). She continued, "I know it sounds incredible, three years later, but it's been really important for me to have worked so hard on that unit, to know the texts inside and out, and to feel comfortable with what I'm doing." While the evidence is circumstantial (besides Melinda, others have made similar claims), I am reasonably convinced that the course-design project ends up being highly valued by students because they have learned practical skills such as how to plan long-term, how to design daily lessons, how to choose texts, but also because they have experienced the process of actively constructing themselves as teachers, making apparent what they believe, what they value, and what goals they refuse to relinquish.

Allow me to illustrate with one example of holistic, self-invested approach to teaching I'm trying to describe—the final examination in the literacy course. Evaluation is the domain in teaching hardest to make consistent with one's teaching style or principles. Perhaps because judging, evaluating, grading, involves the ranking of individuals required by the institution, teachers feel that the methods are immutable or fixed and not subject to transformation. Sometimes teachers feel free to experiment with the nature and content of their courses but act conservatively with respect to evaluation and grading. But for a pedagogy to work well, every action ought to be valuable, not simply expedient.

I prepare students for the exam by explaining what they need to know, but do not inform them ahead of time about what they will be asked to do. The element of surprise is an added bonus (especially since there is unfortunately so little surprise in our classrooms). If students arrive prepared, then the form of the exam poses no problem. You would think that the word would get around, but in the five years I have taught the literacy course, students have maintained the secret, partly because of the novelty of the experience given traditional examination formats. The exam pulls together everything from the course; it is truly a culmination. It covers content as well as process, and requires students to demonstrate not only what they know but what they have learned to do. For instance, can they collaborate, can they design activities, can they transform their beliefs into practice?

During the three-hour exam block, students work in small groups to produce a small book about teaching in their content area. (I arrange for us to take the exam in a computer lab which greatly facilitates the book production but I first conducted the exam before such luxuries were available.) Students receive an extensive set of directions that lists the goals and guides their group process. The book includes an introduction, written jointly by the group, and individual chapters, one for each group member. The groups must go through a composing cycle that includes drafting, responding or feedback, and revising stages, with the goal of making each person's chapter as proficient as possible. Each chapter must be written around a guiding principle, idea, or theory, and contains an explanation as well as an illustration in the form of a lesson or activity consistent with the theory. The book must be produced and assembled by the end of the exam period. Students receive a group grade for the finished book, and an individual grade for their respective chapters. The room hums for three hours; for most of the time, I sit and watch, feeling that in having set them into motion and in being quietly observant I'm doing some of my best teaching. I want them to learn this lesson (how to enact one's beliefs) most of all. If I have not managed to convince my students throughout the semester that this sort of process-based teaching connecting theory and practice is good (and what they ought to be aiming for as teachers), then I have one more shot at it with the exam.

The stakes are high but the payoff is correspondingly fruitful: if I can enact my beliefs even as I design and administer an exam, then I have a chance at being fairly convincing, of persuading students that they too can create an inhabitable teaching space for themselves as teachers. At the very least, I hope to bolster their will to try.

Conclusion

The principle of enactment advocates that we, as teacher educators, put our ideas, beliefs, and feelings into action. Enactment also means instilling the idea that our students (when they are teachers) should follow suit—living out, personifying, actualizing, and embodying their pedagogical commitments. By changing the way we teach prospective teachers, we will end up with better teachers. Field-tested in the laboratory of my own classes, this proposal precedes and indeed overrides the need for formal assessment.

These pedagogical principles are not directives but rather they are characteristics of the learning environment, philosophical lenses through which teachers can look. In this sense, the principles offer a kind of pragmatic theory; they describe an approach, a disposition, a sensibility, or a temperament toward teaching. One final example illustrates how I intend the principles to work in practice. In an interview almost a year after graduation, Elizabeth (while working toward her M.A. in English) tells me that, though she is not teaching high school, she "still sees 'teacher' in the equation." Because of her expertise in teaching writing, she was assigned to assist two faculty members in her university's School of Textiles who were eager to improve writing in their classes. She approached her job as "consultant" by observing and interviewing the teachers and then reporting back to her English department mentor. When he asked what she thought, she analyzed the situation this way: "It seems like their students just are not located in any sort of discourse community. They don't have an overall idea of what they're doing, and so the assignments seem meaningless." Noting how she had connected language's form to its function in her analysis, her mentor, she said, was "surprised and really pleased he didn't have to make that jump for me. He said, 'Just go with your ideas because they seem to be really on target.'" What Elizabeth suggested were writing assignments that incorporated real functions typical of that discourse community.

Elizabeth attributes her ability to assess the inadequacies of this teaching situation to her past experiences relating theory to practice. Still speaking, she raises both hands to eye level and, with opposing thumbs and index fingers, she makes the shape of a diamond in the air. Peering through the frame, she says, "I think I've internalized the theory. I kept thinking of a prism . . . that was the image I had in my head." She pauses, then continues, "I am at one with the theory." For Elizabeth, theory has become transparent, an inconspicuous frame through which she views the world, a useful tool. This incident reveals the versatility and strength of the pedagogy I've described. In essence, Elizabeth demonstrates that these principles, once internalized, become perspectives or dispositions, in effect, part of one's self.

These pedagogical principles evolved while I was teaching individual and unrelated courses in a teacher education program. Their evidence is anecdotal, interpretive, and ethnographic; I intend them to persuade rather than prove. As a group, my students' stories demonstrate the considerable constructive power of the principles even in the limited range of a single course. Imagine what might be possible if the whole teacher education experience were designed and executed based on these principles. Their implementation would be simple in programs where faculty members have the autonomy, freedom, and institutional support to organize a comprehensive teacher education curriculum.

Though this situation is, unfortunately, rare, a unified program could be achieved by faculty working together, selecting principles in common, and allowing disciplinary overlap between methods and content courses. The advantage of my proposal is that faculty could act without having to confront institutional inertia, a perpetual impediment to change.

Reform in teacher education is a difficult and complex process that many other educators who are experts in this area have intelligently and sensibly addressed.[30] While programmatic reform is absolutely necessary, it requires communal effort and collectively held values, conditions that are difficult to achieve. In the meantime, we do not have to remain immobile, waiting for the program or our institution to change. We have the power in our own classrooms to teach as we wish. To improve teacher education, I would encourage any faculty member to begin by reforming his or her own teaching in single classrooms. The next step toward reform would be to enlist another like-minded faculty member and try team teaching or (if teaming is logistically impossible) to plan jointly, but teach independently, two separate courses. My notion is that every teacher-educator can and ought to do something, even if that means simply teaching better classes within the existing teacher-education program. Of course, I advocate using the pedagogical principles described here. This movement toward reform would begin at ground level and work its way upward, spreading through the program, in contrast to top-down reform proposals that encompass the programmatic level. My approach is atomistic and thus *can* work one teacher at a time.

No explicit instructions accompany these principles. While I have provided illustrations, all faculty involved in teacher education would have to invent ways of imbuing their teaching with these features, qualities, or theories. But the power of this pedagogy is that every one can try to be a better teacher and this will improve the situation for prospective teachers. No matter how we as teacher educators are constrained by the nature of individual programs, institutional settings, student populations, or faculty composition, we can at least do things differently in our own classrooms. Relying on these principles of pedagogy, we can actively promote the transformation of students into teachers.

REFLECTIONS

Faith

My passion for language, and especially for writing (though I feared it too), fueled the first writing course I ever taught while I was a graduate student at Berkeley. Like a tidal wave, my fervor swept along my first-year students who had not yet discovered their own same energies in this area. (I had complete faith they all would, and soon, too). It was an emotionally gripping time. I remember reading the essays about writing and language that I was to teach with extreme clarity—Scott Momaday on Native American myths, the story of Helen Keller's simultaneous awakening to word and world, and essays on the Sapir-Whorf hypothesis, artificial intelligence, and the "language" of bees who dance directions to hive members about found sources of blooming plants: was this a language or only a system of miraculous communication?

The intensity arose partly on account of my desire to convey the meaning and inherent lessons of these essayists to my students while at the same time provoking them into writing. But other monumental changes in my life created a surge and surfeit of energy. For a time, I left my house in the Berkeley hills and was temporarily living on Virginia Street, a block away from the north edge of campus in small apartment borrowed from a good friend's ex-lover. The new apartment signified conversion. Day by day, I grew into my new skin, creating for myself methods and reasons for teaching writing. The most difficult part was creating writing assignments that were not completely artificial, that did not entirely depend on students' docility and compliance to produce them. This was not something I learned right away, especially not in the year I spent working with students at Berkeley in remedial composition. But I knew enough to understand that good writing arises from a motivation to communicate, to persuade, to amuse, to educate—different strategies for connecting one person to another. Social interactions and relationships, personal commitments, distinctive differences among people, animate and energize everyday life. Writing is one mode for such enactments.

While a great insight, it did not make things simple or easy. Simultaneously it dawned on me that the context of the traditional classroom—supposedly where real life happened outside of school and assignments given by the teacher were done only to fulfill the requirements—worked against or precluded interpersonal motivations from coming into play. But something more important happened. My insights were interesting and compelling and indicated growth and change in my thinking. I realized one day—caught up in the rush of adrenaline preparing my class—that making writing real for my students was a problem that captivated me completely, leading me to think about associated issues of language and culture, of teaching techniques, of what constituted curriculum, and many other dimensions of teaching and learning language. This charged intensity was a sign that I had changed. It was the sea change that people sometimes talk about, the so-called paradigm shift or the reordering of one's self that occurs when identity is under construction. That is how I got hooked on teaching, digging into the days or even moments when I succeeded at engaging students and realizing our connections are what pleased me most.

CHAPTER SEVEN

Teaching Selves

Process and Patience

For a long time I did not know how to end this book. I realize now that my difficulty stemmed from the realization that there are no conclusions in the work of identity. My own life, and those of my students, has gone on from the moment of our first encounter, and continues to go on; we are perpetually under construction. Change is unavoidable and is, in fact, what is most characteristic about selves and identities.

My goal has been to describe what it means to be a process teacher, one who teaches students a process—how to be a teacher—by engaging them in a process—learning to be a teacher. Identities themselves are always unfinished and in the making; identities develop through continuous processes. There is no one process by which identity comes about, but many. However, the pedagogical principles (proposed in Chapter Six) describe the most effective ways I have discovered as a teacher to enable my students' identities.

Working in this constructive fashion has been nothing but pleasure for me perhaps because I am intuitively drawn to process teaching. There are many "process" teachers out there, though we do not belong to any formal organizations (and none exists). But from the signs, process teachers recognize each other the way members of a club or participants in an activity—chess players, mountain climbers, quilters—know a fellow member whom they have never met). However, not all teachers have the same affinities; but if identities are the goal (as I insist they are in teacher education programs), then teacher educators ought to take process seriously.

This book invites teachers to use a process approach. The idea is not new in education, but has been promoted most vigorously since the 1960s by teachers of writing in other fields. In discussing how best to teach students to write (another process), the writer Donald Murray has this encouragement to offer about becoming a process teacher: "To be a teacher of a process like this takes qualities too few of us have, but which most of us can develop. We have to be quiet, to listen, to respond. We are not the initiator or the motivator; we are the reader, the recipient. We have to be patient and wait, and wait, and wait." Beyond that, he adds, "We are coaches, encouragers, developers, creators of environments in which our students can experience the writing process for themselves" (1997, 4–5). Murray makes our task clear: to be a process teacher—to encourage the process of identity making—one has to be patient and to wait, but only after we have created and continue to generate a sustaining environment. We cannot forcibly make students into teachers because "we are not the initiators or the motivators." There are no guarantees, only sincere attempts.

Failure

If students do not become teachers, has the pedagogy failed? No, because each student has developed new dimensions of identity. Through their work in teacher education courses, students explore seriously and deeply the identity position of "teacher." But this is not the only context or site in students' lives where identity work is occurring. Even in one context, such as the university community, students are subject to multiple identity-constructing forces. To take the simplest example, many students are double majors, studying not only education but also English or history. For students like Howard and Michaela, the attractions of an intellectual identity such as scholar or writer (one being constructed by professors in other disciplines) rival their commitments to be teachers. Meanwhile, in every student, other discourse communities and other social identities, professional or otherwise, are being constructed. A program, even one lasting several years, cannot determine someone's self; no context, organization, program, or institution can induce or control a person's identity. But some environments can nurture identity more than others. A process pedagogy in a teacher education program can provide the space and opportunities for students to actively imagine themselves as teachers. For this or any identity to emerge, envisioning and enacting are essential.

To promote identities, teacher education programs should be situated, authentic contexts where they are an organic part of a discourse community that includes real schools, teachers, high school students, districts, administrators, and any other people usually present in school settings. For students to know what it feels like to be a teacher, to have the experience of being players, they must act (or try out actions) in the actual and present discourse community of teachers (including the university, the public school system, local high

schools, and English teachers in the United States). In practical terms, this
means designing field-based programs where students are taking courses but
spend significant time in public schools. These experiences in and outside the
university should be integrated and coordinated, allowing students to feel the
connections between contexts: the university classroom and the ninth-grade
English classroom should be constituents of the same discourse community.

Students in teacher education courses are preoccupied with the issue of
belonging. They are always asking "Is there a place for me in teaching?" The
question is rarely posed directly, but, in my experience, the need to find a place
motivates and energizes students on their journey through the program. One
way or another, our classrooms have to be laboratories rich enough to provide
numerous options. We provide the middle ground, the place for safe experimentation. Once they're in a teacher education program, our students are no
longer simply observers or onlookers—individuals interested in teaching—
they've made a commitment, but neither are they teachers—they occupy a position somewhere in-between, as apprentices. In this intermediary position,
they must explore and experiment in contexts that are genuine enough to learn
the conventions and practices of the discourse community, but not so completely that the stakes are too high. In other words, the student teaching experience should be challenging but not immobilizing. Students ought to have
experimented enough, been in close enough contact with the joys and difficulties of teaching, and performed enough teaching tasks to know whether there
is a place for them in teaching. Using the pedagogy described in this book will
create experiences that allow students to know if it is possible, likely, a good
thing, or even worth the effort, to belong.

In our students and in our teaching, we are obligated to value openness.
For identities to grow, individuals must be open to the possibility of "becoming." Without the willingness and the determination to try to become a teacher
(or any other identity), then no progress can be made. This decision to try is not
made easily; we must respect the tentativeness of it. Students are not sure when
they enter the teacher education program if they will become teachers. For our
part, as teachers, we must remain open too. We must commit ourselves to ways
of teaching that promote identities while remembering that not all of our students will become teachers. We must be invested in our students yet recognize,
without regret or disappointment, that they may make other choices. By creating an atmosphere of acceptance, we allow students to reveal their fears, worries, concerns, and anxieties about teaching and to consider without guilt other
paths, other lives.

My students found it necessary in the interviews to give accounts of
themselves—detailing instances of satisfaction, joy, and fulfillment, as well as
describing competing moments of ambiguity, tension, and distress. From these

and other experiences, I am convinced that providing many opportunities for students to acknowledge the difficulties and to weigh the alternatives improves the chances of their remaining open to teaching. But as I said before, no matter what we do, we cannot promise that every student becomes a teacher, nor should we regard this provision as a sign of failure. Students have achieved a great deal if they know with confidence, based on experience in authentic contexts that reveal the conditions of schools and teaching, that they do or do not want to become teachers.

Six Students a Year or So After Graduation

Donna Rogers

Hilton Head Island, South Carolina. May 1998. My scheduled visit with Donna is at noon. She looks wonderful, waiting in front of the school, wearing a tomato red dress that looks crisp and professional. The school is small and private, four hundred students in all, K-12. Donna is the resource instructor and also teaches tutorials in English to students with learning disabilities. When I pull up in my van, she steps off the curb; we clasp hands through the open window, too awkward to embrace. I take her photograph as we walk to the football field; she's also the cheerleading coach. One reason she found a teaching job (there are only three high schools on the island, one public, one Christian, and Island Preparatory School at Sea Haven) is because they needed someone for cheerleading. The headmaster inquired after her high school sports and when she reported six years of cheerleading "his eyes lit up" she recalls.

"I'm really content here with my job," Donna says, "although I'd like to be at the public high school. There are no openings now but I'm hopeful about next year." We walk into the main foyer, near Donna's office, and stare at the open space jammed with displayed books and at the art around the walls hung on clotheslines; the light and low ceilings make it feel warm and welcoming. "The atmosphere here and the demeanor of the students and their parents is completely unlike anything I've ever been exposed to." She likes it, I can tell. She's learning a different set of skills, unlike the performing, entertaining, and motivating abilities she developed as a teaching intern while working with crowds of students who felt disenfranchised by school. But there are still those strong currents of social commitment underneath. I can feel them.

"How did you end up coming here, Donna?" I ask.

"My husband is a musician. It is perfect here through the summer months since there is so much work for him. We moved here 'cause of that; I thought I could get a job teaching. I waited all through the summer to hear. By

God's grace, I didn't get anxious about it really. Then a week before school started I got the call about this job. My husband's job is seasonal though, and in January, after December graduation, he started looking for something year-round. Although he could never do anything serious, he's not that kind of person. But he's found a job perfectly suited to him—assistant to the minister at our church. So he spends a lot of time with kids; we're both dedicating our lives to working with teenagers."

She pauses. She seems young but utterly capable, happy, relaxed, managing this life in a year-round golf and boating fantasy resort that's far away from Raleigh, NC, from her parents and friends. Looking out over the green field, I remember my own move across the country from Pennsylvania to California after college graduation; how easy and liberating that was. I mention both these thoughts. She laughs and says her parents constantly ask why she had to move so far away, five hours! "But I'm trying to prepare them," she says. "We both plan to go to Africa in two years and continue our work." (It's mission work she refers to here, though I understand the referent. We've had this conversation before.) "My parents know that's what we intend, but it's not real for them," she adds.

Her office, "my little hole" as she refers to it while motioning me in, is a windowless, small room, off a hall where copy machine and general-use phones are both constantly in use. She has tried to make it hers, covering one wall with a collage, a banner that says, "Reach out!" showing pictures of hands, people of all colors, age, races, maps, and foreign countries. A long institutional table under the collage has three chairs pulled up to it. Donna occupies the end seat, her pad with neat notes (lesson plans) at her elbow. Stephen Crane's *Red Badge of Courage* lies on top. When her student Taylor arrives, Donna introduces me (I sit near the door). Taylor says hi and then slumps into the chair nearest Donna on the long side of the table.

The lesson begins, first with a summary of the assignment, what's been due, and then some instructions about the next one. Donna returns a quiz on the first few chapters of the book and says they'll return to the text to find the answers. Taylor is quiet at first, and, as Donna begins to talk about the book, telling the story, asking simple questions, he fidgets. He pushes back in his chair, and finally scoots it a little away from Donna, who leans across her desk, stretching out her arm toward him for emphasis, trying to draw him into the text. "Involving Taylor in literature has been a challenge," she informed me before he arrived. I want to give you some context."

The simple task of turning to page five and reading alternating paragraphs to discover the answer to a missed quiz question turns into an eloquent demonstration of interpretive reading. They read and talk, Donna in a quiet but certain voice, picking out words and details, rereading a phrase or two, creating the character of Henry and his mother as he leaves for war. Taylor asks a question. That's progress. He offers an idea. Better. By the time I leave fifteen minutes into the lesson, the two of them are close to conversation, almost to a collaborative interpretation of the text. Though he hasn't moved any closer to her (she still looks intently at him and leans into her work, toward him), he has stopped edging his chair away and focuses his attention on the text before him.

It has been a pleasure to observe this joint venture. Although Donna is the star, voluble and fluent, spinning out ideas about what the characters are thinking, posing questions about mother-son relationships, foregrounding what will be salient details later in the novel, her student is less witness than partner in the dance. It is a difficult and valuable achievement for them both.

Elizabeth Tavey

The Crossroads Restaurant, Chapel Hill, NC. May 1998. Elizabeth and I meet for lunch at an outdoor place in Chapel Hill. The garden on this hot May day is lush, green, and blooming. The two fountains bubble and cover the street noise. The tall ring of cypress bushes makes the restaurant seem timeless, insulated from the workday concerns that most of its patrons will soon return to. Across the table, Elizabeth looks happy and energetic; I notice she has cut her hair up to shoulder length.

I open the conversation: "So you mentioned that you broke up with your boyfriend." "Yeah," Elizabeth grins, not looking the least perturbed. "It was the right thing to do, and it happened because I was happy writing all these papers in graduate school. There I was in the midst of an intense week finishing my rhetoric paper and take-home exam, which turned out to be twenty-five pages, and I realized that I just love this. I've made friends, I'm happy living in Raleigh, and I just want to be in graduate school. It's perfect, and I haven't ever been happier."

Elizabeth carries on without prompting: "So as the semester went on I was going less and less frequently to Winston to visit Tim. One night on the phone, he asked me if I was happy, and I said YES! (meaning working on papers and such). Then he wanted to know if I thought we'd ever get married. I hesitated a bit, but no, I said, I didn't think so. We've known each other all our lives, since we were little, we're such good friends and he's such a good person. But no, I didn't want to get married to him. He didn't think we had a future either so we both breathed a sigh of relief."

Elizabeth swirls the ice in her glass, drinks some tea, and continues: "It also means that the only impediment or concern I had about going off to graduate school to get a Ph.D. in rhetoric and composition has been done away with. I was so excited when Dr. Cuthbert, unsolicited, asked me if I was serious about graduate school, since I would obviously be a success and could theoretically go anywhere I liked. He offered to help. I was really on cloud nine. I mean, he hardly knows me. He just had the evidence of my work to judge me on. So his opinion really means a lot to me. No one, besides you, and maybe now my sister, a little, understands what this means to me, or even what getting a Ph.D. in composition is. My sister doesn't know really, but she at least recognizes that I'm very happy about it."

I do know what Elizabeth means and her happiness is infectious. "After all this weeding out, whittling down, starting with my journal, and writing, and teacher education and English, and now finding that I'm fascinated with rhetoric! It's so fabulous to feel that I've found something good, something I really want to do, someplace I feel rooted and comfortable. If Mom were here . . . if Mom were alive . . ." Elizabeth trails off, not able to quite finish the sentence. She has made frequent references to her mother throughout our conversation. About leaving her boyfriend, and her inevitable decision to leave North Carolina to go to graduate school, Elizabeth says that her actions would have upset her mother, shaken her to the very core, since she was so close to everyone in the family and wouldn't have wanted Elizabeth to move away. "But she would have understood," Elizabeth states, "She would have been so proud."

Later Elizabeth brings up the emotional gap between her and her father (who remarried after her mother's death). "My father keeps calling and asking if I'm happy." Though Elizabeth did everything she could think of to reassure him, he continued his frequent calls. This annoyed Elizabeth. "Mom would just know how good things are with me, how happy I am. There wouldn't be this communication problem," she said

When Elizabeth begins talking about her sister (nine years older, who cared for the family through their mother's illness) and her sister's new baby, she said, "Mom would just move right down there to be with them. Or they'd have to move back to Winston-Salem." Several times over the course of the conversation, Elizabeth referred to "oddly enough, the positive effects" of her mother's death, although she was quick to amend, "Not that there really are any good things about my mother dying." She insists that now she feels really independent, something she was forced into from an early age. This strength she attributes to losing her mother: "Since Mom isn't here . . ."

Elizabeth sums up her feelings this way: "I don't really have any burning desire to leave North Carolina, but I'm not committed to staying here either. I told my friend Alice in New York that I'd move somewhere if I had a real reason to. (I'm struck by the real reason phrase, so important to Elizabeth elsewhere). Then we talk a bit about Rick, and how he seems to bring his whole family along with him, his ideas about traveling or going on to graduate school. Out front, where we stand for about an hour more talking about using her experience with the textile school as a basis for her master's thesis, Elizabeth says, "I've had such a nice time. It's so easy to sit around for hours and talk to you." It has been important for me too; when she moves out of state, I will miss her more than I can admit.

Richard Lambert

Starlight Diner, Raleigh, NC. March 1998. "This week was the first time I've ever been threatened by a student in school," Rick says. We are having a mid-week dinner at a downtown restaurant in Raleigh, an evening out to catch up. Elizabeth is along too; she and Rick were good friends as undergraduates and they have stayed in touch. "What happened?" I ask. Rick begins a long story, "Well, I was taking up the homework, and this student says, "I don't have to hand that in 'cause I wasn't here yesterday." I reply, 'Jeffrey, you know the rules. I've told you all a thousand times how you're supposed to come to me and get the work, and you're responsible.' So he got mad at me and says, "Do you know who I am and what I can do to you?" He yells right in front of the whole class, during class, which started about three minutes before. But I stood my ground and traded a few more comments with him until he says, 'So let's go outside right now and settle it.' "

"Things were serious. I asked him to leave the classroom (standard disciplinary procedure) and asked him to report to the assistant principal's office. But as Jeff stood up to leave and as I moved to follow him to make sure he goes where he's supposed to, our feet touched . . . accidentally! At that moment, Jeff turned around to the class and shouted, 'Look at the behavior of this first-year teacher. Trying to trip a poor student.' " Rick finishes; his voice is tight and hard. In telling the story, Rick has become uncharacteristically furious. He explains that he didn't actually feel threatened by the student, but he feels ashamed at losing control of his class. "Everything completely disintegrated and all my students were watching to see how I was going to react. Even though I was so upset, I think I did the right thing." Elizabeth and I are quick to reassure him. I'm even proud: he sent the student on his way, returned to his students, got the class in motion again, then wrote a disciplinary action report, handing it to a student who delivered it to the office down the hall. This sounds more like the unflappable Rick I know.

"But the most incredible part of the day was the reactions of the other teachers," Rick says, shaking his head. "When I told the story later in the teachers' lounge, the other teachers were just outraged by what had happened." They all said to me "Everyone knows threatening a teacher is an offense that leads to suspension from school." One teacher said that sending the report wouldn't make any difference; the principal wouldn't notice from the report how serious the situation was. Bill said I ought to go speak directly to the assistant principal. So later that afternoon, I did or tried to. I went to his office where I waited an hour and a half for Mr. Griffin to emerge from his meeting. But Mr. Griffin says, 'I'm busy, can't talk now.' I kept insisting, and finally, he says, 'Okay, you have three minutes to tell your story while I copy this paper.' "

"As soon as I get started on the story, Mr. Griffin reacted instantly. He kept asking me, 'Did you feel threatened, Rick?' I didn't know what to say. After a few minutes of silence, he repeated the question, firmly. I was hesitating because my thoughts are going in two directions: First, the student is just a skinny kid with braces and I didn't really feel afraid of him. Second, I was very angry at the student, not because of the threat exactly, but because I lost control of the class." Finally Mr. G. says to me again, "Did he *threaten* you?" To this question, I could honestly say yes. Jeff did make a threat. But, as soon as the words are out of my mouth, I realize that Mr. Griffin intends to suspend the student. I get a bad feeling in the pit of my stomach because I feel sorry for the student. This student has been a problem from day one, the class clown, but suspending him won't make anything better or different. I know the student needs more attention not less. But things have once again slipped out of my control, and Mr. Griffin springs into motion. He calls the parents who get angry at the school, the assistant principal, and at me. A two-week suspension is the likely sentence."

"But the very next day, I get a call from Mr. Griffin. 'Ah, look here, Rick. It turns out that Jeffrey has a learning disability, which has to be factored in when we decide how we're going to deal with the situation.' The learning disability falls into the category 'impulse control' and since losing control was the heart of the incident, the student cannot be held accountable for his actions. Jeffrey has been asked to stay home from school for two days, then he'll be back in class the following Monday morning. Mr. Griffin tells me that Jeffrey's parents want me to contact them directly if Jeffrey continues to cause trouble. When he comes back to school, he tries to be as good as gold, very quiet. But I know he can't sustain it. His self-containment is only temporary. That's the boy's problem, isn't it? I'm worried because I don't know how I can prevent another confrontation. But, even more so than that, how can I help the student? How can I teach or behave in the classroom that would help Jeff to learn something?"

I don't really have any answers though Elizabeth and I try to commiserate. The conversation turns back to his former cooperating teacher who worked brilliantly with students with learning disabilities. Rick laments the fact that he is without her experience and watchful eye to help him deal with the current situation. "Mrs. Altman really loved working with new teachers. She was fabulous, really good at it. Sometimes she would sit in the back of the room when I was teaching and do things like draw pictures of how I looked or stood, how I held my body. Later she'd show me (he poses, with a hand on one cocked hip) how I looked during the lesson and tell me that my body's stance communicated to the students how I felt about them. She commented on things I never would have thought about, or things I never would have been able to know without her watching, carefully and with great perceptiveness."

As a new teacher, Rick expends energy on what he regards as technical, organizational, or curricular difficulties because he believes he can change things. He despairs, however, about those problems that have social roots, such as Jeffrey's disruptive behavior, about the difficulties that stem from unstable homes or from poverty, realms that Rick can't even dream of changing as a teacher. The topic, he says, depresses him and he shifts gears. He's been thinking plans for his future: "I'm going to England this summer, to visit and to spend some time writing. Every famous American writer went to England or to the Continent, just to soak up the culture, to be inspired, to write."

After the dinner that night, Rick promised to keep me posted on how things developed. But it was Elizabeth who called one day several months later to tell me that Rick had fallen in love. I wondered how this new relationship might affect his plans. "He is really serious," she said. "Don't tell him you know because I'm sure he'll want to tell you himself." That fall, during his second year of teaching, Rick sent me a long e-mail. About West Norriton County High, he reported: "I realize the gifts I have been given at the school and try, every day, not to take for granted my good luck." About himself, he wrote: "I have fallen in love this past summer, become more focused in my teaching, and grown up a lot. Yet, something else calls from inside. Teaching high school has given me invaluable lessons about society, adolescents, and the field of English, but intrinsically I need to move on soon." He ends by asking my advice about graduate school, which I give easily, wondering what will happen by next year.

Lauren Elkins

110 Waverly Forest Lane, Chapel Hill, NC. May 1998. There are three messages on my phone machine. When I play back the last one, a voice I know says, "Hi, this is Lauren, Lauren *Smithfield*! I have a new number. Call me when you get a chance." She's married now and back teaching at her old high school (two hundred faculty, several thousand students) and having a good year teaching, so she reports when I call later that evening. "The other teachers remember me, they're nice to me, it's neat to be teaching at my old school." Though as I listen to the details, I wonder how that's humanly possible. She describes ninety-minute periods, A and B days, 140 students total. In addition, this semester she is teaching two sections of tenth grade students who participate in the International Baccalaureate program, a voluntary academically advanced curriculum. "So motivation is no problem with them at least," Lauren says.

She and Mathew, her husband, are building a house they're almost ready to move into. Mathew has not had a good year teaching and is looking for other kinds of work, or perhaps he'll try another year. "The big difference," Lauren says, "in our experiences as first-year teachers is the support from our departments and administration." My department has been a tremendously helpful, generous, and attentive. Everyone lends a hand to solve problems and share information, materials, and advice. But Mathew's department has not."

She elaborates: "This semester has been wonderful. If you had talked to me last semester, it wouldn't have been the same story. I started off not knowing how to establish discipline and had a lot of problems with students not respecting me, cussing me out, and failing to listen to me, dancing around the room, and being incredibly disruptive. But half my students changed at midsemester, and by then I had learned how to set the tone and be stricter. It has made a big difference. I'm happier knowing that I can do it right. But with the other half, students who I started off the year with, I just have to cope with the situation I created. But it is teaching the International Baccalaureate kids (on B days) that really makes teaching worthwhile; they're smart, not any smarter than the other kids are, but they're motivated, eager to be there, and wanting to learn. They start things—they wanted to discuss controversial issues, and so I told them about the question box we had in Dr. Upton's class, where we could submit anonymous questions that we'd discuss in class. So they sneak in here and put questions in the box, and then I use them for their journal entries."

She chatters on but I am silent, listening, appalled at the day-to-day conditions she describes. There are only six minutes between classes, and twenty-five minutes for lunch, twelve of which have to be spent on hall duty. Lauren's school is under high scrutiny as a result of the ABC accountability program adopted several years ago by the state of North Carolina to improve school quality. Inspectors arrive regularly but unannounced at school to check that the halls are "safe." Teachers are required to spend the six minutes between classes standing by their doors observing the students and enforcing order. "There's no time to go to the rest room," Lauren says, "we have ninety-minute periods and we're not supposed to leave our classes during that time, but with no breaks, we can't go between classes. It's ridiculous. We're denied the time to use the rest room, something pretty fundamental and necessary. We have no privacy since we have to ask another teacher to watch our classes so we can go to the rest room. It is humiliating and wrong."

The poor environmental conditions are not the only challenge. Some of Lauren's students have been jailed, a few carry weapons, some deal drugs (though she doesn't know how many), and there are a fair number of sixteen-year-old ninth-graders who constantly disrupt her classes. To meet the standards set by the ABC program, student absences have to be carefully monitored.

Teachers must contact parents after a student's second and fourth absence. A great deal of time, Lauren says, is taken up by paperwork, monitoring, leaving less than enough time for instruction, for teaching. "But I love my kids, and I love teaching literature," Lauren says, "They really make the hassles worth it."

Howard Dempsey

Bullshead Bookstore, Carolina Campus, Chapel Hill, NC. December 1998. Soon after graduation, Howard left North Carolina to attend graduate school, a master's program at the University of Tennessee. I hear from the director of graduate studies at Tennessee, a faculty member I know well, that Howard is going to return to North Carolina to do some high school teaching. (He had received a four-year scholarship as a Teaching Fellow.) This information surprises me, not his intention to return, but that Howard has not told me about it himself. I wonder what his omission means. We've been e-mailing on and off during the year about graduate school but he never mentioned plans about teaching.

Over Christmas break, I'm in the campus bookstore at the checkout counter when I see Howard in the paperback section. I call out his name and he comes over to greet me. In a rushed few minutes, with my parking meter running out, Howard tells me he'll be finished with his Master's degree in June, then he'll be coming back to North Carolina to teach to repay his scholarship. He explains he's on campus for a brief stop as he travels home for Christmas to Murfeesboro from Tennessee. Apologizing, since I have no time to talk, I ask him if he will call me to chat after the holiday when he drives back through town on his return trip to Tennessee. "Sure," he says. I turn back to wave, not certain whether he is simply being polite or if he intends to call.

Michaela Morris

110 Waverly Forest Lane, Chapel Hill, NC. June 1997. Gone, that woman, gone like the wind. The last time she visited my office just after graduation, to pick up a letter of recommendation, Michaela promised to send me a new phone number and address, once she had one. The last I heard, she was headed for Washington, DC, to work in the performing arts, onstage.

A Few Necessities

I hesitate to proclaim truth. In this book, I've described a set of practices that are derived from teaching, from thinking about teaching, from reading theory that seems relevant to the processes of learning and being that my students engage in while they're in my classroom. The word *practice* as well as its variants *practices*, *to practice*, or *practicing* is central to my project because it refers to everyday actions and their constructive power. I invoke the meaning spelled out by social theorist Bruno Latour. He declares that "practice is not silent or without theories, on the contrary it speaks endlessly and with extraordinarily subtle concepts . . ." (1998).[1] Thus, the pedagogical principles lay out a way of practicing, not the thing in itself; there are no procedures or methods I can simply describe and say, "Try that." Teachers must go through their own process of thinking through the connections between what they know, what they can do with students, and what their students know or can do. The pedagogical principles I've presented here are not dogmas but the result of process, the real heart of teaching.

As someone known around campus for having an interest in teaching, I am often asked, "How do *you* do it?" There is no simple answer. While I intend to be cooperative, my response is usually longer and markedly different from what is anticipated. "It's a dialectic," I say, "between my goals for what I want students to know or do and various domains of theory related to practice, ideas about authority or agency or collaboration. After I've worked these ideas back and forth many times, I end up with plans of action, with an activity or a lesson format or a project that I trust will lead me and my students in the right direction." This answer satisfies me (if not my interrogator) because it gets the conversation going, and it is as close to truth as I can get.

In moving beyond the question of teaching courses to consider how best to design teacher education programs, my mind traces the same route, follows the same line of thinking. If nothing else, the ideal teacher education program should be

1. *Active.* The program should be student-centered, focused on engaging students through active participation in the process of becoming a teacher. Every aspect of the program should emphasize doing.

2. *Holistic and integrated.* A teacher education program should be conceived of as a whole, a synchronous experience. Individual parts, such as content requirements, settings, or courses, should be designed to fit together; each element should support and extend the others. Courses should be interconnected and include field experience. Students should be conscious of their involvement in a coherent program by requiring them to construct a portfolio, a collection of written work and other artifacts that charts their development from the time they enter the program and represents their emerging selves as teachers as they complete the program.

3. *Embedded in a discourse community.* A teacher education program should exist inside the discourse community of teachers and teaching. A discourse community is a group of individuals who share practices, language,

conventions, beliefs, and in this case, profession. Being a teacher means be-coming a member of the discourse community by learning its conventions and practices. Students need significant contact (besides the teaching internship) with teachers in the field in a variety of professional and school settings throughout the program.

4. *Rich in relations.* Because identities are created in interaction, a teacher education program should be an environment rich in relations between indi-viduals, including teachers to students, and students to students. These recip-rocal "caring relations" (as Noddings defines them) should define the ethos of the program. In belonging to a caring community, students should receive (and give) attention, and feel known and recognized by others. Being connected to others adds intensity and dimension to the work of learning to teach.

5. *Morally engaged.* Teaching is a moral act. A teacher education pro-gram should recognize, celebrate, and honor the intentions of prospective teachers who so often feel committed to improving the lives of others, alle-viating social inequalities, and eradicating discrimination. It is often these ethical concerns that have brought students to teaching. We (as teachers also motivated by social conscience) must demonstrate visibly that we share similar convictions about the importance of values. The teacher education program should overtly reflect social goals and support students in their indi-vidual ethical pursuits.

Principles (One Last Time)

In a book called *Embracing Contraries*, Peter Elbow discusses the difficulty of saying anything definitive about "the rich messiness of learning and teaching." We persist in attempting to try, he claims, because of "a hunger to figure things out, to reach conclusions, to arrive at stable, portable, and even neat insights" (1986, x). My students and their stories attest to the unpredictability, serendip-ity, chaos, and contingency of the endeavor to become teachers. Despite my best efforts to synthesize the words of my students together with the experi-ence of teaching them, none of my offerings are neat. They are, however, emi-nently portable (a partial success).

When it comes to practice however, imperfect or inconsistent thinking is not all bad. Elbow argues further that living with contradiction and forestalling resolution of differences will help us as teachers to adopt multiple perspectives and be inventive when it comes to helping students learn. But he also fears rel-ativism and insists there must be some guides to good teaching: "Surely there cannot only be one right way to learn and teach: looking around us we see too many diverse forms of success. Yet, surely, the issue cannot also be hopelessly

relative: there must be *principles* that we must satisfy to produce good learning
and teaching—however diverse the ways in which people satisfy them" (x, italics his). In response to Elbow's provocative and welcome challenge, I assert
that, yes, there are principles, and they include discourse richness and openness,
dialogue, collaboration, deliberation, reflexivity, theorizing in practice, agency,
recursive representation, authority, and enactment. These principles do justice
to the complexities of teaching and learning; they also contribute to the making of identities, the real purpose of education.

REFLECTIONS

Coincidence

It was at a dinner party at a good friend's house that I suddenly understood how
identity formation happened and saw with some clarity the role that language
or discourse plays in this process of becoming. Experience (and all that it contains) is constitutive. Identities depend upon convergence, on constellations of
persons and actions, on zones of contact among people, things, language, and
space, like the dinner party, where we were all being constructed in the moment. Our selves were such because we had gathered together for the dinner,
because each of us had prepared something for the meal, since we were all anxious, intent, and expectant about what would happen over the course of the
evening, because we would talk, look, and move about relative to one another as
we changed seats during cocktails before dinner and, later, as we moved away
from the table for coffee. We talked and touched, creating one another in gestures and signs—the grave handshakes of the early evening, the welcoming
kisses bestowed on the cheeks of one or two close acquaintances, and the spontaneous and unplanned moments of contact, one hand brushing another as
drinks were passed, or a shoulder tapped to indicate emphasis. Through these
actions, as we talked and listened, asked questions and formulated answers, we
became ourselves and invented the others.

Shortly after that evening, I began writing this book. But I couldn't have
known ahead of time the event would turn out to be so influential. The dinner
party was momentous for other reasons. Bruno Latour (a French sociologist
whose work on modern science greatly intrigued me) was to be one of the
guests, and I was eager to meet him. Judy asked me to make dessert. Though I
had not prepared anything special for a long time, the idea of the evening inspired me, and I began recalling other evenings when I had made food both
beautiful and delicious for guests to consume. During the whole afternoon it

took to bake the chocolate cake (the recipe coming from a California cookbook I had used so often in the past that its spine had long cracked, its loose pages having been pocked and rippled with smears of sauces and batters), I was lost in remembering other kitchens and other people. The most persistent and pleasurable memories were of sharing cooking and conversation with my friend Barbara who taught me twenty years ago in her small kitchen in Berkeley how to make decorative chocolate leaves, the kind fancy bakeries use. We had gathered a handful of the hard, waxy oval leaves of camellia bushes (which grew there abundantly) to begin the process. These leaves are perfect molds, stiff and curved, substantial enough to accept a coating of melted chocolate painted on with a small brush. When the chocolate hardens, the leaves can be peeled away, leaving the perfectly imprinted shells.

As the smell of the cake baking grew stronger and more intense, so did the memories of my past. Scene after scene unfolded of people and pleasures long forgotten. Though I had had no such intention to begin with, I felt a great urgency to make chocolate leaves for the cake we were to eat at the dinner party. Six months earlier, my neighbor had planted a white winter-blooming camellia outside my dining room window. Whether it was purely good fortune or simply the bush's proximity that kindled my desire, I do not know. But a camellia bush was there at hand. Taking the kitchen scissors, I cut a few stems of its glossy leaves, and imagined a cake that, later that evening, would taste better not only because of its beauty but also because it was made of memory (of images that had arrived in my mind, unbeckoned, outside my conscious control), something the guests wouldn't know but perhaps would intuit.

At the dinner table, Latour began to talk about his current work on social technologies, specifically about writing on a computer. "When we sit at the computer screen and write, we are often surprised to discover what we have written there. We are always a little overtaken by the words that appear. So we are not in control." To explain his meaning, Latour brought up the metaphor of the marionette, a puppet controlled by a master or *marionettiste*. This relationship existing between puppet and master, Latour suggested, is similar to that between a writer and her computer. Although the puppet is inanimate, its capacities affect what actions the puppeteer can accomplish. The performance cannot determined by the puppet master alone but results from the two working together. Likewise, what we write when using the computer has been similarly influenced, shaped, controlled by its technological features. Sitting in Judy's living room, the six of us at the table (but not yet to the dessert course), Latour gestured over his shoulder to a shadow behind him (referring perhaps to the hours spent writing on the computer earlier that afternoon) and claimed, "We are always a little overtaken by language, by the words that appear. The words run ahead and are not in our control. We cannot escape the fact that language is always ahead of us," that language is destiny.

In June, a year after Elizabeth's graduation, I drove over to her apartment in Raleigh, finding it easily though the complex is one of those curving, labyrinthine settlements without visible markers on the identical buildings. She likes her apartment on the building's backside because it hugs the edge of the property. In the hundred yards between her building and the railings of the shopping center parking lot next door, a ravine with grass and trees dips toward a seasonal creek, little more than a rocky drainage ditch, then ascends a short slope upward. "The natural space helps," she had said to me on the phone. "Helps what?" I thought but didn't ask. But being sensitive to nature myself, even to the damaged, reduced, and violated bits left in developed sites, I watched for the grassy slope. It helped me find her.

Elizabeth has just finished one semester of graduate school. She speaks easily and happily, describing her courses. Finally, since I've come for an interview, I turn to my questions. "Are you a teacher," I ask bluntly. "No, no," she says laughing. "A writer?" she suggests, adding, "Well, maybe. After writing that paper for Dr. Cuthbert, I'm not so sure." Then, in a few seconds, she changes tack, fast, as if she is caught in a crosswind. "Wait! I am a teacher. Working with Dr. Stevens in Textiles, why it's just like teaching." She pauses two beats, then asserts, "It *is* teaching." Suddenly and soundlessly, the two worlds that she has held distinct for the last year, believing herself to have rejected teaching in favor of graduate school, a decision she had a hard time coming to accept, coalesce.

The world has an efficacy of its own. Selves are made unwittingly in moments of convergence, when there is a strong confluence of forces, or a crossing-over of disparate vectors of experience. We are not in charge. There is great freedom and power in acknowledging our lack of control and in relinquishing that desire. Instead, we can hold on to and exercise our agency, the ability to act. Other influences do the creating and remaking. Knowing this, we need not be anxious. With more energy, we can continue our work as teachers to create environments where discursive experience—with all its potential for convergence—happens. In this respect, the principles of pedagogy are useful guides. Identity arises from the perpetual dialectic between internal states and external conditions. We can encourage "becoming" by making processes explicit, assuring openness, and recalling that all things, including selves, are revisable and subject to negotiation. Latour's words have turned out to be an emblem for this book: "Language (with its power to create selves) is always ahead of us." Sometimes it almost seems as if the words already exist or are out there waiting for us. In speaking them, we invent ourselves and make others, and are always a little surprised at what has happened.

Notes

Introduction

1. Figure quoted in the news story "Teacher Pay Remains Thorny Issue." *Chapel Hill News*, 28 June 1998, A1, A9.

Chapter One

1. To maintain their privacy, the names of the six students who are the focus of this study are pseudonyms. Apart from me, all other persons, including other university students, teachers, administrators, high school students, and so forth, are referred to by pseudonyms as well. In addition, significant details related to dates, places, and events have been changed in all cases to protect those who were not directly involved in this research project. Any perceived resemblances are purely accidental.

2. Though the students in this course include secondary education majors from the disciplines of mathematics, science, foreign languages, music, social studies, I have chosen to focus on those from English, my own discipline.

3. See Paul Smith's *Discerning the Subject* (1988).

4. In 1998, a new program consisting of a one-year MAT program replaced the undergraduate secondary education program that I describe here. The nature of the current program at UNC Chapel Hill is significantly different from the one described here, but the goal and its accompanying challenge—constructing identities as teachers—remains very much the same.

5. Because it involved human subjects, this study (#915-004) was reviewed and approved by the University of North Carolina's Academic Affairs Institutional Review Board.

6. The exception was Elizabeth who had taken the literacy course the prior semester. However, because she was writing an honors thesis at that time under my direction and since she would be completing the practicum with the other five students, I also solicited her to participate in the study.

7. I extend heartfelt thanks to every one of my students who, through their responses and reactions to me and my classes, have contributed to the authenticity of this book.

Chapter Three

1. I am discussing the format of the teacher education program at UNC Chapel Hill as it was configured during the years 1994–1998, when the students in this study were enrolled. In the fall of 1998, a new MAT program for secondary teacher education was introduced, replacing what had formerly been an undergraduate program. The teacher education program at UNC as I describe it in this book no longer exits. However, this program remains relevant as an example since it typifies many teacher education programs across the country.

Chapter Four

1. The quotation is from page 31 of the novel *Cloud Chamber*.

Chapter Six

1. Some of these teachers include Bill Ayers, Mariolina Salvatori, Mike Rose, Ann Berthoff, Peter Elbow, Donald Murray, Patricia Donahue, Toby Fulwiler, Steve Zemelman and Harvey Daniels, Patricia Bizzell, Michael Apple, Janet Miller, Thomas Newkirk, David Bartholomae, James Moffet, Nancie Atwell, and Parker Palmer.

2. I would like to honor and acknowledge Kim Davis at UC Berkeley, Irene Papoulis at Trinity College, Marjorie Roemer at Rhode Island College, Sheridan Blau at UC Santa Barbara, Susan Henking at Hobart & William Smith Colleges, Doug Howard at St. John Fisher College, and Alan Tom and Dwight Rogers at UNC Chapel Hill.

3. From M. M. Bakhtin, *The Dialogic Imagination*, excerpted in *The Bakhtin Reader* (1994) edited by Pam Morris.

4. In a book entitled *Discourse*, Sara Mills writes that as a term discourse "has perhaps the widest range of possible significations of any term in literary and cultural theory, and yet it is often the term within theoretical texts which is least defined" (1997, 1). In narrowly conceiving of the term "discourse," I leave out many other meanings that are neatly explained in Mills's book. She traces the term "discourse," beginning with dictionary definitions (discourse is conversation) and work-

ing through to contemporary usage by theorists such as Foucault (discourse as "regulated practice").

5. I borrow this phrase (and hence its resonance and meaning) from James Moffett's book *Teaching the Universe of Discourse* which I would recommend for teaching literacy by exploring forms of discourse.

6. I don't mean to single out Henry Giroux or to cast his work in negative terms; in this example, he represents that group of theorists producing inspirational and illuminating but strictly theoretical work in education. I merely wish to point out how wide the gap is between these writers and classroom practitioners.

7. About discourse, personal writing, and the self, see Thomas Newkirk's *The Performance of Self in Student Writing* (1997).

8. For a critical analysis of the concept of discourse community, see Patricia Bizzell's *Academic Discourse and Critical Consciousness* (1992).

9. Of the many excellent sources available by and about Bakhtin, three have been particularly useful: Bakhtin's *The Dialogic Imagination*, edited by Michael Holquist (1981); *Voices of the Mind: A Sociocultural Approach to Mediated Action* by James Wertsch (1991); *Bakhtinian Thought* by Simon Dentith (1995).

10. For a critique of dialogic practices, see Elizabeth Ellsworth's *Teaching Positions: Difference, Pedagogy, and the Power of Address* (1997). Some theorists (Ellsworth among them) believe that in actual circumstances, especially classrooms, dialogue can be dangerous or at least not the ideal social process Bakhtin describes. He assumes that partners will be responsible and ethical in responding to each other. But the liability of interaction is that participants are often unequal in terms of status and power, and we cannot control the intentions of others. A skilled and ambitious conversational partner can dominate, control, overpower, disrupt, interrupt, or otherwise act badly toward other participants in the dialogue. This possible tendency is certainly an issue for teachers because of the way classrooms are socially arranged: teachers always have more status and control than students, and the prevailing discourses in the institution of school regulate how teachers and students behave, what gets learned, and who benefits from education in general.

Ellsworth critiques the idea of communicative dialogue as a pedagogical goal in favor of an approach she calls "analytic dialogue." She argues that "dialogue privileges continuity over discontinuity, sameness over difference, and full understanding over the productive paradoxes of misfired communications." She asks, "What kind of knowledge does dialogue proffer? What techniques does it use to regulate knowledge and the relationship of the teacher and students within the dialogue to knowledge and truth? I'm persuaded that dialogue, like other modes of address, is not just a neutral conduit of insights, discoveries, understandings, agreements, or disagreements. It has a constitutive force. It is a tool, it is for something" (1997, 15). Ellsworth is afraid that the 'something' may not be good.

11. For a detailed explanation of my experiences with letters, including the assignment, see my article "Writing Letters Instead of Journals in a Teacher-Education Course," in *The Journal Book for Teachers in Technical and Profession Programs* (1999).

12. For further information about different models of collaboration, see Lisa Ede and Andrea Lunsford's *Singular Texts/Plural Authors: Perspectives on Collaborative Writing* (1990).

13. In choosing a single concept "deliberation" from John Dewey's rich and provocative theories about pedagogy, selves, community, and education, I have merely gestured toward the possibilities that exist for transforming one's classroom. Others have gone much further in enacting Dewey's philosophy in their teaching. See the practical and inspiring book *John Dewey and the Challenge of Classroom Practice* by Stephen M. Fishman and Lucille McCarthy (1998).

14. Alan Tom in *Teaching as a Moral Craft* defines "moral" in two ways: "First, teaching involves a moral relationship between teacher and students that is grounded in the dominant power position of the teacher. Second, teaching is moral in the sense that a curriculum plan selects certain objectives or pieces of content instead of others; this selective process either explicitly or implicitly reflects a conception of desirable ends" (1984, 78).

15. In regard to my thinking about agency especially in the context of pragmatism, I owe much to John McGowan for steering me in the right direction. His essay, "Toward a Pragmatist Theory of Action," describes how individual agency and action are interactive and constructive, a perspective that I have found extremely useful. In addition, the volume *Classical American Pragmatism* edited by Sandra Rosenthal, Carl Hausman, and Douglas Anderson succinctly summarizes the pragmatic movement.

16. John McGowan (1998) clarifies the role of interaction in relation to self: "If our definition of "world" and "situation" is not limited to an individual facing a nonhuman environment, but also encompasses others and social arrangements, the interactional model . . . is quadrilateral (self facing nature, others, and social arrangements)" (294).

17. John McGowan offers a clear definition of the pragmatist model: "[T]here is a pluralism of response and possibility. Pragmatist interactionism refutes determinism. Pragmatism identifies four elements (the agent, other people, the things of the world, and social meanings/arrangements) in any situation. The keys to the pragmatist model are the insistence that none of these elements is determinant and that each of these elements has no independent standing, but is an interactional product of the encounters among the other four " (1998, 295).

18. Response is a key feature in Oakeshott's definition of agents: "Doing, identified as *response* to a contingent situation related to an imagined and wished-for

outcome, postulates reflective consciousness; that is, an agent who inhabits a world of intelligible *pragmata*, who is composed entirely of understandings, and who is what he understands (or misunderstands) himself to be" (1975, 36, italics original).

19. Other theorists working on issues of identity have considered the role of repeated acts in creating identities. While I regard repeated representation as contingent acts—anything can happen and no two representations can ever be identical— others regard repetition as a process of rigid inscription. For example, in both *Gender Trouble* and *Bodies That Matter*, Judith Butler proposes that repetition stabilizes or inscribes onto a body, or into a person's self, identities that are predetermined by the culture. However, Diane Dubose Brunner, working in performance theory, suggests in *Between the Masks: Resisting the Politics of Essentialism* that self-representations in public spaces (like classrooms) are always open-ended, and thus are potentially acts of identity construction that exceed or extend beyond given identity categories.

20. Ann Berthoff, in an essay called "Recognition, Representation, and Revision," writes that although language has "an indicative function," if we are interested in students' learning or being, then the most important function of language "is its power to represent our interpretations of experience. . . . No thinking—no composing—could happen if we had no means of stabilizing images of what we have seen, of recalling them as forms to think about and to think *with*" (italics hers) (1990, 35).

21. *Raisin in the Sun*, a play by Lorraine Hansbury.

22. For more information about the classroom as workshop, see the following sources: *A Rhetoric for Writing Teachers* by Erika Lindemann (1995); *A Writer Teaches Writing* by Donald Murray (1985); *A Community of Writers* by Steven Zemelman and Harvey Daniels (1988).

23. In defining power as a network of relations, I am relying on Foucault's definition of power, not so much as fixed commodity, an obstacle to be overcome, but rather as a set of shifting relationships. See *Power/Knowledge* (1980).

24. For more information about voice and its definitions, see *Landmark Essays on Voice and Writing*, edited by Peter Elbow (1994).

25. I use the conference format described by Donald Murray in *A Writer Teaches Writing*.

26. Ahead of time, Elizabeth had received the appropriate permission from involved teachers and the school.

27. For a start on alternative feedback and evaluation systems, see Peter Elbow's essay "Ranking, Evaluating, and Liking."

28. On the topic of teacher education programs, one way to forge single courses into a coherent program is to use a portfolio system based on broad goals. Students begin the portfolio as soon as they enter the program, carry the portfolio through from one course to another, constantly adding to and amending this

collection of work that represents their learning and development as teachers. An outstanding example of what's possible with this sort of system is the COT (Community of Teachers Program) at Indiana University, directed by Tom Gregory.

29. For an excellent collection of the "best" ways of teaching subject matter, see *Best Practice* by Steven Zemelman, Harvey Daniels, & Arthur Hyde (1993).

30. In contrast to my suggestions, there are several existing proposals for reforming teacher education that take a more radical and macroscopic approach. John Goodlad in *Teachers for Our Nation's Schools* (1990) lists thirteen areas (such as the presence of students of color) that could be evaluated in the process of reforming teacher education programs. In addition, Alan Tom in *Redesigning Teacher Education* (1997) proposes a series of principles (such as grouping students into cohorts) for recasting teacher education programs. Others have described qualities of effective schools. See Tom Gregory's book *Making High Schools Work* (1993). For inspiration about curriculum reform, I recommend *The Curriculum: Problems, Politics, and Possibilities* (1998) edited by Landon Beyer and Michael Apple, as well as *Official Knowledge: Democratic Education in a Conservative Age* (2000) by Michael Apple.

Chapter Seven

1. For a more evolved published argument see Bruno Latour's *Pandora's Hope: Essays on the Reality of Science Studies* (1999), especially chapter 9, "The Slight Surprise of Action: Facts, Fetishes, Factishes," p. 266–92.

WORKS CITED

Apple, Michael, ed. 2000. *Official Knowledge: Democratic Education in a Conservative Age*, 2d ed. New York: Routledge.

Bakhtin, M. M. 1981. *The Dialogic Imagination: Four essays by M. M. Bakhtin*. Ed. Michael Holquist. Trans. Caryl Emerson and Michael Holquist. Austin: University of Texas Press.

———. 1986. *Speech Genres and Other Late Essays*. Eds. Caryl Emerson and Michael Holquist. Trans. V. W. McGee. Austin: University of Texas Press.

Bartholomae, David. 1985. "Inventing the University." *When a Writer Can't Write: Studies in Writer's Block and Other Composing Process Problems*. Ed. Mike Rose. New York: Guilford, 134-65.

Becker, H. S., B. Geer, D. Riesman, and R. S. Weiss, eds. 1968. *Institutions and the Person*. Chicago: Aldine.

Berlin, James A. 1988. "Rhetoric and Ideology in the Writing Class." *College English* 50: 477–494.

Berthoff, Ann E. 1990. *The Sense of Learning*. Portsmouth, NH: Heinemann.

———. 1981. *The Making of Meaning*. Portsmouth, NH: Heinemann.

Beyer, Landon and Michael Apple, eds. 1998. *The Curriculum: Problems, Politics, and Possibilities*, 2d ed. Albany, NY: State University of New York Press.

Bizzell, Patricia. 1992. *Academic Discourse and Critical Consciousness*. Pittsburgh: University of Pittsburgh Press.

Bourdieu, Pierre. 1984. *Distinction: A Social Critique of the Judgement of Taste*. Trans. R. Nice. Cambridge, MA: Harvard University Press.

———. 1990. *The Logic of Practice*. Stanford, CA: Stanford University Press.

———. 1977. *Outline of a Theory of Practice*. Cambridge: Cambridge University Press.

Britzman, D. P. 1991. *Practice Makes Practice: A Critical Study of Learning to Teach*. Albany, NY: State University of New York Press.

Brooke, Robert. 1991. *Writing and Sense of Self*. Urbana, IL: National Council of Teachers of English.

———. 1987. "Underlife and Writing Instruction." *College Composition and Communication* 38: 141–53.

Bruffee, Kenneth A. 1984. "Collaborative Learning and the 'Conversation of Mankind'." *College English* 46.7: 635–52.

Brunner, Diane Dubose. 1998. *Between the Masks: Resisting the Politics of Essentialism*. Lanham, MD: Rowman & Littlefield Publisher.

Butler, Judith. 1990. *Gender Trouble*. New York: Routledge.

———. 1993. *Bodies That Matter: On the Discursive Limits of "Sex."* New York: Routledge.

Carter, Ronald. 1995. *Keywords in Language and Literacy*. New York: Routledge.

Clark, Gregory. 1990. *Dialogue, Dialectic, and Conversation*. Carbondale, IL: Southern Illinois University Press.

Cooper, Marilyn and Michael Holzman. 1989. *Writing as Social Action*. Portsmouth, NH: Boynton/Cook.

Crystal, David. 1987. *The Cambridge Encyclopaedia of Language*. Cambridge: Cambridge University Press.

Danielewicz, Jane. 1999. "Writing Letters Instead of Journals in a Teacher-Education Course." *The Journal Book for Teachers in Technical and Professional Programs*. Eds. Susan Gardner and Toby Fulwiler. Portsmouth, NH: Boynton/Cook, 92–105.

Davidson, Donald. 1984. *Inquiries into Truth and Interpretation*. Oxford, Eng.: Clarendon Press.

Dentith, Simon. 1995. *Bakhtinian Thought*. London: Routledge.

Dewey, John. 1994. "Deliberation and Choice." *The Moral Writings of John Dewey*, Ed. James Gouinlock. Amherst: Prometheus Books, 139–43

———. 1963. *Experience and Education*. New York: Collier. First published 1938.

———. 1922. *Human Nature and Conduct*. New York: H. Holt and Company.

———. 1980. *Theory of the Moral Life*. New York: Irvington Publishers. First published 1908.

Dorris, Michael. 1997. *Cloud Chamber*. New York: Scribner.

Ede, Lisa, and Andrea Lunsford. 1990. *Singular Texts/Plural Authors: Perspectives on Collaborative Writing*. Carbondale, IL: Southern Illinois University Press.

Elbow, Peter, ed. 1994. *Landmark Essays on Voice and Writing*. Davis, CA: Hermagoras Press.

———. 1986. *Embracing Contraries*. New York: Oxford University Press.

———. 1993. "Ranking, Evaluating, and Liking: Sorting Out Three Forms of Judgment." *College English*, 55.2: 187–205.

Ellsworth, Elizabeth. 1997. *Teaching Positions: Difference, Pedagogy, and the Power of Address*. New York: Teachers College Press, Columbia University.

Faigley, Lester. 1992. *Fragments of Rationality: Postmodernity and the Subject of Composition*. Pittsburgh: University of Pittsburgh Press.

Fishman, Stephen M. and Lucille McCarthy. 1998. *John Dewey and the Challenge of Classroom Practice*. New York: Teachers College Press, Columbia University.

Freire, Paulo (with Ira Shor). 1987. *A Pedagogy for Liberation: Dialogues on Transforming Education*. New York: Bergin and Garvey.

Foucault, Michel. 1972. *The Archaeology of Knowledge*. Trans. Sheridan Smith, A. M. New York: Pantheon.

———. 1979. *Discipline and Punish: The Birth of the Prison.* Trans. Alan Sheridan. New York: Vintage.

———. 1976. "The Discourse On Language." *The Archaeology of Knowledge.* Trans. A. M. Sheridan Smith. New York: Harper & Row.

———. 1980. *Power/Knowledge: Selected Interviews and Other Writings.* Ed. C. Gordon. Brighton: Harvester Press, 172–99.

Friesinger, Randall. 1994. "Voicing the Self: Toward a Pedagogy of Resistance in a Postmodern Age." *Landmark Essays on Voice and Writing.* Ed. Peter Elbow. Davis, CA: Hermagoras Press, 187-212.

Gadamer, Hans-George. 1975. *Truth and Method.* New York: Seabury.

Gale, Xin Liu. 1996. *Teachers, Discourses, and Authority in the Postmodern Composition Classroom.* Albany: State University of New York Press.

Giddens, Anthony. 1984. *The Constitution of Society.* Berkeley: University of California Press.

Giroux, Henry. 1997. *Pedagogy and the Politics of Hope: Theory, Culture, and Schooling.* Boulder: Westview Press (HarperCollins).

———. 1988. *Schooling and the Struggle for Public Life: Critical Pedagogy in the Modern Age.* Minneapolis: University of Minnesota Press.

Giroux, Henry, and Peter McLaren. 1986. "Teacher Education and the Politics of Engagement: The Case for Democratic Schooling." *Harvard Educational Review* 56: 213–38.

Glesne, Corrine and Alan Peshkin. 1992. *Becoming Qualitative Researchers.* White Plains: Longman.

Goffman, Erving. 1959. *The Presentation of Self in Everyday Life.* London: Allen Lane. Reprinted 1969.

Goodlad, John. 1990. *Teachers for Our Nation's Schools.* San Francisco: Jossey-Bass.

Gregory, Tom. 1993. *Making High School Work.* New York: Teachers College Press.

Grimmett, P. P., and G. L. Erickson, eds. 1988. *Reflection in Teacher Education.* New York: Teachers College Press.

Hall, Stuart, ed. 1997. *Representation: Cultural representations and Signifying practices.* London: Sage/The Open University.

Hall, Stuart. 1997a. "The Work of Representation." *Representation: Cultural Representations and Signifying Practices.* Ed. Stuart Hall, S. London: Sage/The Open University.

Hansen, David. 1995. *The Call to Teach.* New York: Teachers College Press, Columbia University.

Head, F. A. 1997. "Student Teaching as Initiation Into the Teaching Profession." *Anthropology and Education Quarterly* 23.2: 89–107.

hooks, bell. 1994. *Teaching to Transgress: Education as the Practice of Freedom.* New York: Routledge.

Holt-Reynolds, D. 1995. "Preservice Teachers and Coursework: When Is Getting It Right Wrong?" *Educating Teachers for Leadership and Change. Teacher Education*

Yearbook III. Eds. M. J. O'Hair and S. J. Odell. Thousand Oaks, CA: Corwin Press, 117–37.

Jenkins, Richard. 1996. *Social Identity*. London: Routledge.

Joas, Hans. 1996. *The Creativity of Action*. Translated by Jeremy Gaines and Paul Keast. Chicago: University of Chicago Press.

Kent, Thomas. 1989. "Paralogic Hermaneutics and the Possibilities of Rhetoric." *Rhetoric Review* 8: 24–42.

Labaree, D. F. 1994. "An Unlovely Legacy: The Disabling Impact of the Market on American Teacher Education." *Phi Delta Kappan* 75: 591-95.

LaBoskey, V. K. 1994. *Development of Reflective Practice: A Study of Preservice Teachers*. New York: Teachers College Press, Columbia University.

Latour, Bruno. 1999. *Pandora's Hope: Essays on the Reality of Science Studies*. Cambridge: Harvard University Press.

———. 1998. "Touching the Untouchable Factishes, or Can We Do Politics Without the Critique?" Unpublished Conference Paper.

———. 1993. *We Have Never Been Modern*. Trans. Catherine Porter. Cambridge, MA: Harvard University Press.

Lindemann, Erika. 1995. *A Rhetoric for Writing Teachers*, New York: Oxford University Press.

Liston, D. P. 1991. *Teacher Education and the Social Conditions of Schooling*. New York: Routledge.

Mayher, John S. 1990. *Uncommon Sense: Theoretical Practice in Language Education*. Portsmouth, NH: Heinemann.

McCutcheon, Gail. 1992. "Facilitating Teacher Personal Theorizing." *Teacher Personal Theorizing*. Eds. E. Wayne Ross, Jeffrey W. Cornett, and Gail McCutcheon. Albany, NY: State University of New York Press, 191–206.

McGowan, John. 1998. "Toward a Pragmatist Theory of Action." *Sociological Theory* 16.3: 292–97.

Miller, Janet L. 1990. *Creating Spaces and Finding Voices: Teachers Collaborating for Empowerment*. Albany: State University of New York Press.

Mills, Sara. 1997. *Discourse*. New York: Routledge.

Moffet, James. 1983. *Teaching the Universe of Discourse*. Boynton/Cook Publishers. (First published 1968.)

Morris, Pam, ed. 1994. *The Bakhtin Reader: Selected Writings of Bakhtin, Medvedev, Voloshinov*. London: Edward Arnold.

Murray, Donald. 1985. *A Writer Teaches Writing*. 2nd ed. Boston: Houghton Mifflin.

———. 1997. "Teach Writing as a Process not Product." *Cross-Talk in Comp Theory*. Ed. Victor Villanueva. Urbana, IL: NCTE, 3–6. (first published in 1972.)

Newkirk, Thomas. 1977. *The Performance of Self in Student Writing*. Portsmouth, NH: Boynton/Cook Publishers.

Noddings, Nel. 1984. *Caring: A Feminine Approach to Ethics and Moral Education*. Berkeley: University of California Press.

———. 1992. *The Challenge to Care in Schools: An Alternative Approach to Education.* New York: Teachers College Press, Columbia University.

Oakeshott, Michael. 1975. *On Human Conduct.* Oxford: Oxford University Press.

Palmer, Parker. 1983. *To Know As We Are Known: A Spirituality of Education.* San Francisco: Harper & Row.

Popkewitz, T. S., ed. 1987. Critical Studies in Teacher Education: Its Folklore, Theory and Practice. London: Falmer Press.

Qualley, Donna. 1997. *Turns of Thought: Teaching Composition as Reflexive Inquiry.* Portsmouth, NH: Boynton/Cook Publishers.

Rich, Adrienne. 1993. *What Is Found There: Notebooks on Poetry and Politics.* New York: W.W. Norton and Co.

Rorty, Richard. 1979. *Philosophy and the Mirror of Nature.* Princeton, NJ: Princeton University Press.

Rosenthal, Sandra B., Carl R. Hausman & Douglas R. Anderson. 1999. *Classical American Pragmatism.* Urbana: University of Illinois Press.

Russell, T. and H. Munby, eds. 1992. *Teachers and Teaching: From Classroom to Reflection.* London: Falmer Press.

Russell, T. and H. Munby, eds. 1995. Teachers Who Teach Teachers: Reflections on Teacher Education. London: Falmer Press.

Salvatori, Mariolina R. ed. 1996. *Pedagogy: Disturbing History, 1819–1929.* Pittsburgh: University of Pittsburgh Press.

Scott, Joan W. 1992. "Experience," in *Feminists Theorize the Political.* Eds. Judith Butler and Joan W. Scott. New York: Routledge, 22–40.

Shanahan, Timothy. 1994. *Teachers Thinking, Teachers Knowing: Reflections on Literacy and Language Education.* Urbana, IL: National Council of Teachers of English.

Shapiro, E. 1988. *Teacher: Being and Becoming.* New York: Bank Street College.

Smith, Paul. 1988. *Discerning the Subject.* Minneapolis: University of Minneapolis Press.

Taylor, Charles. 1991. "The Dialogical Self." *The Interpretive Turn.* Eds. David R. Hiley, James F. Bohman, and Richard Shusterman. Ithaca: Cornell University Press, 304–14.

Thomas, Gary. 1997. "What's the Use of Theory?" *Harvard Educational Review,* 67.1: 75–104.

Todorov, Tzvetan. 1984. *Mikhail Bakhtin: The Dialogical Principle.* Trans. Wlad Godzich. Minneapolis: University of Minnesota Press.

Tom, Alan R. 1984. *Teaching as a Moral Craft.* New York: Longman.

———. 1997. *Redesigning Teacher Education.* Albany: State University of New York Press.

Ward, Irene. 1994. *Literacy, Ideology, and Dialogue.* Albany: State University of New York Press.

Wertsch, J. 1991. *Voices of the mind: A Sociocultural Approach to Mediated Action.* Cambridge, MA: Harvard University Press.

Williams, Raymond. 1983. *Keywords: A Vocabulary of Culture and Society*, 2d. ed. New York: Oxford.

Woodward, Kathryn. ed. 1997. *Identity and Difference*. London: SAGE Publications.

Yancey, Kathleen Blake, ed. 1994. *Voices on Voice: Perspectives, Definitions, Inquiry*. Urbana, IL: NCTE.

Zemelman, Steven, and Harvey Daniels. 1988. *A Community of Writers: Teaching Writing in the Junior and Senior High School*. Portsmouth, NH: Heinemann.

Zemelman, Steven, Harvey Daniels, and Arthur Hyde. 1993. *Best Practice: New Standards for Teaching and Learning in America's Schools*. Portsmouth, NH: Heinemann.

Index

action: personal theories of, 9, 105, 106, 193; as "doing," 167, 202–203n; pragmatist theory of, 202n
affiliation: and collective identity, 113–114; definition, 114; examples of, 115–127; and mentor teachers, 113–114
affiliation patterns: differentiation, 117–118; identification, 115–116; joint problem solving, 119–120; oppositional, 120–121; substantive role, 118–119
agency: concept of, 2, 11, 35, 51, 54, 61, 75, 163–165, 167, 197; cultivating, 165–167; defined as teaching principle, 164; described, 163–167; and identity, 163–164; in teachers, 163–164. *See also* principles of pedagogy
agent, 75, 163–165
Altman, Roberta (Rick's mentor teacher), 102, 117–118, 189–190. *See also* pseudonyms
answerability, 145
Apple, Michael, 200n, 204n
assignments: classroom letters, 146–147, 166, 202n; collaborative final examination, 175–176; course design project, 160–162, 168–169, 175; integrated units, 175, 204n; interviews, 167; learning centers, 154–155; portfolios, 162, 174, 203n–204n; teaching philosophy, 142–144, 156; thesis project, 172–174; workshop model, 169–170; writing-to-learn project, 150
Atwell, Nancie, 158, 200n

authority, 17, 141; cultivating, 173–174; defined as teaching principle, 170; described, 170–174; institutional, 172; and power, 170; and self, 171–172; and voice, 171–174. *See also* principles of pedagogy
Ayers, Bill, 200n

Bakhtin, Mikhail, 134, 139, 145–147, 200n, 201n
Bartholomae, David, 200n
Barton, Bill (Rick's mentor as first-year teacher), 103–105. *See also* pseudonyms
becoming, 1, 2, 75, 106, 133, 168, 197; a teacher (or not), 3, 12, 37–38, 127, 142, 183–184
belonging, 183–184
Berthoff, Ann, 200n, 203n
Beyer, Landon, 204n
Bizzell, Patricia, 200n, 201n
Black English Vernacular (BEV), 147
Blau, Sheridan, 200n
Bourdieu, Pierre, 36, 61
Britzman, Deborah, 10, 113, 132
Bruffee, Kenneth, 149
Brunner, Diane Dubose, 203n
Butler, Judith, 203n

caring: defined, 165; as philosophy, 165–167
case studies: Lambert, Richard, 91–107; Tavey, Elizabeth, 66–91
Clark, Gregory, 146
collaboration, 17, 141; defined as teaching principle, 148; described, 148–152;

211

teaching: demands of, 9–10; messiness of, 194–195; as a moral craft, 153, 202n. *See also* moral teaching; process

teaching practicum, 12, 48, 59, 86; discourse of, 135, 137; Elizabeth's 76–85; and identity development, 112–113

theorizing in practice, 17, 141, 177; described as teaching principle, 159–163; modeling theory, 161–162; personal theories, 105, 159–163

theory: and action, 159; defined, 159; and pedagogy, 15, 159; and practice; 73, 80, 140, 160–161; and teaching, 15, 140, 174

Todorov, Tzvetan, 145

Tom, Alan, 200n, 202n, 204n

undergraduate students: in courses, 12; desire to be teachers, 8, 13; differences between, 8. *See also* participants (in research study)

University of North Carolina: M.A.T. program, 199n, 200n; secondary teacher education program, 4, 5, 12, 48, 70. *See also* School of Education

voice, 171–174. *See also* authority; self

Vygotsky, Lev, 139, 159, 161

whole language, 68, 76–77, 88, 157, 158, 173

Williams, Raymond, 11

Woodward, Kathryn, 36

workshop: classroom as, 169–170

writing, 22; as developmental mode, 71–72. *See also* process; process approach to teaching writing

writing-across-the-curriculum, 13

writing-to-learn activity, 150. *See also* assignments

Yancey, Kathleen Blake, 171

Zemelman, Steven, 200n, 203n, 204n